What others are saying about

Dancing on Raindrops

"In a special and startling way, Lucky Mike has created a masterpiece. His extreme adventures will enthrall and motivate you, and his **7** secrets will ensure your success. **A Must Read!**"

- **Robert G. Allen.** *Millionaire-Maker. Author of New York Times bestsellers: Nothing Down, Creating Wealth, Multiple Streams of Income, Multiple Streams of Internet Income and co-author of The One Minute Millionaire.*

"You will be thrilled and uplifted by this wonderful compilation of one man's **amazing tales**. Lucky Mike certainly delivers."

- **Hanne Svensson.** *Extreme Sports Specialist.*

"Lucky Mike lives a life of extreme adventure. His thought provoking teachings and unique style of writing made this book **immensely enjoyable**."

- **Mark Boxshall.** *International Mega-Yacht Captain.*

"I thought I was an adventurer until I met Lucky Mike. He is a true adventurer. He controls paralyzing fear in situations of great accomplishment and exhilarating fun. Thus, he overcomes the odds against great peril and hardship. What is even better, he tells his stories so that you can live the excitement and adventure with him, second by second! At times I got goose bumps and hair raises, and yes, I emitted spontaneous screams of surprise and joy late one night.

I read it non-stop. I could not put the book down. What fun *Dancing on Raindrops* is. A life worth living is a life worth sharing, and I am so happy that Lucky Mike has shared his life with me in his wonderful book. A must-read for anyone with a spirit of adventure and love of life."

- Joycebelle [Edelbrock.] *Author, publisher, Love Your Beauty, Freedom Forever, Raefon in the Land of WOW! Sea Otters--Our Friends and dozens of kids e-books.*

"Lucky Mike will leave an incredible impact on your heart. You will love the excitement and triumph, hope and inspiration, as he so skillfully shares the attitude required to: **Step out of line and get what you want out of life!**"

- Brian Delport. *Artist, creator of the 'Zak Mural.'*

Dancing

on

Raindrops

EXTREME ADVENTURES
REVEAL THE 7 SECRETS TO YOUR SUCCESS

LUCKY MIKE

Publisher's Cataloging-in-Publication
(Provided by Quality Books, Inc.)

Lucky Mike.

    Dancing on raindrops : extreme adventures reveal the 7 secrets to your success / Lucky Mike. -- 1st ed.

    p. cm.

    "Extreme adventures. Short stories."

    Includes bibliographical references and index.

    LCCN 2003095418

    ISBN 0-9743476-4-7

    1. Success--Psychological aspects. 2. Conduct of life. I. Title.

BF637.S8L83 2003   158.1

              QBI03-700566

Published by M42 Corp.

P.O. Box 740852, Boynton Beach, FL., 33474 – 0852 USA.

Printed in the United States of America.

10 9 8 7 6 5 4 3 2 1

First Edition

FOREWORD

Passage-immediate passage! The blood burns in my veins.
Away, O soul! Hoist instantly the anchor!
Cut the hawsers-haul out-shake out every sail!
Have we not stood here like trees in the ground long enough?
Have we not grovell'd here long enough, eating and drinking like mere brutes?
Have we not darken'd and dazed ourselves with books long enough?
Sail forth! Steer for the deep waters only!
Reckless, O soul, exploring I with thee, and thee with me,
For we are bound where mariner has not yet dared to go,
And we risk the ship, ourselves and all.
O my brave soul!
O daring joy, but safe! Are they not the seas of God?
O farther, farther, farther sail!

(Walt Whitman: "Passage to India," 1871)

I met Lucky Mike several years ago while cruising the Caribbean Sea. I had decided to make a visit to Oyster Pond in St Martin. Getting in there was like a Lucky Mike story itself – I had to maneuver my 20 tons of sail-boat through the breakers and between a couple of reefs, and then make a hard right to avoid colliding with a rather aggressive looking group of rocks that lay dead ahead, as I came surfing down the swells. And, like most everything else in life, once you've done it, it's easy!

The water was calm inside and the pond was packed with charter boats, cruising boats and sailors from all over the world. It didn't take long to meet Lucky Mike himself: he was the most successful skipper in the place, with the best disposition, the best boat – a beautiful steel vessel he built himself in South Africa – and he was having the best time.

Over the next few years there were some remarkable knocks, some of which you'll shortly be reading about and even more remarkable are the recoveries. In fact, I often wonder if the knocks themselves are not the catalysts or stepping-stones to bigger and better recoveries. With Lucky Mike at the helm, each recovery becomes an adventure of gargantuan proportions, and would probably suffice as a whole life for a lot of the dwellers on our planet. But not for you and me. No, we want a little more. In fact, a whole lot more.

Now, if you feel you already are a successful human being with little to gain, just reading this book for pure enjoyment will be a wonderful experience. It'll take you to places you've never even dreamed of, and offer you insights that only you and the other readers will ever be privy to. And in the end I'll bet it might just refuel your tanks and give you the urge to fly again. Why not? If Lucky Mike can dream it, do it and enjoy it - so can you!

On the other hand, if you're feeling a little lost, or are just looking for some new ideas to really get up and going again, you have come to the right place! It's here you'll begin to see a whole new you, doing things you never thought possible and reaching ever higher and higher. And the best thing about it is that it's all fun, the most fun you'll ever have – really. Yes, there's nothing more fun than success, and achieving success in many different ways is what this book is all about. But that's enough from me: *Dancing on Raindrops* is far more entertaining than any introduction will ever be and I wish you well on the coming journey. Enjoy!

Peter Heath. International film director.
Winner, CLIO Awards and Cannes Film Festival.

To my mother, Ann, without whose support and guidance, I might never have come to know the true power that lies within each of us.

To my son, Orion, and your future adventures in life's wonderful journey.

To you. You who have a desire to create a better life for yourself. You who hold your dreams in your head.

GIVE YOURSELF MORE:

More time.
More money.
More love.
More control of your thoughts.
More in touch with your inner self.
More power to follow your heart.
More dreams coming true.
More fun in your life.
No more fear!

How can you dance on a raindrop?...

ADVENTURES

* * *

"The thoughts you hold in your head, create your reality."

Dancing on Raindrops

INTRODUCTION

Often I hear people remark as to how lucky I am. Yes, I am very lucky, but I have noticed that the more I use the principles laid out in these **7** secrets; the more I focus my mind on the things I want to happen - the luckier I become.

Should you choose to apply these principles to your life, they will enable you to achieve anything you want; for a principle is a truth, something that works the same for everyone, no matter who, what, or where. Take gravity for example. Here is a principle to which we are all accustomed, so much so that we never give it a thought – unless of course we find ourselves at the top of a ladder! Yet gravity is applying its force to everything on this planet, every instant of every day, it is unchanging it in its uniformity and persistence.

There are many such principles in our world; science, mathematics and life are filled with them, so much so that it is only the existence of principles that allows them to be. For example, how could mathematics exist if two plus two only sometimes equaled four? No, it always equals four, it has to.

These **7** secrets are ancient teachings, but they are still as valid today as they were in the beginning - they are timeless. However, as with most things in life, unless you really want success with a desire that is strong enough to hold your thoughts aligned like the needle of a compass, it will be hardly worth your while to attempt this life-changing act. These strategies are for **You**, but only if you are prepared to give of the action required; for to change the way you think, or the things you think about, is always a challenge - but it is a fact that anyone who controls their thoughts has the ability to control their future. Those who wish to keep you in your place, or maintain the status quo, deny this concept. But should you find the courage to take action and begin to consciously hold your thoughts in a specific direction, then the abundance of nature will become an inseparable part of everything in your life. The more you practice using this power - the luckier you too will become.

Taking charge of my thoughts and emotions has undoubtedly saved my life many times, but more importantly this action has enabled me to live the life I choose. From extreme fear to extreme tranquility, enjoy the adventures I have experienced and the lessons I have learned - for every one is a true story.

Lucky Mike – October 2003
Home

*"Step out of line
and get what you want out of life!"*

AFRICA

IN THE LION'S DEN

The first European voyagers to set foot on what is now known as South Africa, must have been awed by what they saw. A place of such beauty and splendor; home of earth's most diverse plant population and the land of the big five - lion, elephant, rhino, leopard and buffalo.

In the south, the Cape of Good Hope is the meeting place of the Indian and Atlantic oceans. The cold Benguela current comes up from the frigid Antarctic and goes off to the west coast, while the warm Mozambique current flows southwards on the eastern side, bringing with it the tropical delights of the Indian Ocean. Spectacular mountains rise out of the sea, their bases covered in a carpet of trees.

Table Mountain, with its famous 'tablecloth' - the cloud that covers the top of the flat mountain and as the southeast wind blows, it falls below the vertical face and dissipates, giving the impression of a white tablecloth.

To the north, the land rises up to over six thousand feet - a huge plateau, under whose dusty earth lie vast fortunes of gold.

On the west coast, the dryness increases as you go north, up to the desert land that is now called Namibia; a place where diamonds lie scattered on the ground.

In the 1600's, settlers began arriving from Europe, but it was not until the early 1800's that they had established outposts in the interior. The influx continued and the wildlife population took a dramatic turn for the worse. Trading in skins and ivory increased as people moved north and soon the once endless herds of game were becoming decimated. It took years of slaughter, disease and land clearing for farming, before President Paul Kruger realized the danger, and in 1898, took steps to form what is now five and a half million acres of unspoiled African bush; an area larger than Massachusetts, Wales or Israel. The Kruger National Park.

The park is surrounded by unfenced reserves, and it was in one of these that I learnt the ways of the bush and the animals that inhabit it.

My childhood had been one of travel and as my parents could not decide where to live, we moved between South Africa, England and Ireland. After thirteen schools, I became accustomed to having to deal with the new and sometimes surprising situations that seemed to come my way.

Wet and dreary, the English winters were too drab for me and the Irish saying of 'when you can see the Wicklow mountains it's going to rain, and when you can't it is raining' - made me long for the heat and dust of the Africa I remembered.

When I was sixteen and back in Africa, I decided I wanted to work with wild animals, so through the contact of a friend, I found a job as a ranger on a private game reserve. My experience with Africa's wild animals was limited to a few trips to game parks and spending some time growing up in the country. I did however have some shooting experience. Since I was a young boy and in happier times with my father, we had been shooting pheasant and grouse together. On the twelfth of August for many years (the glorious twelfth as it is known), we would be in Scotland for the opening day of the grouse shooting season.

The guns would be evenly spread up the side of a hill and we would hide behind a sunken stone emplacement, a butt. Each butt would have two guns, a shooter and a loader and once ready, the beaters, who were spread out in a line across the heather covered hills, began to walk towards us.

The birds were fast and would come screaming above the heather, but often it was possible to have two shots at a covey as they approached from in front, change guns and then fire two more shots as they disappeared behind. Sometimes only a pair of hot barrels and a brace of grouse were all there was to show for a drive.

From the grouse we would move on to the pheasant. Here the birds were a lot slower but much higher, as they were beaten out of the woods and rose up above the tall trees. The guns would simply stand in a long line, in a field on the edge of the wood and shoot the birds as they passed above. I used to shoot a lot of things, there were also the rabbits and hares, ducks and geese and of course deer. After shooting my first stag on the moors of Scotland, the gamekeeper smeared its blood on my face. At first it was quite a shock, for I was not expecting his hand to be full of blood, as he poured it onto my head and began to rub it over my face. A mark, a rite.

When the salmon fishing season opened we would make another trip to Scotland and fish the Tweed, the Spey and my favorite of all, the river Tay. It was deep, dark and full of salmon. Yes, I knew a little about guns and the great outdoors, but I knew nothing about lions.

The Timbavati Reserve, famous for its pride of white lions, borders the park on the western side and catered to the needs of wealthy tourists who wished to enjoy the luxuries of life, deep in the African bush. The camp itself had no fences and wild animals often wandered over the green lawns, some in search of grass and some in search of meat.

Twice a day we took the guests on a game drive in an open Land Rover. Morning and evening, the times when animals come to water holes to either ready themselves for the heat of the day, or replenish the lost body fluids that the scorching African sun had depleted.

Besides catering to the guests, we were also involved in the conservation of animals. Poachers were constantly trying to kill elephant for ivory, rhino for their horn and big cats for their skins.

On occasion we would find a dead animal that was caught in a snare, perhaps a rhino with only its horn removed; the rest of the carcass lying rotting in the sun, as the vultures circled above waiting for us to leave. Such an ignominious death for some of the last great beasts to inhabit the earth.

The rains come in the summer and after the first wetting the landscape turns to green. The tall African grasses sprout quickly and soon the bush becomes so thick that it is impossible to see even a few yards ahead. The air fills with the scents of trees and bushes growing and multiplying during the short rainy season. An earthy yet sweet smell that always reminds me of a time of plenty. Fruit trees hang low with the weight of their crop and all the animals look fat and healthy. When the marula tree comes into fruit, it is time for a jungle party. The small yellow fruit has a ropey texture and inside, the big seed looks like a small skull and when it falls to the ground, it begins to ferment and forms alcohol.

One afternoon I came across a half a dozen elephants and a troop of monkeys, feeding in a grove on the edge of a ravine. The party was in full swing by the time I arrived and the elephants looked as though they were enjoying themselves immensely. The monkeys on the other hand, seemed as drunk as any sailor on a Friday night bender. As I watched the spectacle, one large male monkey stood on the edge of the cliff, his face covered in the remains of his feast. He stood upright, smiled and then fell over backwards, out of sight down into the ravine.

With the onset of winter, the ground begins to dry once again. The rivers cease to flow, the trees lose their leaves and the grasses wither. Winter is not a cold affair, but occasionally a light frost covers the ground in the mornings. This is the best time for viewing the animals, as the bush is clear of undergrowth and there is no cover for them to hide behind.

It was in the reserve that I met Ben. He was a tall man for his tribe, the Shangaan, and although he had spent his entire life in the bush and was only in his late forties, he carried an aura of knowledge and dignity. At first sight I could see that there was something special about him. His short-cropped hair, graying on the edges and his beaming smile made him instantly likeable, but it said nothing of his inner-self and his powers in the spirit world. We bonded immediately and he took me under his wing and guided me through many of the dangers and fears of Africa.

Like most Africans, he believed in the power of the fifth dimension; spirituality and the evil intentions of the Tokolosh - a small 'spirit person,' who would come to their beds while they were sleeping and steal their souls. (Legend has it that only young children, who have yet to reach puberty, can see the Tokolosh.) At night, sitting around a fire, he would teach me of the ways of the African spirits. He loved to tell of how we are all able to subdue any of the spirit forces, simply by using the power that is within our minds to overcome them.

Ben's connection to the 'other world' was close and intimate. Often he would know the outline of some up coming event long before it actually happened, and he would delight in sharing that knowledge with me in the form of parables. Coming so close to telling me what he believed was about to happen, yet leaving out the punch line and thus causing me to think about the outcome, rather than the situation.

One month before I arrived, I was told that the Sangoma (witch doctor) had been in the camp and had cast a spell on one of the young men; telling him that in seven days, he would die. Sure enough, seven days later the young man was found dead in his bed. It was not an event that anyone seemed to find incredible.

"Such is the power of the mind," Ben said when I asked him how such a thing could happen. "The young man believed in his fate with such conviction, that he created it."

The camp covered perhaps two acres and white rondavels (circular thatched cottages), formed the perimeter in the shape of a horseshoe, with all the other buildings in the middle. They were made with local stone, dug from the edge of the riverbed and painted white. The roofs were long wooden poles that all joined at the top and were then covered with eight to ten inches of thatch, the khaki colored grasses that grew over most of the country.

In the center, the main building was huge. The floors were a dark polished slate and on the walls hung the skins and heads of various wild animals. The ceiling rose to thirty feet and allowed the room to stay cool in the heat of summer. Breezes wafted in through the large glass doors in the front, the air already cooled by the trees next to the building.

The dining room was in the boma. An outdoor, circular enclosure. It was open to the sky, with thick bamboo stalks making up its perimeter. Skulls and the horns of animals hung from the sturdy poles and the floor was dirt, walked on so many times before it became smooth and hard like concrete. Around the circumference, dozens of oil candles tried in vain to shed their orange light into the bush beyond, giving an eerie effect. The tables were set in a semicircle and covered in starched white tablecloths, silver cutlery and fine crystal glasses. It seemed almost too refined and elegant for its surroundings. In the center was the bonfire and every night we would dine under the stars, to the dancing light of the flames.

Most often we would have a braai (barbecue), cooking perhaps an impala that had been shot that day, or sometimes the chef would create one of his masterful dishes of bobotie; a local favorite made from ground meat, curry, apricots and egg custard, then served on a bed of rice. In addition to the local fare, there were always the lobster, mussels and oysters flown in regularly from Cape Town.

In the evenings, each of the guests had to be escorted to their rondavels in case there was a lion in camp, or a leopard waiting in a tree; so the rangers were always the last to go to sleep. One night, as I made my way to my room, far in the distance I could hear the sound of thunder and the sweet smell of rain began to hang thick in the air. I readied myself for bed as the rain began to fall in one of the last thunderstorms of the season.

Between the bright flashes of lightning and that huge African thunder, I eventually managed to fall asleep. The door and windows of my room were both wide open, as I slept soundly within the unfenced camp. Sometime during the night, I awoke to the sound of something walking up and down outside my room. In that half awake and half asleep state, I assumed it was one of the local rangers sitting out the storm under the shelter of my balcony and without another thought, I was fast asleep.

I woke early in the morning and fumbled my way out of bed as usual. I kept my clothes and rifle on a chair by the wall, so I scratched and yawned my way over there and began to dress. Then, almost dressed I reached down to put on my boots and there below me, on the polished slate floor, was the paw print of a lion. It was a lion that had been walking up and down outside my room, while the storm was raging outside. He had come in with his paws all covered in mud and left a trail that went first to the edge of my bed, then around the bed to the other side, into the bathroom, back to my bed and out the door.

His head would have been right above mine as he stood next to the edge of my bed - and with that reflection I suddenly realized what might have happened while I was sleeping. Wow! I took a deep breath and looked more closely at his tracks, the blood beginning to pump in my body. Waves of energy flowed through me, from my head all the way down to my feet, and in that moment I knew for sure that someone or something had been looking after me the previous night. It reminded me of the biblical story of

Daniel in the lion's den and I remember smiling, happy to be alive.

The dusty porch in front of my rondavel had turned to a mud bath during the night and as the lion walked up and down, the mud had become thicker and thicker. By the time he decided to come into the room, his paws were covered in a golden muck that stuck wherever he walked. I finished dressing and went to the main kitchen to get some coffee.

Once the camp had found out about the lion in my bedroom and everyone had looked at the paw prints, Ben walked over to me.

"Haaw Numzaan," (Sir) his teeth gleaming as he smiled hard, "Simba almost get you!"

Yes, the lion could have had me any moment he chose. In the blink of an eye I could have been in his jaws, out of my room and into the bush, before I had realized what was happening. Ben stood there and stared at me. Not actually looking at me, but rather through me, as if I was not there. For a long while I waited for him to speak.

"At the last full moon I told you about this," he said in a hushed tone, almost a whisper. As I remembered, we had walked to the top of the kopje (hill) that was behind the camp and while we sat under a huge full moon, he had told me many stories. Wondering which one he was referring to, I was still pondering the question, when Ben nodded.

"Yes, now we go find him," he said and with that he turned and went to fetch his spear, leaving me none the wiser. In the company of guests Ben had to carry a rifle, but when alone, he was free to choose his own means of protection. Picking up the spoor at the side of my rondavel was easy and the large paw prints were clearly visible in the soft mud, but fifty feet further on, I lost the trail.

As we came to the edge of the clearing, all that lay ahead was the bush - tall grass and trees. Ben, with his phenomenal tracking ability took the lead and we followed the spoor. Sometimes a paw print was visible in the soft dirt, but most of the time it was a bent blade of grass, or a bruised leaf that showed him the way.

For the first part, we chatted as we walked, because Ben was sure the lion was still far away. I broached the topic of which story he was referring to, but all he would say was, "You will remember."

Two hours later we were getting close to the lion, so not a word was spoken between us. We communicated through hand signals and watched carefully where we stepped, in order to keep our approach silent.

He stood on the edge of the thicket in a dry riverbed and looked at us. A mature male weighing well over four hundred pounds, his long black mane flowing in the breeze. Most all of the creatures in the bush, either gave homage to, or warned of his approach. Yet there we were, less than one hundred feet apart. I looked at Ben and he had a solemn expression on his face.

"Mike, yes you are very lucky," he said as he nodded his head and the same old smile returned. "Yes, I shall call you Lucky Mike." He began to chuckle.

I stared at the lion. He was a magnificent creature in the prime of his life and seemed totally indifferent to our presence. I looked directly into his eyes and as he stared back at me, those same waves of energy that passed through me earlier that morning, washed over me again. It dawned on me which story Ben had been referring to.

"Come, we must go," Ben said and with that he turned and began to walk back to the camp. We were half way home before I broke the silence.

"It was the story about the spirits, the one with the little girl and the mean old maid," I said.

Ben looked at me and smiled, but offered no comment.

EYES IN THE DARKNESS

The idea was to run outside of the beam of lights and approach from the darkness, as the impala stood blinded in the spotlight. With as much speed as you could muster, you would dive at the animal and try to tackle it to the ground, being careful of the dangerously pointed horns and the kicking hooves. It was late at night and a new ranger had joined us, so it was time for some fun. It was his turn to try to catch an impala. Seated in the open Land Rover, not long after dinner, we drove through the bush looking for eyes.

"There at two o clock," someone said, as half a dozen eyes lit up in the beam of light. Our new recruit was eager and he waited, ready to jump from the vehicle. No, it was a herd of kudu. Such graceful animals with their long spiraled horns, they stared into the light not knowing what to do, mesmerized and much too big for what we wanted.

We were looking for impala, but somehow on that particular night all the other animals of the bush were out and about, except for the ones we wanted. We drove for an hour but still could not find any impala, so we decided to call it a night and head back to the camp.

There, on the edge of the camp behind one of the rondavels, were eyes - lots of eyes. Our new friend could not stand the strain of waiting. These were sure to be impala grazing in the darkness on the edge of the open camp.

He leapt from the moving vehicle and started to run in an arc, just outside the beam of light. He overtook us and zeroed in on his prey. The eyes were only about fifty feet away, but because of the bush it was still impossible to see clearly. We continued forward and twenty feet away, we all suddenly realized what was about to happen. The eyes did not belong to impala.

The young ranger was on his last step before launching, when he finally saw his prey. He stopped dead in his tracks, ten feet from the nearest animal and in the same instant he was airborne traveling backwards, back towards the open Land Rover. His feet touched the ground once and he landed on the back seat, easily clearing the high sides of the open vehicle. The eyes belonged to a pride of lions.

The few guests we had in camp at the time had gone to bed and I was doing the rounds to make sure that everything was in order. I went to my room and looked out of the window to see if the lions were still in the bush behind, but they had moved on. The holster belt for my revolver, a .44 magnum had been hurting me all day. It dug into my hip where I had cut myself on a piece of wire, so I took it off and put it on the bed. I picked up my rifle, slung the strap over my shoulder and walked out onto the grass by the swimming pool to enjoy a little of the night. Looking out over the bush, it was dark and only the sounds gave any idea of what was out there.

The sky was clear and the moon had long gone. I could hear a herd of impala in the tall grass nearby and I realized they must have been waiting for me to leave, so they could resume their nighttime grazing on the green lawns by the pool.

How strange I thought, *that we had spent an hour this evening looking for impala and had not seen a single one. Yet here they were, on the opposite side of the camp to where the lions had been.*

A path led to the dry riverbed at the far side of the clearing. It was about a ten minute walk and I had not intended to go all the way, but somehow I became caught up in the night. The Southern Cross was brilliant in the sky and as soon as my eyes adjusted, I could see from the light of the stars. The river was lined with trees, most having lost their leaves for the winter. They looked stark against the backdrop of the night sky. I put my rifle down next to me and sat on the trunk of an old dead tree, enjoying the peace and quiet. It felt as though I was becoming a part of the night.

A call of nature prompted me to move, so I got up and wandered beyond the big tree that stood between the edge of the riverbank and me. The dry leaves crackled beneath my feet as I relieved myself onto the sand below. Finished, I turned and as I did so, a movement caught my eye. Something was in the tree. I froze and blinked, as I tried to focus on the branches to see what it was that had attracted my attention.

It was then that I thought I saw a leopard, a silhouette blended into the lowest branch of the tree. The tree I had moments before walked under, and the tree which stood between my rifle and me. I felt my heart begin to thump in my chest and I consciously made an effort to stop the emotion. The last thing I needed was the smell of adrenaline wafting on the night breeze.

The big cat looked as though it was a part of the tree, and I began to have second thoughts as to whether or not it really was a leopard in the darkness. Then his tail moved and I knew I had a problem. My rifle was only sixty feet away, but the leopard was directly in between - on a branch ten feet off the ground - and waiting. I could not think of anything else to do besides staying still, so I froze in that exact position and waited. At times my breathing seemed so loud that I tried to slow it down. I contemplated crouching, trying to blend into the ground, but he knew where I was and if he wanted to wait, then so would I.

After ten minutes I could feel my arms and the soles of my feet begin to ache. We were stuck in a game of wills. He who moves loses, but if I lose - I die. In the distance I could hear the sound of baboons screeching, a powerful and desperate noise. I knew that it was more than likely the presence of a leopard that made them react with such vigor.

Twenty minutes and nothing had changed, except for the millions of thoughts going through my brain like an endless stream. I started to concentrate on them, picking out the positives and ignoring the gory negatives. It was hard at first, as the idea of a bloody ending was not easy to ignore; but the more I concentrated on the fact that I was all right and the leopard would not attack, the more it became the predominant thought in my mind.

For perhaps two hours we were immobile, staring at one another. My breathing had quieted, but my mouth was dry and it seemed as though the standoff could go on forever. The baboons had stopped their noise and the night was still.

He who gives up loses. The very idea of it gave me the strength to stay exactly as I was, in total silence and wait. Perhaps with the dawn the big cat would go away.

I spent some of the time scanning the ground for a stout piece of wood nearby, or some other object to at least attempt to protect myself with, but except for a few dry little twigs, there was nothing. I tried to remember what Ben had told me about leopards, but the only thing I could remember was him saying that if a leopard wanted me, then I would more than likely not know about it until the last instant - and by then it would be too late.

My mind wandered back to the story that Ben had referred to, on the day the lion had come into my bedroom. A little girl was doing her chores and went to the river to fetch some water. She was having a wonderful day and she sang as she walked. The more she sang, the more her spirits rose and by the time she reached the river, she was so at one with herself and nature, that the spirits entered her mind. A little way behind her, an old maid also walked to the river - but her mind was filled with bitterness and revenge. She created a wall about her and filled it with bad thoughts. Nothing could get in or out.

During the night, the small stream had dried up and all that remained was a sandy riverbed. Without noticing, the young girl scooped her pot into the sand and when it was full, she placed it on her head and began to walk back to her village. It was not long before she met the old maid, who peered into her pot and saw that it was full of sand. The old maid laughed and told the little girl how stupid she was to fill her pot with sand, but the little girl did not acknowledge the malicious words, because the spirits were in her and her thoughts were pure.

Returning to the village, she removed the pot from her head and put it at the door of her mother's hut. Her mother looked into the bowl and saw that it was filled with sparkling, crystal clear water. She congratulated the child, and told her how clever she was to find such beautiful water when the river was so dry.

"So what happened to the angry old maid," I had asked when he seemed reluctant to finish the story.

"She was never seen again," he replied.

"If the girl was in a trance and the maid was never seen again, then how come anyone knew of the story?" I asked, not understanding.

Ben stared at the full moon and the light cast soft shadows on his dark face. The air was clean and the bush danced in shadows far away. Besides the occasional scurrying of a dassie (a rock rabbit), the night was quiet and the light bright enough to see for miles onto the plains below.

"The maid told me," he said softly.

I was suddenly startled from my thoughts, as a lion roared somewhere far in the distance, the sound echoing in the darkness. Normally I loved it, so majestic and powerful, but right then it tried to take away my will; just as the sound of crickets chirping in the nearby bushes tried to distract me. The leopard had not moved.

Lights from a vehicle arriving in the camp swept through the darkness. Bright and penetrating, the strong beams of the Land Rover's multiple spotlights lit the night, as it made the last turn to enter the camp. Like a lighthouse, the beam hurtled towards us from one side, getting brighter until it shone directly at us. It was dazzling in its brilliance, my eyes having become so accustomed to the dark.

I quickly closed my eyes to stop any further damage to my night vision and as I did so, I remembered how on occasions I had seen a leopard in the spotlight. The glare from two eyes was instantly changed to one, as he closed one eye to protect it from the light, while keeping the other open to see by; so I forced myself to open one eye when the light was still upon me. The vehicle completed its turn and as the night rushed back to fill the void, I switched eyes. It was then that he made his move, as I expected he might. He raised his body off the branch and turned in my direction.

Oh no, I thought to myself, *it is not going to end like this.* My body was stiff and sore from being immobile for so long and it was only in my mind that I could ready myself for the attack. My heart started beating faster, an instinctive reaction to get ready for a fight for my life.

In slow motion the leopard dipped his head, bent his front legs and dropped silently out of the tree. As he landed on the ground, I readied for the next leap to be in my direction. From that distance his feet would have to touch the ground only once and he would be close enough for a last leap to my throat. I braced my body as best I could and hoped. In my mind I was still trying to contain the positive thoughts that I had been repeating to myself, but in the face of such a threat, it was hard not to fall into the trap of negativity and fear.

In one fluid movement, he turned and disappeared into the thin bush without a sound. Relief swept over me, but I knew it was not over yet. That might be his way of coming back from behind, to take me when I least expected it.

I tried to move towards my rifle, but I was not sure my legs would work, so I slowly stood in an upright position first and then tried putting one foot gently forward.

Then the other, then the other, trying to move as fast as I could, all the while being aware of what was going on around and behind me. The sixty feet I had to cover seemed to have stretched itself, and at any moment I half expected to see a blur out of the corner of my eye. I moved as fast as I could, but at the same time I wanted to keep my movements natural, so as not to look like a lame duck, an easy prey.

The feel of the cold barrel on my palms was most welcome. I chambered a round into the breech and looked back in the direction the leopard had gone, but the night was still; even the crickets were silent. Not wanting to hang around there any longer I started walking back to the camp and had not gone but a couple of paces when I heard a sound behind me. I spun around expecting to see at least something, but the only sight that greeted me was that of a dark and empty night.

Several times I heard the same noise close behind. A dry leaf cracking, or a small twig being stepped on and each time I turned, the hairs on the back of my neck stood up and my scalp tightened. Although I could see nothing, I knew that something was following me. Resisting the urge to run, the walk back seemed a lot longer than the walk there. I turned my head and body around as far as I could, and walked almost sideways as I scanned the bush behind.

It was a great relief to once again be on the green grass by the swimming pool, well in the open where I could not be stalked. I went into the main building and there on the table was a powerful flashlight. Then filled with the bravery that comes from having both a gun and a light, I walked out onto the edge of the bush and began to shine the light into the darkness. The beam was strong and I swept it from side to side, but nothing reflected back at me. I was about to give up and go to bed, when I noticed a pair of eyes about two hundred feet away on the outer edge of the clearing, and as I put the beam back on the same spot - there was only one eye to be seen. I moved the light away for an instant and the eye was gone. I never did see it again.

THE FACE OF FEAR

Sometimes we would shoot a couple of impala. One for the pot and one for the lions, then at night after dinner in the boma, we would treat the guest to the sight of lions having a snack. That is assuming they were in the area, or even felt like a snack. For a pride of perhaps a dozen large cats, an impala certainly was nothing more than a snack.

While the guests were being escorted into an enclosure, I would take the carcass of the impala and wire-tie it to a stake in the open ground. The enclosure was walled on three sides and the front was covered in a layer of wire mesh. Wooden benches allowed people sit, as they watched flesh and bone being chewed and swallowed. Occasionally the lions were waiting in the bush as I tied up their treat. I hauled the impala from the back of the Land Rover and began to drag it on the dry ground, over to the clearing in front of the enclosure. The night was hot and clear. A million stars shone brightly above and the air was thick with the scents of an African evening.

The impala was not heavy, so I was able to hold the horns in my left hand and still leave my right hand free in case I should need it to get to my revolver. By the time I reached the front of the enclosure, the ten or so guests were seated and Grant, the owner of the lodge who was visiting for a few days, stepped out of the door and came to walk with me to tie down the bait.

So far I had not seen any lions waiting and there was always the chance that they would not show. If they had killed something large in the last day or so, then their bellies would still be full and an impala snack would not be tempting.

About fifty feet into the clearing, I let go of the impala. There was a steel stake driven far into the ground. I had with me a few pieces of thick wire and I set to the task of securing the buck, so that it would not be dragged away. I took my knife from its sheath and cut holes thorough the tendons of the legs; then I threaded the wire through the holes I had made and attached them to the stake. I was bent over, working away when Grant said that he was going to walk back to the enclosure. No problem, except that I would have to then keep an eye on the dark bush, but I was only a few minutes away from finishing and there were no sign of any lions.

A few weeks prior, I was doing exactly the same thing and the lions were waiting hungrily in the bush. All of a sudden, a lioness charged towards me from out of the darkness - such power. Still crouching, I reached for my revolver then stood and leveled it at her. *Please don't jump*, I thought as she came on, her eyes glowing in the light from the enclosure. Fortunately it was only a mock charge and still some twenty feet away, she broke off and turned back to the darkness of the bush. My heart was beating in my chest as I holstered my revolver and continued to tie the impala; glad that she had not pressed home the charge and jumped, for that jump surely would have been her last and was not what I wanted. Like most wild animals, the big cats are highly attuned to the smell of adrenaline. The scent seems to be picked up in an instant and in the case of a lion, it can be reason to press home an attack. Therefore in moments like those, I was always trying to control the natural fear that comes from seeing a huge cat hurtling towards you.

I was making the last twists on the wire, when I happened to notice a movement in the bush. The lions had arrived and that night was to be a show night. As I looked back down at the impala, the lioness began her charge. She broke into the clearing and headed directly for me, her long powerful strides closing the distance between us at an alarming rate.

My reactions were quick and I reached for my gun, but as my hand groped, I realized that my holster was empty. For a split second I fumbled once again, but there was nothing there, only the feeling of hard and empty leather. On she came as my world slowed and each stride became longer as she accelerated.

If you don't have it, you may as well fake it, I thought as I started to stand and held my hand out as though there was a gun in it.

The lioness was still charging, her ears flattened against her head and a purposeful look on her face. Her eyes were unmoving, focused intently on her prey. There I was with pointed finger, trying ever so hard to stop my fear from showing itself. One more stride and she would have been close enough to leap - then she stopped. Stopped in an instant, the dust rising around her as she stood and looked at me. Her eyes penetrating, looking for signs of weakness. We were twenty feet apart, playing the game of cat and mouse, except that this mouse had no intention of running. That would be suicide.

Five seconds felt like an eternity, and all we did was to look at one another and try to read the intent. I stood still, with my hands holding the imaginary gun in front of me and waited. My fear tried to raise its ugly head from within me, so I turned my concentration outward, towards that magnificent animal before me.

She snarled and seemed confused, as her tail flicked from side to side. The hot and rotten smell of her breath overcame all the other scents around. There was nothing for me to do, but stand there as though I had a gun and felt nothing by her presence. Both of which were totally untrue. I averted my eyes from hers and looked to the ground, so as not to invoke a challenge. Somehow I must have managed to convince her that I was armed and fearless, so at last she turned and walked back into the darkness, without so much as glance in my direction.

As soon as she was gone, I cautiously headed back to the enclosure. *Grant must have taken it from me when I was not watching*, I thought while keeping a wary eye behind. I rounded the corner of the enclosure and there was Grant, laughing away with my gun in his hand. I was not amused!

My draft papers arrived shortly after my encounter with the lioness and for the next two years, I was to become the property of the South African Navy. Compulsory draft was in force for the entire white male population and no matter how much I detested the idea of conforming to a military life, I had no choice in the matter.

Saying goodbye to Ben was hardest of all and I knew that I was going to miss his teachings and friendship. I did not realize just how much I would miss him, until I heard a few months later that he had been killed by a terrorist's land mine, as he drove to Mozambique to see one of his sons.

Dancing on Raindrops

HOME

PRESENT DAY

Driving up the hill I can't see my house, for it is tucked away behind the huge pine trees. Off to my left, way down in the valley, the lake is shimmering in the late afternoon sun. The sky is clear and a gentle breeze moves the treetops. It is one of those perfect days, the ones we would like to remember forever; yet with the passing of time, they fade with the evening light and are all too soon replaced by the brightness of another day.

My car takes the steep incline in its stride and as I raise the window, the lovely smell of leather fills my senses. Slowing down, I take the right turn into my driveway. On the side of the entrance is an old driftwood log with the word CALISTE – (Greek for most beautiful amongst others) carved into it. The brick driveway curves and winds in front of me and the sight of the pristine forest makes me smile. Somehow it seems almost surreal, the old forest with a carpet of sandstone lining its floor and winding between the huge trunks.

Rounding the last bend, there in front of me is my house. Built of stone, with two large oak front doors, it seems quite part of the forest. Pushing a button on the remote, a garage door opens, the white metal folding up to the ceiling. Open sesame. I park and walk out of the garage as the breeze ruffles my hair. The air is scented with the sweet fragrance of jasmine, mixed with the sappy smell of pine.

The house is only a single story, and the large stones in the front wall give it the appearance of strength and permanence. Walking to the front door, I put my hand on the large brass door handle, shiny and cool to the touch, push down and it opens effortlessly without a sound. Aah, I'm home - that warm feeling of being where I belong.

Now it is time to continue working on the presentation I have to give at noon tomorrow. I consider it more of a workshop, as I like to interact with my audience and get them involved. That after all is my subject; getting involved with your life and getting what you want out of it. By using my adventures as parables, I try to get my audience to relate to the fact that they are responsible for their lives, and that it is their thoughts that take them wherever it is they are going.

I have seen in my own life, countless times where my thoughts created my reality, be it good or bad. This is the work I have chosen for myself, to show people that we all have the ability to live any life we choose. Sometimes it can be hard, as we become so wrapped up in our daily drudge and so accustomed to our routine. But by changing our thoughts, we change our habits and this then changes our lifestyle.

The speech will be for a group of people who are interested in taking control of their lives, and I can feel the excitement grow within me. Hopefully there will be some with open minds, some with a belief in themselves and a desire for a better life. These are the people I love to work with, for they truly do hold their future in their heads.

I kick off my shoes and the wooden floor is cool on my feet. The house is quiet, only the sound of my breathing and the faint hum of the refrigerator. But that smell, yes I would always recognize that smell. My tummy rumbles; a chicken is roasting in the oven. I glance over and see that the timer still has an hour to go and realize that I must have just missed my mother, who had said she would stop by for a quick visit.

The room is large and almost round with a fireplace in the center, its brass chimney flue, an oversized inverted funnel, glows golden from the light streaming in from the large glass doors overlooking the front lawn. A seating area forms a semicircle around the fireplace. Created in the style of an African safari lodge, the ceiling rises to twenty feet in the center with large round poles supporting the roof. The floor is partly covered by a hand woven mat made from African bush grass, giving the room its unique odor, somewhat earthy yet with a faint tinge sweetness. On the walls are large photographs of 'the big five'. The leopard is my favorite and he seems to be looking at me no matter where I stand. Staring into his eyes, my mind is captivated and wanders to a time in Africa, a time of great learning for me. It was there that I began to understand fear and the influence it can have on our lives. Oh Africa, so beautiful and yet so harsh and violent...

To my left is the kitchen, from whence that mouth-watering smell is coming and to my right, the office and it is there that I head. Two computer monitors sit atop a large yellow wood desk in the shape of a raindrop and it looks out onto the lake in the valley below. The far side of the room has a built-in bookshelf that covers the entire wall. Hundreds of books, each adding to a particular smell that is found only where there are lots and lots of books; somewhat musty, yet exuding their richness in knowledge.

On the edge of the desk is a note. 'Just popped in to say hi. Thought you might be busy tonight so I put a chicken in the oven!! – Love you. Mum. xxx'

I bend over and turn on the computers, smiling. The room fills with the light sound of wurring, the unmistakable hum of tiny electric fans. Thinking about my lecture tomorrow, I sit down at my desk. The soft leather chair feels as though it was made for me, as I relax into the well-worn shape and open the top drawer. For the last few days I have been working on this presentation. I want it to be simple enough to be understood by everyone and hopefully it will sow a seed into the minds of my audience; to help them find the courage to look deep within themselves and set a course to creating the life they choose to live, not simply the one they have been living. To do this takes courage, lots of it.

Lifting the thick yellow folder from the drawer, I place it on the desk. Here are the thoughts I want to convey and all that remains is to put them into a logical and easy to understand sequence. This is knowledge that I have learned in my life, mostly from personal experience, but some through the teachings of others. On top of the pile is a rough list of the points I want to cover. Writing fills the page and arrows lead to the different headings, but in amongst the mess are the seven keys to success. Taking a couple of blank sheets from the bottom drawer, I pick up my favorite soft lead pencil and write a column of numbers on the left-hand side of the new page. 1-7.

I begin to glance over the pages in front of me and as I do so, it dawns on me that none of this is taught in our lives - it all has to be learned after our so-called education is complete. Perhaps the most fundamental and important aspects to life, have to be acquired at a time when our formal learning days are over.

Dancing on Raindrops

1. SECRETS TO YOUR SUCCESS

ATTITUDE

Thinking back on my experiences, I realize that the seven key principles are all very much interlinked. They weave a tangled web between one another, but perhaps the most fitting way to begin any journey, is to be sure you have the correct attitude. Your attitude is created from the sum of your thoughts and experiences, it is the way you look at life - and the way you look at life is exactly what life will give you.

It is the conscious mind that holds your thoughts and gives you the ability to operate the way you do, on a day-to-day level. You have the ability to control these thoughts and although it is often hard, by doing so, you can take control of your life. If you can hold true to this principle, not only will you be able to control your attitude, but you will also be able to influence your future, both physically and financially. It is however so much easier to look at your surroundings, see a lack and believe that this is your lot - but if you do that, it surely will be your lot.

An abundant attitude will place its power on anything it touches; magnifying, enhancing and increasing. It is more than a passing deliberation or comment. It is a deep-rooted belief that no matter what happens, there will always be more.

Ben told me a story about an African king called Shaka, literally translated to mean 'the beetle.' Shaka was the son of a chief and his mother was an orphaned princess. When he was small, his parents separated and his mother took him to live with another tribe, but soon they were cast out from that tribe and left to fend for themselves. As a young man Shaka excelled in the army and soon his genius at creating and implementing new types of warfare, led him to great power. He became the chief by forming his own army, then killing his half-brother.

When his mother died, he went mad and the noon sun was taken from the sky. (An eclipse.) He burned the crops and slaughtered all the cattle, turning an abundant nation into a wasteland. Everyone was held responsible for his mother's death and he killed mercilessly. He even went so far as to kill his own son, but in the end it was his half-brothers Dingaan and Mhlangane who stabbed him to death.

"It takes great courage to reach great heights," Ben said in his rough charcoal voice, "but if you do not have the right attitude, it is easy to become giddy and fall into the darkness." He believed that everyone could achieve the things they want in their lives - that is if they want them badly enough. "It is this 'want' emotion that can give you the state of mind required to have anything," he said.

I smile, as I remember that my life was not always as good as it is now. Prior to my adventures as a game ranger, my future seemed headed towards finishing school, then going to college to become an accountant. All that took an unexpected turn one day, for within the span of a short conversation, the experience of which sorely tested *my* attitude, every semblance of my previous reality was shattered. My life headed in a direction I would never have imagined.

BE AWARE OF THE POWER OF YOUR ATTITUDE.

* For more information visit:
  www.dancingonraindrops.com

Good luck or bad luck,
it's still luck...
and better than no luck all.

Dancing on Raindrops

DOWN AND OUT

Before my sixteenth birthday and three years after my parents had divorced, I was home from school one weekend when my father called me into his office.

"It is time for you to experience life, so here is one hundred pounds, now go and pack yourself a bag and I shall have Liz take you to the station. Don't ever come back," said the voice of a mad man. That was it, that was the only explanation I received. That too was our last communication for many years.

Liz was my father's new wife who was pregnant at the time, and it seemed to me as though it was out with the old litter and in with the new. I went up to my bedroom, took my rucksack from the cupboard and tried to decide what to take with me, but I seemed incapable of making such a big decision. In the end I simply stuffed a few odd clothes into the bag and stumbled down the stairs to meet the car. I remember clearly the only words that were spoken on the short journey were as we stopped at the station.

"I'm sorry it has to be like this," she said. *Me too*, I thought, but I couldn't manage a reply, so I simply closed the door and made my way to the platform - my mind was a mess.

Winter was well on its way and the bitter wind would not let up. I was dressed in only a pair of jeans, a light sweater and a thin jacket. I tried to find shelter behind a pillar, but nothing kept the wind away. After what seemed like an eternity of waiting in the cold (something like ten minutes), the train arrived. A one-way fare was supposed to cost forty pounds. That meant forty percent of my total cash, there had to be another way, so before I boarded without a ticket I made sure to locate the conductors, for I did not want to be in one of their coaches. The train pulled off and I was on my way. The warmth inside slowly thawed my cold body.

Fortunately it was a slow train that I was on, so that meant that we stopped at every station. It also meant that I was continually getting up to see where the conductors were. As they moved down the train towards me, I began to formulate a plan and it was with perfect timing that we arrived at a busy station, so I moved to the end of the train that the conductors had come from. Good luck was with me that day and soon the train stopped at Kings Cross station in the heart of London, and hundreds of people began to make their way to the exit.

I noticed what was happening. All passengers were being made to show their tickets at the exit, before being allowed out of the station. That was potentially catastrophic to my plan, so I raced to the line that was forming and placed myself near the front of it. A frightfully un-British sort of thing to do, but no one said anything. My idea was to have lots of people behind me, people who were in a rush to get somewhere. My turn.

"Ticket please," said the ticket collector.

"Ek is jammer, maar ek het nie 'n kaartjie nie," I replied in Afrikaans, a South African language.

"Your ticket please sir," he said once again. Fortunately, as I had hoped, the people behind me were becoming agitated.

"Come on come on," shouted someone at the rear of the line.

"Ek is jammer, maar ek het nie 'n kaartjie nie," I repeated, trying to look as dumb as possible.

"Hurry it up!" Someone boomed in a loud voice. The ticket collector was weighing the possibilities in his mind and it did not take him long to make a decision, as all the while the cries of exasperation were slowly growing.

Dancing on Raindrops

"Bloody foreigners," the collector mumbled to himself and with that he waved me through.

Oh yea, I had made it to London and it was time to look for somewhere to stay. My new situation was so unexpected and so off the wall, that I had not even had time to think about a plan. One moment I was attending a fine private school; I had a home, friends and family, but in the next I was down and out in London.

On the train, I had thought of the possibility of trying to get a job in a hotel. That would give me somewhere to stay and an income. Bellhop, baggage boy, whatever, I did not care. In days gone by, I had spent time in some of London's finest hotels and so it was to these that I headed. The Dorchester was my first stop.

Trying to look as smart as possible, I entered the main lobby and the smell of warm air and money greeted me. It was a smell to which I was accustomed and it seemed strange to have only one hundred pounds in my pocket. I put my shoulder bag in a corner out of the way and went to the reception desk.

"Good afternoon, I'm looking for work and thought you might have something for me," I said trying to sound as up beat as possible.

"Yes, we may well have something available," the kind lady behind the counter said. I was beginning to like her more and more. She continued to ask questions and fill in the answers on her sheet of paper. Then it came, the dreaded question that I had been hoping to avoid.

"How old are you?" she asked. That lovely smile from moments before had transformed into the look of a vampire. To my eyes anyway.

"Sorry son, but we are not allowed to employ anyone of your age, it's against the law." So it went for the next five hotels, each with the same song. You are too young to be employed.

The early winter evening was upon me and still I had nowhere to stay. Snow began to fall, as I wandered down some street in a daze. There in front of me was a church and an idea sprang to mind. *Yes, surely I will find shelter there.* I walked up to the rectory door and knocked. In fact I think I put my hand against the door and as I was shaking so badly from the cold, that in itself would have done the knocking.

Creeeek, the rusty or frozen hinges squeaked as the door opened. A wall of hot air rode over me and standing in the doorway, was the pastor. He was a portly man in his mid fifties and dressed in a pair of cream slacks and a light shirt. I explained my plight and asked if it were possible for him to give me shelter for the night.

"No one is allowed to sleep in the church," the old man said in a high pitched voice, as he closed the door on me.

Oh well, the best part of that experience was the fifteen seconds of hot air, I thought as I continued to walk aimlessly down the street once again. Soon, I noticed a police station on the other side of the road and I crossed over and went inside. I knew that in some parts of the world, if you went into a police station and asked for a cell for the night, you would usually get it - sometimes along with breakfast in the morning.

"No, you have to commit a crime first," the police officer behind the counter informed me. Of course I begged and pleaded, but he was having none of it. I threw my bag over my shoulder and went outside, where as it happened there was a construction site next door. A brick seemed to be looking up at me.

"Me, me, me," it shouted, so I picked it up and went and stood outside the station window. I had fully intended to throw it.

How long will I get for this? I wondered, but before I had a chance to act, the police officer was at the door.

"You lob that through my window and I'll lock you up for years," the miserable, mean, horrible and nasty man said. Years were not what I had in mind.

By then it was dark and along the way I had stopped at a couple of what looked like cheap hotels, but their price of fifty pounds for the night was well out of my league. I knew that I could not keep on walking all night, as I would soon freeze to death on the sidewalk. I passed the entrance to the Marble Arch subway station and the warm air wafted up from the tunnels below. Eureka, that was the answer to my prayers; they had been all around me, but I had failed to notice. I headed down into the subway.

The first level was busy and there were people sleeping on the benches, so I headed lower and with each level there were fewer people, until at last I found one that was deserted. I walked to the very end of the platform and sat on the concrete floor. I was exhausted, wet and hungry, but oh so happy to be out of the bitter cold. As I sat, I wondered why I had chosen London of all places. I certainly knew that a big city could be a most inhospitable place.

Why didn't you go north to some little village, somewhere where the country folk live? I asked myself, but I was too tired to continue my interrogation, so while feeling very lonely, I rolled out the few clothes that remained in my bag, lay on top of them and went to sleep.

It seemed like only minutes later that someone kicked me and I woke with a start. People were everywhere. The platform was crowded with commuters going off to work and there I was, lying down amongst a forest of legs, trying to wake myself enough to get up. Moments later the train arrived and people were shoving and hustling to get aboard, as I tried to rise to my feet. I picked up my few belongings and headed outside. It was still cold and dark, and although the snow had stopped, it had turned to slush in the gutters. I found a temporary sanctuary in a coffee shop and the hot liquid felt fantastic, as the caffeine set to work immediately on my empty stomach.

What to do? In less than twenty-four hours I had had enough of the city. Work, that was my main priority, anything that would pay, so I set off and started asking. Butchers, bakers and candlestick makers, I stopped at them all but everywhere the answer was the same.

"You are too young to work."

For lunch I bought a pint of milk and a loaf of bread, then I sat in a park and fed the pigeons and myself. Half the loaf certainly filled my empty stomach, so I saved the rest for dinner. It was still cold, but the wind had stopped and the sun was trying to peak through the English grayness above. All afternoon I continued my search for work and a place to stay. I inquired at a couple of small bed and breakfasts, but everywhere was too expensive, so I had to resign myself to another night in the subways.

So it went for the next five days and then the evening paper changed everything. There was a yacht race in Southampton. *That's it,* I thought as I saw the sign. *In the morning, I will catch a train to Southampton and get a job aboard a race boat when they come back into port.* The fact that I knew nothing at all about boats did not even enter my mind! It was just a feeling inside that that was the right thing to do at the time.

My final night in the subway was much the same, cold, damp and heartless, but at last I had a plan - a plan that took me away from the city. The next morning found me heading west aboard the first train to Southampton. I had to pay for that one.

The darkest hour is right before the dawn.

2. SECRETS TO YOUR SUCCESS

THOUGHTS and VISUALIZATIONS

THOUGHTS

The thoughts you hold in your head create your reality. This is one of the most powerful statements in the universe. All power is directed and molded by your thoughts, and everything that has ever been created was first a thought.

I wish I could have truly grasped the supreme importance of that concept earlier in my life, but fortunately, even as a very young man, I have always looked on the bright side of life and expected things to work out for the best. They do, even though they may not seem to at the time. There certainly were moments of despair, as I wandered the streets of London looking for somewhere to sleep. Thoughts of *what if I can't get work*, or *what if I run out of money,* would enter my head and instead of dwelling on them, I concentrated on how I wanted to change the situation. The cold, that was the first thing I wanted to change, but my immediate need was an income.

In Southampton, again lodging was a problem, because due to the race all the small hotels were full, but I found a place to stay in an attic. A bare double mattress lay on a sheet of plywood nailed to the ceiling beams and even the fact that I had to share the bed, did not detract from how good it felt to be out of the cold and the subways.

The Fastnet yacht race is renowned for having plenty of wind, but that year it was different, the boats were becalmed at sea and were taking much longer than expected to finish the course – around Fastnet Rock and back, a distance of about six hundred miles. Every day I had to pay the landlady twelve pounds, so after three or four days I was getting desperate and at the same time, longing to be back in Africa.

I found work in a boat yard well before the race finished and still with twenty pounds remaining in my pocket. Then shortly after, I received word from a friend that there was an airline ticket waiting for me at Heathrow airport. A one-way from London to Johannesburg, a gift from my mother who had somehow heard of my situation, for we had not spoken since before I was tossed out of the house – she's the best.

Africa, that was where I wanted to be and so with a most welcome ticket beckoning me, I set off the next day back to London and my spirit truly soared. At heart I am an African, not because I was born in Africa, but because Africa was born in me.

Returning to Africa was exactly what I had wanted to happen. That was the thought I had held in my mind, day after freezing day, then out of the blue it happened. It is a concept of which I had no knowledge at the time, but throughout the experiences in my life I have come to see that time and time again the things that happen to me and the way I deal with them, are the result of my thoughts. Maybe being trapped under a sunken barge in a crocodile infested river, or perhaps wanting to sail around the world when I had no job and no money, will be the story that helps you understand the supreme importance of your thoughts.

Those thoughts that are held in your conscious mind for long enough and with enough belief, will soon make their presence known in your subconscious universe. When it is repeated, it begins to take on a force of its own and the more confirmation it receives from you, the more it is able to stand alone. Soon it can begin to exert its own influence, but it is interesting to note that the subconscious does not differentiate between fact and fiction, it is all simply information.

When you focus your mental energy and feelings towards your dreams, they will become so real within your mind that they will create a void or an imbalance. This imbalance is at the very root of creation itself, because when you think something that is not in existence, nature by design tries to make it so. Behind the scenes, unknown to your conscious-self, that energy is trying to create a balance. There is a state of disequilibrium, which due to the laws of the universe, must be brought back to stability.

It can happen in two ways.

Firstly, the thought can become overpowered by your other thoughts and then it will be forgotten. If you take your eyes off your dreams, you will loose your way and thus restore the balance. At some time or another we all fall victim to losing sight of our dreams, usually because something else gets in the way, something that seems far more important at the time.

However, if you refuse to let that happen, then the only other available alternative is to make it so and to restore harmony. Nature has no option, in a universe that is constantly seeking equilibrium, but to create your wishes - because you were just too darn stubborn to give up or become distracted.

Your mind is rather like a garden, for if you plant specific seeds, you will get exactly those flowers. That is if you plant seeds at all, for most people leave the tending of their mental gardens to the winds of fate, which bring with them a variety of weeds and unwanted growth. That is exactly the unkempt garden you will have, if you do not put in the effort required to plant, weed and fertilize. You have the ability to think about whatever you want, but most of the time your thoughts are those that are suggested by your surroundings. To think of these things is easy, as the suggestions are constant and often overwhelming. It is far harder to think the thoughts of your dreams and desires, regardless of present appearances. To think of the life that you want to live when you are not actually living it, is difficult, but if you persevere you can accomplish this and can have anything you want.

"Who you think you are is only a thought."

VISUALIZATION

Visualization is the ability to see a clear picture in your mind's eye. It is not enough to have a vague idea of what you want.

"I want more money," is too vague - what do you want, a dollar, or a million dollars? You cannot hope to transmit an idea unless you have a clear picture of it. If it is a new home that fills your thoughts, then cut out a picture of the same or a similar house and place it where you will see it often.

Like the helmsman of a ship, keep your eyes on the compass of your desires and once you can picture your idea, begin to add your other senses. Smell the flowers, hear the birds, taste the air, imagine how you will feel, until it becomes so real and you can see the desired result so clearly in your mind's eye, that your visualization will begin to take on an existence of its own. The more you think about your visualization, the clearer it will become, for it is the details that produce the desire and faith necessary for your action.

After my time in the African bush and still with Ben's death very much on my mind, I was drafted into the South African Navy. Over the next two years, I learned first hand the power of a thought. One thought in an extreme situation, could save your life, but Ben had already told me that.

The Navy was not a career that I wished to pursue, so it was not long before all of us new recruits were talking about what we would do once we were out of uniform. It was at that time that I began to form an idea of exactly what I wanted. Sail around the world in my own yacht. Yes, that was it!

...But that is still many adventures away.

BE AWARE OF YOUR THOUGHTS AND THE IMAGES YOU HOLD IN YOUR MIND.

* For more information visit:
  www.dancingonraindrops.com

Dancing on Raindrops

EXTREMELY WET

THE FEW

The new Navy recruits including myself were sent to Saldanha Bay, a dry and dusty fishing village on the west coast of South Africa and home of the Navy's basic training camp. There we learned the rudiments of seamanship and of course being the Navy - how to hurry up and wait. It was not a course that could be failed and one of the objectives was to get us into the habit of obeying orders. Something I have never been good at.

Basic training was three months of running. No matter where you went, you had to run there. It was easy enough once I found my feet and became used to the routine. The normal military obsession for neatness prevailed and even our beds had to be exactly square, so much so that for daily inspection we would iron the corners of the bed, to make a sharp and rigid angle.

Walking on the floor of the dormitory was done with the aid of 'taxis,' small pieces of blanket placed under our boots and upon which we would slide over the sparkling floor. That helped to keep it polished and prevented footprints on the glossy surface. Once basic training was completed, we had to choose which specialty to pursue. I had heard that the divers were the elite of the Navy, but owing to both the physical and mental strains, very few managed to finish the course, however, once you were qualified, life was supposed to be a breeze.

Simonstown lies at the foot of some of the Cape's most magnificent mountains. Rocky peaks rise quickly from the shoreline and the quaint little town is steeped in naval history. On the shores of the warm waters of False Bay and home to the Navy's diving school, it is only a few miles from Cape Point; the meeting place of the Indian and Atlantic oceans.

We started the course with one hundred and twenty-five aspiring divers and day by day the numbers dwindled. The first three weeks was nothing but physical and mental torture, designed specifically to weed out the weak and the unfit, both physically and mentally. The day started at five am with a three mile run to warm us up a little. Twenty minutes for breakfast and then back to hell. A ten mile run up the side of the mountain with a sixty pound backpack, followed by a mile swim - all before lunch.

The afternoons were the worst. We would kit up in full wetsuits, complete with weight belts, hood, mask and snorkels and then choose a friend; a wooden log weighing fifty pounds and head for the beach. Breathing through the snorkel was bad enough, but when the instructors threw sand into both the snorkel and mask, it became more than just uncomfortable. Two or three hours of that extreme exercise was often enough to send some into tears, or have others pass out from heat exhaustion. Every day there were those who succumbed and gave up, opting rather to spend the next two years as gate guards. Preferring anything to get them away from their present hell.

After dinner, the torment continued well into the night. We would be allowed a few hours sleep, then were abruptly woken in the wee hours of the morning, to continue with more swimming and exercises. By the end of the first week we were down to sixty, the second week forty and as the first month ended, only twenty-five men were left.

I had met Georgeo at the beginning of basic training and we instantly became friends. When we started divers' course together, we made a pact that neither of us were allowed to quit. Should one of us wish to give up at any stage, then it was up to the other to either carry him, or kick him so hard that the pain would make him continue. It never actually became necessary, but the belief of it often kept us going when others were falling by the wayside. His calm attitude, even in the most frightening of situations, was a rare and desirable trait and not once did I ever hear him speak of giving up. He had made up his mind and no matter what, he was going to pass. I was glad to have him as my friend.

It was only in the second month that we actually started to dive and then there was but one cardinal rule. Surface for air and you were immediately disqualified. The instructors went to great pains to try to get the remaining few to surface, using every trick they knew of. Such as turning off your air and removing your mask, ripping the mouthpiece out of your mouth, then punching you in the stomach. Trying to get you to panic and rather than asking your buddy for air, heading straight for the surface. Sure enough, the tactic worked and almost daily someone would be sent packing, feeling dejected and holding his head low in shame, having come so far only to fail.

Simply removing your mouthpiece from your mouth, meant that you had to go through a series of procedures before you were able to put it back and take your next breath. The twin hose regulator had no non-return valves, so by the time you put the mouthpiece back in your mouth, both the inlet and exhaust hoses had filled with water. You would then have to grab the exhaust hose with your left hand, turn your body to a horizontal position and slowly rotate to your left, almost onto your back, while pulling down on the exhaust hose and blowing out. You would have to be careful in taking that next breath, as sometimes there was still water left in the hose and if you had used up all your breath – well, then there was no option but to drink the cupful of water before you could breathe.

Sometimes we would do an endurance dive and the idea was to spend as long as we could underwater, using only one dive tank. It was incredibly boring, as we slowly moved up and down a two hundred foot line that was laid on the shallow bottom. Barely moving to conserve our oxygen, Georgeo and I made our way up the line for the umpteenth time, as we tried to break the record of three and a half-hours. In front, I noticed another group swimming towards us and behind them, an instructor with a two foot octopus in his hand was almost upon them. He came up behind one of the unsuspecting divers, pulled his mask forward, deposited the octopus on his face and let go the mask.

The octopus clung around his head and would not let go, as the mask pushed it harder onto his face. The diver ripped off his mask and tried to remove the creature, but as he pulled one tentacle and released it to grab another - so the tentacle that he had removed would again wrap around his head. He reached for his knife and began to sever each tentacle in turn and shortly there were octopus parts floating in the water beside him. When it eventually came off his face, the diver's unmasked eyes were large and I am sure the adrenaline pumped through his body, but he had not surfaced.

It could be worse, I thought to myself, as Georgeo and I continued on our way. *It could have been me!*

The doctors too, did their share of weeding. We were all given a brain scan, an EEG and those who failed due to having latent epilepsy were perhaps the most dejected of all, for they did not even know of the condition before the scan.

I was worried about the hearing tests. For years I had done a lot of shooting and I was so concerned that it might have dulled my hearing, that when we went into the silent underground bunker, I pulled Georgeo aside and asked for his help. The plan was that whenever the doctor pressed the button to send the sound to my headset, he would give me a signal. I was not about to be kicked out after so long an ordeal, simply because of a possible slight hearing impediment. I went into the glass-lined, sound-proofed booth and put on my headset.

Behind the doctor, I could see Georgeo was in position and as the doctor pushed his button, Georgeo scratched his head and I pushed my button; indicating that I had heard the sound. The first few were easy and then the sound became more difficult to hear, until I could hear nothing. I simply waited until Georgeo scratched his head and then pushed the button. My test seemed to take longer than anyone else's, and when it was over the doctor was amazed. My hearing was so good that I could hear things that even dogs can't hear!

The dentists also had a chance to practice their trade. Most fillings needed to be removed and replaced in the shape of a cone. Should air get behind the filing during a dive, on surfacing the tooth might explode. By having them all refilled, the idea was to allow the filling to pop out, rather than losing the whole tooth due to the pressure difference between the bottom and the surface.

At the end there were only fifteen of us left - all of whom had been close to hell and back. Gone were the days of starched shirts and shiny boots; but on the other hand, our work then included extremely dangerous and life threatening situations. A far cry from the boredom of guarding a gate. It was both with pride and relief that I hand-sewed the divers' badge onto my shirts at the end of the course and when I was done, I went to get some dinner. It was a strange feeling at first, walking to the front of the line and being served immediately, then sitting at a reserved table, no more hustling for a seat. The perks were beginning to come our way.

SUNKEN TREASURE

One hundred and twenty feet below the ocean surface, it was cold. A mind numbing cold. Georgeo and I were looking for something metallic. The Navy's sonar had picked up a metallic object on the seabed and it was our job to find out what it was - then remove it. All week we had been doing the same thing and had found an array of treasure in the form of old anchors, chain and even the odd metal bucket.

At that depth, our neoprene wetsuits were squeezed so thin, that it was almost like being wrapped in a sheet of paper. The slightest scratch on the surface of the neoprene and it would tear all the way through. Visibility was not good and because of our depth we had lost the red, orange and yellow colors from the spectrum. Everything was a murky gray, as small particles of 'stuff' hung suspended and immobile in the cold water.

We had placed a stake in the seabed, then taken a line from there out about one hundred feet and started swimming in a large circle. Once the circle was complete, we would take in about twenty feet of the line and repeat the process. A circular search.

Georgeo and I were connected by a six foot long piece of rope attached to our upper arms, and hopefully that would prevent us from becoming separated.

Slowly kicking and with arms crossed on our chests to conserve body heat, we floated about four or five feet off the sandy bottom, scanning the surface below for any signs of the metallic culprit. Breathing slow and controlled, the noise of the air passing from the tank to our lungs made a high-pitched sound as we breathed in, and a throaty low one as our exhaled bubbles raced to the surface, expanding with every foot. The large ones break apart to form smaller bubbles, these then expand and so the process keeps going, all the way to the top.

When I get home I'm going to sit in a hot bath for a week, I was thinking to myself, when I felt a tug on my arm. *Great, we have found it.*

I turned my head to the left to look at my partner. His eyes seemed to fill his mask. Georgeo was an avid collector of old bottles. He would find them from time to time while we were diving, so the first idea to go through my frozen brain was, *bottles - a huge mountain of them.* Octopus love bottles too and often they will collect them and make a home for themselves on the desolate seabed. But that made no sense; not from eyes that large.

Treasure, it must be treasure and the image of a cask laden with pearls, gold and diamonds shot through my mind, as I scanned the bottom trying to make head or tail of what he had seen. Georgeo by that time had realized that I had not seen the 'thing', so he pointed, arm outstretched and up at about thirty degrees. He opened and closed his fingers against his thumb - a munching and chomping - the biting signal; followed by the same action, but with his fingers pointing up - 'I'm scared.' I lifted my vision to the angle he was pointing at and there it was, a silhouette in the murky depths. I blinked and tried to focus my salty eyes, as my heart began to pound. The cold had gone.

The shark was about twelve feet long and its outline instantly distinguishable. A sharp pointed snout and smooth white underbelly, the unmistakable shape of a sleek killing machine - a great white. The mother of all the predators in the ocean, an eating machine so perfect that it has not changed for thousands of years. Jaws - even the word evokes fear in the hearts of most people.

I watched, fascinated by the sight as the fear began to rise within me. It seemed so serene and harmless on one hand and yet so dangerous and terrifying on the other. Swimming on the outer edge of our visibility, the shark crossed in front of us and as it was about to disappear from our view, it turned. One flick of its tail and it was speeding towards me, so quickly that I did not have a chance to react. The power, beauty and grace of that monster was not lost to me in that instant. The next however was quite different. It slammed into my shoulder with the side of its nose, jerking my body around from the force of impact. It was the eyes that caught my attention and remained as an image in my mind. So cold and devoid of any emotion or feeling, as if its heart were made of ice. Yes, the fear was now real.

Often a shark will taste its prey before taking a bite and that is exactly what was happening. We composed ourselves, pulled our puny knives out of their sheaths on our legs and sank to the bottom, watching as it circled slowly at the outer edge of our vision. If it liked the taste of the first pass, then the next one would be with jaws wide open. Both of us knew that. So there we sat, with our knives tucked under our arms to avoid any reflection of the shiny steel, feeling totally helpless. What chance did we have? Surely none.

After a while it was not there anymore and it seemed as though the shark had moved on. We looked at each other, breathing half a sigh of relief. The half that signaled we were still in one piece. The other half knowing that if he did return, the odds of us both getting out alive were slim.

An old divers' joke passed through my mind. *Why do divers carry knives and always dive with a buddy?*

So if you see a shark, you can stab your buddy and swim away!

Time was moving on. At that depth we only had about twenty minutes of bottom time. If that were exceeded, it would mean that we would have to spend a great deal of extra time at a shallow depth, waiting and breathing while the excess nitrogen was slowly released from our bodies. Failure to do so, would likely give us what is commonly known as 'the bends.' The high concentration of nitrogen is not a problem when you are under pressure, but as soon as you return to the surface, the reduced pressure causes the gas to come out of solution and form tiny bubbles. These little bubbles of nitrogen can get stuck anywhere in the body and if it happens within the muscle tissue it is extremely painful, but in the brain it is often fatal.

I looked at my watch and we had five minutes of bottom time remaining, so we decided to finish the search. Neither of us wanted to go back to that cold and desolate place again, but most importantly it gave us both a bit more time to see if the shark would return, before we started our ascent.

When a large shark is about and the water is murky, the place I hate to be is in the middle zone, between the surface and the bottom. Here there is twice as much area to look at, up, down, left, right, back and front. A shark can just as easily attack from any direction.

We continued on our way, but there was no dreaming of bottles in the sand, or caskets laden with treasure. Our progress was slow as we kept a wary eye out for the shark to return and as our bottom time came to an end, we could see the spike in the ground. The search was complete and we had found nothing.

Georgeo pulled the orange metal spike out of the sand and secured the loose line floating about in front of him, while I kept a look out. Now was the moment. We looked at each other and signaled that it was going to be a fast ascent, both content to accept the problems that that can potentially cause.

One, two, three and we pushed ourselves off the bottom and started kicking for the surface. Long powerful strokes; breathing out, always breathing out. As the surrounding pressure became less, the air inside our lungs expanded, so we had to breathe out in order to keep the same volume in our chest. Our rate of ascent was such that not once did either of us have to breathe in.

Looking up, down and all around, we swam back to back. The higher we went, the lighter it became and at about thirty feet, we could just make out the bottom of the boat. Thank heaven it was where it was supposed to be.

Twenty feet, ten feet and we adjusted our aim for the stern, for there was the dive ladder and safety. As we approached, so our kicking took on a sense of urgency and the faster we ascended, the faster we had to breathe out. On breaking the surface, our momentum carried our bodies half way out of the water and before we fell back, we grabbed onto the edge of the step, pulling and kicking with all our might to get aboard. In one motion, we flopped onto the deck like fish out of water, but safe.

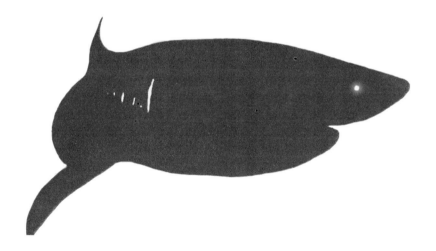

UP IS OK

My job for the next few days was to teach helicopter aircrews how to jump out of a helicopter and into the sea. If a situation arose where people were in trouble in the water, the aircrew would then be able to reach them quickly.

It promised to be an interesting time, as I had never jumped out of a chopper before. The highest jump I had done up until then was about ninety feet, from the mast of a destroyer. Wow, that gravity sure is powerful stuff. On that day, someone lost his front teeth and another came up coughing blood, all a result of not striking the water correctly. Straight in, toes pointed down and head looking horizontally, legs pushed together and hands firmly by your side. Simple enough on a calm day, but we were about to try it with the downward rushing wind of a helicopter's rotors.

Eight o'clock in the morning and we were ready. My class consisted of six students, all new to the air force. We had spent the previous hour going over the what and how, then practiced by jumping off a nearby table. Our chariot was a French helicopter, a Wasp, a collection of nuts and bolts trying to shake themselves loose.

Our pilot, a veteran in his forties, looked upon his machine as a total extension of himself; whatever he thought, that is what the machine would do. The doorman was an older man who had no intention of jumping out of a perfectly good chopper - and was quick to say so on our first meeting.

I discussed the itinerary with the pilot and his doorman. We were going to start slow and easy, the first jump to be made from no more than ten feet, with zero forward speed. Simple enough and if anyone did get it badly wrong, at least they would still be okay. We broke the class into two groups, so as not to overload the small helicopter. That would mean three students on each load.

Soon we were airborne and heading for the ocean about a half a mile away. False Bay was crystal clear with hardly a ripple on the surface. We could not have chosen a better day to begin. A boat was waiting exactly where planned and their task would be to collect the jumpers and take them back to the shore, then return for another load. Also, in case of any problems, it would be good to have them at hand.

Hovering at ten feet, I waved to my friends in the boat and they knew we were ready to go. I removed my headset, as the first student cautiously placed his feet on the landing gear and looked back at me. Oh yea, he was nervous all right.

"Keep your head up and remember to step off. Do not jump," I shouted at the top of my voice, not sure if he could hear above the din of the motor.

"Ready, set, go!" I yelled. Nothing happened, he stood there frozen to the fuselage. I tapped him on his shoulder and he looked over at me, eyes wide. I then gave him the thumbs up signal and nodded at the same time. Poor guy he was scared, but he took a deep breath and leapt off the chopper. As he jumped, so he leaned forward and the down draft hit his back, tilting him even more. Ouch, but a great belly flop. He was all right and his wetsuit kept him buoyant as he looked up and waited for his buddy to jump.

I hand signaled the doorman to pass on the message to the pilot to move forward a little, to be above clear water. Looking at the next guy, I gave him a hand signal lecture about the errors of his friend.

You have to keep your body vertical, I mimed and wished I could have verbalized the instructions once again. He slid to the edge and placed his feet on the strut. I tapped him on the shoulder and nodded. Oh perfect. He stepped off the strut, body vertical and disappeared beneath the surface of the ocean, soon returning to give us a thumbs up signal.

Moving forward, we repeated the process and by the time I had my headset back on, the boat had picked up the three jumpers and was ready to head for the shore. We took a little joy ride low over the beach, our pilot enjoying himself immensely. Touching down on the helipad, the next three came aboard and we repeated the process. All morning and three jumps apiece, we kept static at ten feet and soon everyone was making a perfect entry into the water. After lunch, we would try a little forward motion and see how they handled that.

Ten knots forward and ten feet of height had its initial problems. Due to the forward speed, the body had to impact the water at a slight angle. The faster the speed the more the angle, but the guys were getting the hang of it.

By the end of day two, everyone had made ten jumps, the last of which were from twenty feet with ten knots of speed. They had done well and as the final student left, I put on my headset and spoke to the pilot. For two days I had been watching other people jump, but I had not done a jump myself. It was my chance.

"Hey captain, I'm going to jump out if that's all right by you." I spoke into the microphone.

"Sure no problem. What height do you want," he replied.

"Oh whatever, give me a nice high jump and thanks again for the help," I said as I took off the headset and felt the chopper begin to climb.

Gee this looks good and high, I thought as I looked out the door. I glanced at the altimeter and we were at seventy feet. Nice one.

Crawling to the door, I gave the doorman the thumbs up. *Yes, this looks perfect.* As I was about to jump, the old man grabbed my arm. 'Wait,' he motioned. Without the headset I could hear nothing, but seconds later the chopper began to rise.

Yea, very funny. I looked over at the altimeter once again and it was reading one hundred feet. The doorman had a quizzical expression on his face as he looked at me and he gave me a thumbs up. I returned the gesture.

All right here goes. I took a deep breath and prepared to jump. Once again, the doorman grabbed me by the arm and motioned me to wait. The chopper climbed.

These guys are crazy. I glanced at the altimeter. One hundred and forty feet. *You lot are nuts and I am out of here*, was my last thought before I leapt out of the doorway.

The wind outside was a violent, living thing. As if gravity by itself was not enough, I accelerated faster than I would have believed possible. *Keep vertical*, I repeated to myself, looking at the horizon and seeing out of the corner of my eye, the surface of the water below. Far, far below.

My arms were doing the 'wax on - wax off' routine, flailing wildly to try to keep myself stable and my stomach felt as if it had risen into my throat. Every millisecond the water came closer and I was constantly adjusting my body to keep my balance. About half way, the downdraft dissipated and for an instant there was no wind at all - then it began to come from below. Slight hand movements kept me in tune and the corrections became finer as I neared the water. The afternoon sun made it sparkle and dance, as I approached at a frightening speed.

Okayyyyyy......NOW, I judged the moment of impact and straightened my body. Toes pointed, head horizontal, hands and feet welded into position. I waited an instant, knowing that there was nothing more that I could do besides hoping that my entry was going to be perfect.

Impact was silent, but for the shock that ran through me. My eyes closed. A loud noise exploded in my head as it went below the surface. Down and down I plunged and began to feel pressure on my eardrums. I waited to bleed off a little speed, before putting out my arms to slow my descent. The pressure in my ears was building to a painful level and still with closed eyes, I tried to estimate how fast I was traveling. Not in miles per hour, but rather am I still going so fast, that lifting my arms would tear them out of their sockets.

Water is a wonderful thing for slowing a moving object, and only because I was starting to worry that I might go so

Dancing on Raindrops

deep that I couldn't make it back to the surface before I drowned, I moved my elbows away from my side. For a moment it felt as if they were to be torn from me, but that motion slowed me enough that I was able to put a great deal more effort into stopping.

By then the pain in my ears was screaming. The first thing I did was grab my nose and blow hard. With a loud screeching sound the pressure in my ears equalized and the pain was released. Eyes open and not a moment to spare, I started clawing my way to the surface. I was deep. Forty, fifty feet? I didn't know, but the fact I had a wetsuit on made the ascent much easier - as I was very buoyant. Out of the depths I came, longing for that first breath of air.

That night I headed for the local bar, my body feeling as though I had been through a washing machine. All I wanted to do was relax with an ice-cold beer. Walking to the counter, who should I see in front of me, but the pilot.

"Hey Lucky," he shouted out as I approached. "You are crazy man, totally crazy. What do you want to jump from that height for?" he asked.

"Yea right," I replied. "I say okay and give your doorman a thumbs up, then he tells me to wait so you can go higher. You're the crazy ones!"

He studied me for a moment, then burst out laughing.

"So that's what happened," he said in a broken voice, between the racks of laughter. At that point, I was not amused. I did not catch the joke. He eased up on the laughter and looked me square in the eye.

"This is OK," he said loudly, raising his hand and touching thumb and forefinger together in a circle. Then he gave me the thumbs up signal.

"This means I want to go up," he said, as he broke into laughter once again.

Communication with others is just as important as communication with yourself.

TERROR IN THE MUD

I rolled out of the dinghy into the dark and cold liquid. The water was rough and it was an oily harbor, so I was sure to put my mouthpiece into my mouth before I entered. That way, I avoided having that oily taste in my mouth for the next hour.

Eight of us hit the water at about the same time. Our mission was to check the under water parts of a supertanker, as it was believed that there might be mines beneath the ship. Earlier that night, someone had apparently seen bubbles on the surface and because of the war that was going on against terrorism at the time, it had to be checked. It was dark in the shadow of the huge hull and the only light, a dim yellowish hue, came from the pier on the other side of the harbor. The tide was very low and in the distance moisture glistened on the barnacle encrusted concrete pilings, as the howling wind turned the tops of the waves to spray. Up and down we bobbed, as the small waves came crashing by. The familiar, rhythmic sounds coming from my regulator, as I breathed in and out.

We assembled at the side of the hull, three quarters of the way aft. It was here that we would start our 'J' search. Called that because we would form a row of divers from the keel of the ship, all the way to the surface. The keel swimmer would clip onto a line and slowly head for the bottom of the hull. As the line went down, every six to eight feet, another would clip on. So on and so forth, until we were all evenly spaced down the hull. The person on the bottom swam on his back and those further up swam on their side. Both hands were used to sweep the hull, feeling for lumps or bumps that could be a mine.

That night I was to be the keel swimmer, so I reached out and took the first clip and hooked it onto the short line that was attached at the top of my arm. The cold water ran into my armpits and I winced, I hate cold water. Breathing out, I began to sink. Slowly I went down into the cold and wet darkness, the others clipping on one by one and following. To begin with, my descent was vertical, but soon it flattened out as I passed the rounded corner of the hull and the huge flat bottom of the ship lay in front of me. As I came horizontal and onto my back, water filled the tiny air spaces against my eardrums and what little hearing I had to start with was reduced.

Each weld I came across, I would check my direction to make sure I was not swimming at an angle and adjust my course if necessary. I could feel the welds in the steel plate as I moved along, the little ridges running fore and aft. My goal was to find the center weld. That is the weld that runs down the middle of the hull, all the way from the bow to the stern. In front of me was a flat steel surface the size of a football field, with no points of reference as to how far along it I was.

I came across what I hoped to be the center weld. It seemed a little larger than the others and also I reckoned I had traveled about half the width of the hull, so I stopped and gave the signal up the line that I was in position. While I waited, I kept one hand on the weld and let my legs fall under me, as if I was standing.

My heart skipped a beat, as my feet touched the muddy bottom. Not three feet below the ship was the slimy, oozy, grunge that covers the bottom of most commercial harbors. With a point of reference, I could feel the ship slowly moving up and down as she rode the swells of the storm above.

From then on, communication was solely by means of specific pulls on the rope. Each person repeated the message to the next, until it reached the end of the line. If someone in the middle needed to stop, he would pass the signal both up and down. It would have been easy enough if you could see the person next to you, but in the total darkness, upside down and under the water, it was no simple feat. Messages would fly back and forth when someone came across something that needed checking. The huge inlet and outlet fittings had to be inspected by whoever had come upon one and that would take time, so everyone had to stop to keep the line straight. Then, the signal to move was sent and we would all resume our search.

Moments later the go signal reached me, so I kicked my fins, turned on my back and started off down the weld. My job was made all the more difficult because I had to search with one hand and keep the other on the weld. To lose that reference point could turn the dive into chaos, as there would be no anchor at the end of the line.

The minutes went by slowly in that cold and dark world. As I kicked, I began to feel the ooze against my heels and it was not long after that, my dive tank pulled on my shoulder straps and I slowed to a stop - trapped between the hull and the bottom. Meanwhile, everyone else was moving on and the line attached to my arm was beginning to pull. Still keeping my one hand on the weld, I tried to reach the line with my other hand, but before I could get there, I was free. Kicking as hard as I could, I managed to catch up and keep the 'J' intact, but not ten seconds later I was stuck again. As the ship rose and fell to the swells, so it pushed me into the mud and released me. Pinned to the bottom, the steel hull pressed against my chest and face, and I felt like a fly between the fingers of a giant; the tiniest squeeze and everything would turn to mush. It was a very strange feeling, lying on my back and having a tanker above, push me down into the mud.

On and on it went, to the rhythm of the ocean. Squashed into the mud, then racing to catch up. Sometimes my mask became dislodged, as the hull pressed hard against me, my eyes smarted as the cold and muddy water poured in. Then, as I raced forward, I breathed out through my nose and some of the water at least would be blown out.

It felt like forever before the signal to turn around reached me. We had arrived at the bow and would now check the other side on the way back to the stern, which meant I would have to run the gauntlet once again. That time I managed to lose the weld, as I was pushed into the mud at an awkward angle. The ship let me go and I raced forward, both hands sweeping the hull, feeling for my reference. Fortunately I had the line to tell me where the next diver up was and as long as I kept it taut and at right angles to me, then I should have been roughly in the right position.

A minute or so of frantic searching and I came across a weld. It felt smaller than the one I had had before, but nonetheless, I stuck with it. I knew that we were getting towards the stern when the water became deeper, or in my case, the land became deeper. I was exhausted by the time we reached the propellers. The added effort of having to catch up all the time, combined with the adrenaline from the fear of being crushed, made me wish it were all over.

The propellers were always a tricky part of a ship to search in the darkness. The multidimensional shapes made it hard to keep everyone together. Each of the four blades needed searching on both sides, then the rudder and the remaining stern section, but finally it was all over and the signal to surface arrived.

My head was the last to break into the wild night and the dinghy was perhaps eighty feet away, with a line of shimmering wetsuits and tanks heading towards it. I put my head down and kicked as hard as I could against the wind and the waves. Enough was enough and I wanted to be out of the water.

Dancing on Raindrops

TRAPPED AND DROWNING

The whole reason for us going there was to find a capsized barge in the river, then recover it and whatever bodies were still trapped underneath. That was how we came to find ourselves in the middle of a war zone, with a difficult and dangerous task ahead.

Six days before Christmas, we boarded an air force C130 Hercules transport plane. It was a great start, as we carried a whole heap of gear. Dozens of dive tanks, two large compressor units on trailers, portable decompression chambers, dinghies, outboard motors, air bags for lifting things in the water and spares of every part we may need in the event of a breakage. Then of course there was our personal equipment and us. Being chosen for the mission seemed the easiest part of all. You, you, you and you. That was it.

Five aircraft personnel and five divers lifted off early one morning from a military airport on the outskirts of Cape Town, and headed north. Passenger comfort was not a prerequisite in the design of that aircraft, yet she was perfect for our needs. Several tons of equipment and more than enough room to swing a cat, - an expression that comes from the old sailing days, where the cat was the whip used to inflict punishment and it often had nine tails, - gave us all the chance to create whatever seating accommodation we chose. I went for the soft bags on the floor and soon, way before the dawn, I was fast asleep with the miles ticking away below.

The Botswana government had asked the South African Navy for help, because one of their grain-carrying trucks had capsized a river barge and some of their people were still inside, trapped at the bottom of the muddy Zambezi

River. The barge had overturned at a major crossing point, which happened to be at the convergence of four international borders; Zambia, Namibia, Botswana and Zimbabwe and to top it off there was a war going on. Our job was to remove the barge, the vehicles and whatever bodies we could find. It sounded simple enough.

Around mid-morning we started our descent, even though we were still hundreds of miles from our destination. Yes, our flight was cleared at the highest levels and we were assured that it was safe to be in the region, but what would happen if the message did not get through to some small group on the ground, waiting with a SAM missile? Our pilot, who flew that route all too often, was having none of it. I imagined this scenario:

"At eleven hundred hours tomorrow, there will be a C130 coming in from the south, be sure not to shoot at it," said the terrorist leader into the old radio's microphone.

"Whaaat you say? Say again I didn't hear," replied the lone terrorist.

"I said tomorrow, beep, squelch, hummm, hummm." Yea, you get the picture...

Down we came as we approached the border. Down and down indeed, until we were so close to the treetops, occasionally we would remove the top few feet of some lofty pine. Changing course every minute also added to the fun, as the wingtips would dip below tree level, then rise again as we assumed a new course. The whole point of that approach, was that anyone wanting to shoot us out of the sky wouldn't hear or see us, until we were overhead or gone; then, as we were so low, hopefully a tree or hill would get in the way of their aim.

Two hours of tree chopping and we were on short final. The dirt runway ahead looking about the length one might need to land a small Cessna. STOL - short take-off and landing. That bird really had her act together. Chee chee, the wheels were on the ground and all four engines in full reverse, even the ABS on the wheels were working overtime to get us stopped before the end of the runway.

"Ha, piece of cake", the pilot remarked as we taxied over to the ramp to begin unloading. Slowly the rear door was lowered and the 110-degree outside air was quick to make itself known inside the aircraft. Hot, dry and dusty. Welcome to nowhere land.

Within minutes the cavern of the fuselage was empty and with the help of a dozen soldiers, a five-ton Bedford truck bore the weight of our equipment. The plane was on a quick turn around and before we had boarded our new transport, the rear doors were closed and it was heading back to the runway. Off to find some better lodgings for the night, hopefully some place where she was less likely to die from a mortar or missile. Hot, hot, hot.

The ride in the back of the Bedford was mercifully short and soon we were parked in the shade of a baobab tree, where we began to unload our kit. This over here, that there and so it went on for a few hours as we sorted and checked our equipment. By late afternoon, as the heat was beginning to ease, we were done. Everything we would need for the next day was loaded in the truck, checked and rechecked; the rest secured in a locked room.

A jeep pulled up and an officer climbed out and introduced himself. He seemed quite surprised at first that no one saluted him. An offence in the army, punishable by slow death - well almost. Fortunately, he did not take the matter to heart and he soon realized that although none of us were officers, we did not care. You treat us with respect and you will receive the same in return. Simple as that, rank meant nothing to that outfit of crazy divers.

"My name is Major Sykes," he said matter of factly. "I shall be looking after you lot, so anything you need, let me know and we will see if we can get it."

"Yea, how about an ice cold beer?" Georgeo shouted out, as he climbed into the back of the Bedford to recheck his gear.

"Okay," said the Major. "Put these number plates on the truck and I'll see you in twenty minutes in the officers mess for a beer." Way to go Major, he was our kind of officer - we were going to get along just fine.

Someone had come up with the idea that it would be better for us to cross international borders as civilians. Yea right, five burly divers, a five-ton truck and equipment that most civilian divers could only dreamed about. What kind of a hoax was that supposed to be? Anyhow, we changed the plates and our brown military truck became a 1969 Morris minor. We were tired from a very long day, but first and foremost, we were thirsty.

"Officers only," said the young soldier guarding the door of the mess.

"Go and call Major Sykes, we've been invited," our leader of the moment replied. Seated at the bar in an air-conditioned room, we were introduced to the rest of the officers. A few lieutenants, a couple of majors and even a colonel - about a dozen in all. Yea, let the festivities begin.

Our pay for that kind of work was fantastic. We received a basic salary of twenty-seven Rands per month. (About $3.00 U.S.) Because of the nature of our mission, we were all receiving danger pay and that almost doubled our basic, so we felt rich.

Aaaaah the first ice cold beer did not even touch sides, nor I'm sure did the next half a dozen. What the hell, if you may die tomorrow, you can at least party the night before. The bar had a ship's bell next to the counter and whoever rang the bell would have to buy a round of drinks for everyone. Being sailors and all we took a great liking to that beautiful brass bell, so the more we drank, the more we rang the bell. In the wee hours of the morning, it was only our major and the five of us left standing. This guy was all right. Perhaps the finest compliment we would pay anyone, especially an officer.

Young, fit and able to leap tall buildings in a single bound? Perhaps, nonetheless there were six sore heads the next morning, as we were up once again before the dawn to start day one of our mission.

The main highway, that's what they called it. Miles upon miles of dirt road, special dirt road, as that road was swept daily for land mines. Yea, it sure made me feel better and in addition we had an armored truck accompany us for the first leg of the journey. Their large cannons would be of much help, if needed. Three hours of boredom and we reached the first border post, our armored companion a memory in the dust behind. A mud hut with a grass roof in the middle of nowhere. Half a dozen soldiers lazed about, all carrying automatic weapons - AK 47's. Thanks to the Russians, they were as easy to acquire as a loaf of bread. The truck slowed and our following dust overtook us. It was our first moment of truth, would they let us through, or would we all be stood up against a tree and shot?

No one seemed too interested. We tried to initiate a conversation, as we would be passing through here often in the next week or so, but they were not bothered. A look at our phony registration papers, a glance in the back of the truck and we were waved through. It was all too easy.

Standing on the edge of the mighty Zambezi River, I thought of a mud bath. The water was light brown, thick swirling mud. Nowhere to be seen was the barge or its contents. As we studied the river, with its four knots of current, it became apparent that there were swirls in areas that should have been calm water. Midway across, the water was being forced to the surface and here it churned and boiled, dissipating as it continued on its way downstream; oblivious to the fact that in a few short miles, it would be airborne as it fell over the Victoria Falls.

An inflatable dinghy with a fifty horsepower motor was ready to go at the water's edge and we were all making final checks on our gear, when we heard the first shot. An instant before, a 'whup' close by, then the unmistakable metallic sound of an AK 47. There were two more shots, but our area was already deserted. Everyone had dived behind trees, or into ditches, anything just get out of sight.

"Hey stop shooting...come to fix the barge...no shoot...," followed by the usual profanities that one tends to come out with when someone is trying to shoot you!

"Ooh, okay," came the muted reply from the other side of the river. A few more terse lines of conversation and then laughter followed. It sank home the reason the pilot kept so low for the final part of our flight. Communication in Africa is not known for its reliability, or even its availability. Small groups of terrorists were often out of contact with their bases for long periods of time. How was that lone man supposed to know who we were, or what we wanted?

Four of us were ready to dive; the other diver and the major would handle the boat. We motored out into the middle of the river where the current was strong and turbulent, then we threw an anchor about two hundred feet upstream of what we thought might be the barge and waited to see if it would hook on anything. Bingo, first time lucky.

Georgeo and I volunteered to be the first two in the water. We were to go down and try to get an idea of what was below the surface. Was this the barge or simply a few rocks? How was it lying? Was the truck about?

Wetsuits were put on, not for the cold, but for protection against scratches and scrapes in an unknown environment. Everyone was busy with something or another, as I glanced over to the far bank and noticed the crocodiles. About a dozen of them were sunning themselves on the water's edge, huge creatures - ten to twelve feet long and as we watched, two decided to go for a swim. Slowly and lazily, they pushed themselves into the water and disappeared beneath the muddy surface.

We might not salute officers, but we get the job done, I reflected to myself, as the water covered my head and I was plunged into a blackness that I was not expecting.

Visibility was zero. No, beyond zero. I took my heavy diving light and shone it into my face from about a foot away, but I could not see anything, not a glimmer. At six inches I was able to make out only a glow from the powerful flashlight. We certainly were in a mud bath. We descended on the anchor line, kicking hard to offset the current. Down and down we went, into a realm of total darkness. A world where light was non-existent. Our hands were our eyes and as always, we were attached by a line to each other's arms.

The anchor had caught on the edge of the upturned barge, so the bottom of the vessel was then on top. We tied a line to the guardrail near the anchor and slowly let ourselves drift downstream, feeling as we went. We communicated by a code of 'bells and whistles,' slow pulls or short tugs on the rope that connected us. Everything took a long time, for when we wanted to communicate, first we would have to hold on securely with one hand, then use the other to pull or tug on the line, all while the current was trying to tear us loose.

Ouch! It felt as though someone had stuck a needle into the exposed flesh on my wrist.

Ouch! once again. I held onto the line with one hand and with the other signaled Georgeo to stop. Stop and wait. My useless flashlight was tied to my waist, so I undid it and lifted it up to my face. Holding the beam shining across my mask, I brought my wrist up to try and see what had happened. A small fish, about five inches long, came into view in the muffled beam of the powerful light. Tiger fish, here we were diving in crocodile infested waters, getting eaten by baby tiger fish. It certainly was not a normal day at the office!

Sure enough, the truck was downstream of the barge, lying on its side. The windows were open and we checked inside for bodies. Nothing, between the crocodiles and the tiger fish, no flesh would last long in those waters. My head was coming out of the cab of the truck when I felt Georgeo's hand in my hair. He tugged a bit then suddenly let go. *Whatever*, I thought.

On returning to the surface, the darkness prevailed until the last few inches, when dim light was once again visible. Another inch or so and my head was out of the water and in the bright African sunlight.

"So why were you playing with my hair down there?" I asked Georgeo as we climbed into the dinghy.

"Wow, you sure gave me a fright," he replied and began to laugh. "I figured it was a body, so I was trying to pull it loose - then it moved!"

As the second pair of divers made their way below the surface, I looked over at the bank to where the crocodiles had been sunning themselves and there were only four left.

"Yes," said the Major reading my mind. "Every few minutes one gets up and makes its way to the water, but don't mind the crocs, it's the hippos you will have to watch out for."

Coming between a mother hippopotamus and her young will almost certainly get you bitten in half. The hippo, being fearless of humans, accounts for more deaths in Africa than any other animal. At least with the crocs we stood a chance. We had two knives apiece, one strapped to each leg and unless both of your hands were tied up, there was always a chance of being able to get to one of the knives to even the odds a little.

The rest of the day was uneventful. We had found the barge and the truck, so we could begin to formulate a plan to get them out of the river. We packed up our old Bedford and shouted our good byes to the sniper on the other bank. With an audible chuckle, but still out of sight, he wished us well and we set off on the four hour drive home.

The border guards paid us no mind as we arrived and that time we offered them some cigarettes, real cigarettes. I doubt any of those 'officials' moved that fast all day long. From that moment on we were not simply a truck full of unknowns, no, we were the bearers of gifts, very fine gifts indeed.

It was late by the time we returned to camp, but the thoughtful cook had put food aside for us. We ate like a bunch of starved men, showered and as the major was off to bed, we went to make some new friends in the NCO's mess.

The bar was reserved for non-commissioned officers, still way above our rank. Everyone it seemed had more rank than all of us combined. The sergeant major and I had already met early that morning, as I walked across his parade ground on my way from the sleeping quarters to our truck. All of a sudden there was a roaring voice breaking the early mornings stillness.

"Get the X*^$% off my parade ground, you useless piece of shit!" he shouted in Afrikaans. My understanding of that tongue was limited at best, so I looked at that crazy man who was going ape and continued walking. The more I ignored him, the crazier he became, so I changed course and walked over to him.

"Bla bla bla," I'm sure smoke was about to come out of his ears. Then he must have realized who I was and he changed to English. Aaaah that was better, instant comprehension. Apparently no one got to walk over the parade ground - not unless there was a parade going on. Well you live and learn, and it was late into the night that we partied together - and yes, they also had a bell.

Christmas day was much like the preceding days, except we quit early and made a detour on the way home. The Zambezi River Lodge used to be a place that film stars and other celebrities would visit. That was history. It was in shambles and used only as a truck stop, a meeting place for truckers traveling up and down that barren part of Africa. They did however have good food and cold beer, so we spent the rest of the afternoon sitting on a shaded porch, drinking beer and watching Africa.

A herd of elephants drank and cooled themselves on the opposite side of the river, and occasionally the shrill cry of a fish eagle could be heard in the distance. Such a tranquil scene, it was hard to believe that not far away people were trying to kill each other.

Our mission was almost finished. The truck was the first to make it to shore. Our new friends on the opposite bank, Mr. Sniper included, organized a couple of D6 bulldozers and enough steel hawser to reach from the shore to the barge. Where in the middle of nowhere, did they come up with two huge bulldozers? We had no idea.

The dozers were tied together, one in front of the other and began to pull the truck from the muddy depths, up onto the bank. That event gave the newly formed crowd of locals reason to celebrate, and we were the heroes because some of them had lost friends and family when the barge overturned. They collected fruits; mangoes, papaya and bananas, then deposited a large pile into our boat for us to take home. One more dive to make and that would be the end of our task.

The barge, since it was upside down, had on the underside, a large flat steel surface with railings all around. Hence there was only one entrance or exit and that was the gap in the railings. The plan was that I would go down through the tiny opening, then, once under the barge, I would work my way to the far side, about one hundred and fifty feet away. There, someone else would pass me the thick steel cable between the gap in the ramp and the hull. This I would then pass around the cleat and back to the diver on the other side.

One potential problem was air. During the course of the day we had used up most of the air in our tanks and were left with only two bottles - both a quarter full. Go for it and finish the job, or come back tomorrow for only one quick dive? Moreover, the two bulldozers were waiting on the shore. Get it done.

I descended once again into the now familiar blackness, slowly easing myself into the gap between the railings and underside of the barge. A large flat surface was above me and I had to make my way on my back, pulling myself through the mud, as there was not enough room to swim between the steel ceiling and the riverbed. Slowly I headed onwards, reaching out in front to feel the next stanchion, taking hold and pulling myself forward.

My journey down the length of the barge seemed to take forever and in the darkness it was hard to retain any concept of distance; but I was happy in the knowledge that when the dive was over, I would never again have to find myself at the bottom of that dangerous river.

I bumped into the ramp at the end and began to make my way upstream to the other side, where my buddy was supposed to be waiting with the steel cable. Yep, there it was and after much fumbling and feeling, I took the end of the wire and while trying to brace myself in the mud, I passed it around the cleat and back to the other side. Mission accomplished.

It was hard work and I was breathing heavily. I helped the other diver pull a little more wire through the gap, enough so that it could be clamped on the other side and that was it, my task was finished. That too was the last breath I ever took under that barge. I exhaled and went to breathe in again, but there was nothing - no air. I let go of the wire cable in a panicked attempt to reach my reserve rod. (This was a piece of steel wire that ran from the valve on top of the tank, all the way down the side.) In the event of running out of air, we simply pulled the lever and would get a reserve supply, enough to give us a few minutes - and that was exactly what I needed. I pulled on the handle, but it would not budge, so I pushed it back up and sure enough, it moved easily. Oh no, that meant that somewhere I must have bumped the reserve rod and had unknowingly been breathing all my reserve air.

When I let go of my handhold, I began to roll and tumble under the barge as the current took hold of me. I pushed both arms up and braced myself against the steel plates, pushing my body into the mud. I was disoriented; disoriented and without any air in my lungs.

Think quickly. I eased my brace against the steel and the mud and allowed the current to slowly take me downstream. Seconds later I bumped into the railings. I need air. Which way was out? Taking a moment to be sure I was headed in the right direction, I started using the stanchions to pull myself along. Hand over hand through the mud and one hundred and fifty feet to go. I desperately needed air.

Pull; pull faster! I tried to make my way to the exit - the only way out, but I was not quite half way, when the thought entered my head that I was not going to make it. I could hold my breath no longer and the desire to breathe was becoming overwhelming. Having only half a lung full of air to start with, was not enough and the heavy exertion of pulling the steel cable was taking its toll.

Pull faster damn it! My arms too were beginning to tire and my consciousness was slowly losing its hold. A memory came to me. Years ago my good friend Zak, while teaching me to dive, had remarked that if ever I ran out of air and was about to breathe, I should start to drink water. As you drink, so you cannot breathe. As long as you keep drinking, breathing is impossible. I spat the regulator out of my mouth and began to drink. I drank like a camel home from a long journey. The water tasted foul, lots of soft lumpy bits and it was not easy to stop myself from vomiting. That would be a sure way to drown.

Pull you lazy sod, pull. I urged myself on, drinking faster and faster, as the desire to stop and breathe almost overcame me. One hand out, grab the stanchion, pull, next hand.

I'm going to make it, I'm going to make it, I kept repeating to myself. *I'm going to make it, I'm going to make it.* Every cell in my body was screaming for air and I could feel the adrenaline coursing through me. I was wide eyed, on the verge of panic and a breath away from death.

Drink drink, I'm going to make it! I forced the thought into my mind and I could feel myself shaking, as I clawed my way through the darkness.

Oh no, I've lost the feeling in my arms. I put out my hand and could not feel the next stanchion. From somewhere far away, an idea came to me.

It's the exit! Drink, drink, drink. I put one hand up outside the barge and pulled myself through the mud and out of the tiny gap. As my body cleared the exit, I passed out.

My next sensation was that of light and something pulling on my arm, as I was hauled out of the water and into the dinghy. Coughing and vomiting, I took my first breaths of air, still not sure yet if I was alive or dead. When I was done and had my breath back, Georgeo helped me to sit against the pontoon of the inflatable dinghy. I noticed that we were still at anchor in the same place. Somehow I had assumed that I would have floated on down the river.

"What happened?" I said out loud. The Major was the first to reply.

"You certainly are lucky," he said with a grin on his face. "Georgeo was in the bow of the dinghy when you popped above the surface right in front of him and we hauled you out."

I felt weak, as I related my side of the story while the guys helped me out of my wetsuit. The sun shone brightly and warmed my cold skin. On the far bank, only one crocodile remained.

It was good to be alive.

Dancing on Raindrops

A MONSTER SHARK

It was a perfect night for a night dive. The sea had not a ripple on the surface and the sky was clear, a small sliver of moon starting to rise. Fifteen of us sat on deck and waited for the boat to come to a stop on the edge of the reef. This was not a work dive, and everyone was looking forward to a nice relaxing swim amongst the nocturnal creatures of the ocean.

We dropped anchor in eighty-five feet of water and began to get ready. The routine was familiar to everyone and it was simply one of the dozens of night dives we had done in the last few months. People milled about the deck sorting out gear and putting on their wetsuits. There was no rush, it was supposed to be a fun dive after all. Voices carried on the still air and I could hear the reef crackling through the hull.

Night diving is the best, as all the fish, crayfish included, come out to feed and leave the holes that they normally inhabit during daylight hours. The ocean comes alive and the fish population seems to soar. Many an hour I have spent enthralled by the presence of some tiny little fish, as they would guard their territory, or try to catch some dinner as an even smaller fish passed by. That night had the ingredients of a perfect dive.

It was subtle at first, but the atmosphere had changed. In the space of a few minutes, as everyone was ready to jump in, a feeling moved through the group and without words or a conscious decision, everyone started to delay getting into the water. It was crazy, here were a dozen divers, all with hundreds of hours of underwater experience and no one wanted to be the first to go in. A few comments were thrown about as to how things did not feel right, but the speakers seemed foolish after voicing their fears. The night was perfect and the sea calm, clear and inviting.

"Oh what the hell," someone said, as he jumped into the water, the concentric ripples clearly visible on the surface. That seemed to break the spell and soon everyone was in the water and preparing to go under. Georgeo and I swam to the anchor line and started to descend the rope. Our powerful flashlights penetrated the clear water and the bottom was barely visible in the dimmed light.

Down we went, slow and easy. Still the strange feeling had not left me and occasionally I was spooked by some shadow or movement. Something did not feel right. We reached the bottom and sure enough, it seemed as though the entire reef population had come out to greet us. Crayfish were walking on the sandy floor and fish were everywhere; it was a perfect night to be under the water, but my uneasiness persisted. Somehow I could not find the motivation to catch crayfish and spent most of my time looking into shadows and thinking spooky thoughts. I was not having fun and I could not understand the reason for my apprehension.

It was then that I noticed something floating in the water, at the outer edge of my beam of light. It seemed about three feet long and hung motionless, ten feet off the bottom. I tapped Georgeo on the shoulder and pointed, then slowly we swam towards the object, our lights beginning to illuminate and define it. A chill went through my body and I'm sure I stopped breathing for a while. The object of our curiosity was a dolphin's head. It had been bitten off cleanly only moments before and blood still oozed from the raw, lifeless flesh. It looked so sad to see one of my favorite ocean friends hanging immobile, eyes still open, yet lifeless. There was the result of the fear we had felt - and the cause was close by.

False Bay is renowned for its great white shark population and in summer, the waters have among the highest concentration in the world. Normally however they stay in the vicinity of Seal Island, a small outcrop of rock in the center of the bay that is literally covered in seals, as that is their staple diet.

We looked at each other and without a sign or signal, we both knew that a great white had done that and that it was somewhere close by. The sound of our breathing seemed so loud, as we turned and started slowly kicking in the direction from whence we had come, back to the safety of the boat. Our eyes scanned the blackness that surrounded us and our hearts beat faster. Somewhere out there in the darkness was a monster shark, something large enough and fast enough to catch a dolphin and then sever its head from its body in a single bite. No, I no longer wanted to be there and I felt a huge sigh of relief when I saw the anchor rope in the pale glow of the flashlight.

We went up the anchor line and climbed into the boat without incident. Most of the others were already back aboard and the talk was about how weird everyone felt on the dive. No one seemed to understand why that was - until we related the story of the dolphin's head.

Dancing on Raindrops

A WHALE'S TALE

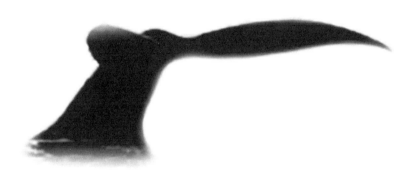

It was a beautiful day on the Cape Peninsula and I had been diving with a couple of friends in the chilly ocean off Cape Point. We were just having fun, trying to get a couple of crayfish for the pot. Afterwards, while heading back to Simonstown late in the afternoon, we spotted a whale blowing on the surface. Effortlessly it rose out of the water, breathed and headed back under.

During the summer, the Southern Right whales come into the Cape waters to give birth to their calves and often they can be seen close to the shoreline. We slowed the boat and watched for a while, as the two whales continued on their way.

Imagine swimming with a whale, I contemplated to myself. These huge creatures grow to a length of forty-five feet and weigh in at a whopping sixty tons. There they were, fifty feet from the boat and it had to be done. It was my chance to swim with a whale and I was not about to miss it. I zipped up my wetsuit, put on my weight belt and fins and rolled over into the water with my mask in hand. They were moving deceptively fast and by the time I had my mask on, they had already moved well away from me, so I put my head down and began kicking towards them, catching up as fast as I could.

Slowly they came into view under the water, two giants swimming peacefully together. As I approached, I almost expected them to move off or to sound, but they seemed unfazed by my presence and continued in their slow methodical way. I swam alongside the larger of the two, barely ten feet from it and as I looked over it seemed to take up all of my field of view. I had to come to the surface for air, as I did not have a tank, so was limited to the length of time I could spend under the water. I went closer and closer until I was touching the huge beast. Swimming up to his head, I looked into his eye; large as a shiny saucer, his face was encrusted in barnacles. My heart was pounding in my chest - what a magnificent sight, literally eyeball to eyeball. Still the gentle giant paid me no mind and after coming up for air, I held on to his lateral fin and he dragged me along through the water.

It was time to go and have a look at the other end, so I stopped kicking and that huge creature moved away beneath. As the tail came below me, I took a deep breath and swam down, taking a hold at the center of his fluke. Up and down we went as the motion propelled him forward. Up and down, it was the ride of a lifetime; a slow rhythmic motion and he seemed to ignore my presence. On the way up my body was pushed against his tail and on the way down I had to hold on as I floated above his fluke.

In an instant the serenity of the moment evaporated. One flick of his tail was all it took to remove that annoying bug that was pestering him. For me, it felt as though I was in a washing machine, as I tumbled backwards in the powerful current that he had created; not knowing which way was up or down and powerless to do anything except wait for the water to subside.

It seemed like forever until I was able to start kicking for the surface, but something was wrong - not only had I lost my mask and snorkel, but my fins had been torn from my feet too. I used my hands to try and claw my way up towards the air that I needed so badly. Even that was difficult, as it felt as though I had armbands on and I could not bring my arms near to my body; they were stuck out to the side like the Michelin Man.

Kicking and clawing, I made the surface and noticed that my thick winter wetsuit had been rolled up my arms and legs by the force of the water. The whale had not moved off, but had simply glided about a hundred feet away and was carrying on as though nothing had happened. I rolled down my wetsuit as best I could, at least enough to be able to swim and headed back to the boat, my heart still pounding, but a huge smile on my face.

Dancing on Raindrops

3. SECRETS TO YOUR SUCCESS

WORDS and DESIRES

WORDS

Affirmations (a meaningful set of words that you say out loud), can be of great help in creating and maintaining your thoughts. We all know the power of the spoken word; it is 'said' - to be able to move mountains.

The spoken word repeated, creates a belief and soon your subconscious becomes flooded with specific thoughts, as you verbalize your dreams. Write down your affirmations and keep them handy, or until such time as you can repeat them from memory. Then use the spoken word to nurture your dreams and most of all, be aware of the things you say.

So often you say things that you don't mean, or things that you don't necessarily want to happen - we all do - but it is these seemingly insignificant comments (be they positive or negative), that can cement your thoughts enough to make them happen. Even little sayings, repeated, can have a profound effect on your life.

Oral 'prayer,' (asking and thanking) is a good place to begin and will have the effect of clarifying your thoughts; but it is not simply the occasional repetition of words that will get you what you want. It is rather by using the words to constantly enforce your vision - that will get you what you want!

When I told my friends that I had decided to build a yacht and sail around the world, they thought it was only a passing fancy and laughed, for they knew that I had no money and no job. That didn't stop me, I told everyone, but their reactions were all much the same.

I had spent most of the previous two years either underwater, or being ordered to do things by others and I had had enough of it. I wanted to live free on the ocean, so I began to design my yacht in my mind - the one on which I was going to sail around the world. I imagined what the hull would look like, with its two thin red stripes below the toerail and the places I would visit. It was all a figment of my imagination and existed only in my mind as a fantasy, but it was fun and would sometimes make me feel like a child again. If nothing else it helped pass the time, creating new adventures to my voyage. How to make them a reality? I did not have the faintest idea, so I concentrated only on the fun parts. The adventure, beautiful women, the freedom to come and go as I chose; to wake in the morning and decide what part of the world I would like to visit next. That was what I wanted to do.

The last few months of my Navy service were quiet, the war against terrorism had abated and the military embarked on a process of change; the draft was being reduced to one year, black Africans were allowed to enlist and everything was being downsized. The fleet had too many ships to maintain, so we were given the task of turning an old destroyer into a reef. We towed the magnificent old lady to a deep bay near Cape Point, set explosives in her keel and watched in awe as she sank below the surface.

DESIRES

All desires represent the possibility of something to come and within each desire lies an enormous potential. For you to pursue something without desire would make it a worthless task, for desire is a force, a very real force and if you follow it, it will give you the motivation to overcome whatever problems you may encounter in your pursuits. Desire can keep you going when you are tired after working a long day, or give you the courage to take that next step when the fear seems too much. Moving out of your comfort zone will only happen if you have a desire for something else - and that desire has to be stronger than your fear.

Coming out of a military life was a huge adjustment. I had to find a place to stay, cook all my own meals and earn an income. Some of my friends had found work diving for diamonds on the barren West Coast. They would spend hours underwater sucking the sand off the seabed and with it would hopefully come the diamonds. They kept a crow bar handy and when they spotted a glittering rock in a fissure, they would pry it open and put the stone in their wetsuit. At night in the local bar, the divers would take the diamonds they had found and lay them in a pile on the counter. It was quite a sight, but the work was cold and certainly not in line with the tropical life I wanted, so I decided to keep looking. Somehow I knew I would find a way to earn the money I needed.

The thought of sailing around the world was becoming so vivid in my mind, that I could hear the voices of the vendors as I bought a hand of bananas in the local market. I could smell the fruit and feel its smooth yellow skin, as I looked out into the bay and saw my yacht riding at anchor; the hull gleaming in the tropical sun. The beach was covered in clean white sand and small waves of clear water lapped against the shore. Puffy clouds hung in an endless sky and the mountain behind me was green, as green as I could imagine.

It felt great!

BE AWARE OF THE POWER OF YOUR WORDS.

* For more information visit:
  www.dancingonraindrops.com

*"Follow your heart,
for those are your true desires."*

PRESENT DAY

I lift my eyes from the page and my body tells me it is time for a break; so I stand and walk past my note board, a cork wall covered in paper - some hand written, some printed, some neat, some scribbled.

A part of my mind lives there, I think as I head out of the room. Stopping at the music center, I glance for the play button, push it and hope for the best. Yes, it's my lucky day, as the sweet sound of Mozart's music fills every room.

Walking to the large glass doors that look out over the valley, I open them and the fresh, cool evening air pours in, bringing with it the scents of the forest. A low wooden deck lies between the front lawn and me. To my right is the barbecue, a stainless steel drum cut in half length-wise, with a neat pile of logs beside it. Not tonight, but many a summers night I would sit out here with some friends, cooking dinner and watching the sun set over the mountains, then see the stars light up the sky.

As the Milky Way came to life above, We would watch in awe and ponder the size of the universe. There was our galaxy, the Milky Way, with its one hundred billion stars, yet it is only a small part of more than one hundred billion galaxies. M42, the great nebula in Orion, appears as nothing more than a dim smudge in a huge sky; a small dot on Orion's sword. Yet it is there that stars are born. Huge masses of gas collide at incredible speeds, sending powerful shock waves into the universe and new worlds come to life. A true display of abundance.

Leaving the door open, I turn and walk through the arch into the main bedroom and change into a pair of warm flannel pants. Pulling a light sweater over my T-shirt, I then head for the kitchen to carve the chicken and make a quick salad to go with my meal.

Once ready, I look in the fridge for some wine and sure enough, there is a bottle on the top shelf. I open it, a bottle of "Goats do Roam" from the Fairview vineyard in South Africa, one of my favorite rosé's. I pour myself a glass and return the bottle to the fridge. A knife and fork from the drawer and I am ready to eat. As I pick up my plate and return to the office, I notice outside that day has given way to night and far in the valley I see a few lights flickering. Aaah, the chicken is excellent and the dry, smooth, palate of the wine excites my taste buds.

On the side wall of the office is a large picture of a yacht sailing by a tropical volcanic island. A thin black frame surrounds the glossy surface. The water is a crystal-clear light blue and in the background, the sky has a few cotton clouds scattered about. The white hull shimmers in contrast to the dark green of the island behind; Morea, perhaps the most beautiful island on earth. It seems almost as if the boat is moving, as the white water at the bow comes alive and sparkles in the sunlight, the sails fill with wind and I find myself reminiscing past adventures.

ALL AT SEA

A POCKET FULL OF DREAMS

It was late in the afternoon by the time I made it to the Harbormaster's office. All morning I had been shopping for the last of my essential items, a sextant and a book on celestial navigation. I was ready to leave; Tapestry was provisioned and her tanks were full - all that remained was a clearance from the Harbormaster.

I entered his office high above Cape Town harbor, with a magnificent view of the ocean. He looked over my paperwork and then started questioning me with a suspicious eye.

"So how much sailing have you done before?" he asked. It was a simple question and I gave him a simple answer.

"Maybe a hundred miles sir."

"You mean to tell me that you have only one hundred miles at sea and you want me to sign you out to cross an ocean?" I could tell he was not impressed. "And what is that?" he asked, looking at my sextant box.

"It is a sextant and a book on how to navigate," I replied.

"So have you done much celestial navigation?"

"No Sir, I have never taken a sight before, that is why I bought the book, so that I can learn out at sea."

Then he really did not want me to leave, but as it turned out there was nothing he could do to actually prevent me, except to try and persuade me not to go and I was having none of it. He suggested that I delay my departure for a while and take a course on celestial navigation, perhaps also a few sailing lessons. No, my mind was made up; I was leaving with or without his consent. The old sea dog was having a hard time understanding. He had perhaps a million at miles at sea and could not comprehend someone setting off with no experience whatsoever, but later rather than sooner, he relented.

As I left his office, I let out a cry of joy. I was finally ready and the following day would see me setting off to cross the Atlantic. First stop, the island of St. Helena.

Eighteen months earlier, after being discharged from the navy, I had decided to build a yacht and sail it around the world. The very first obstacle that had to be overcome was money, but I believed my dream would happen, so I was not surprised when I received a phone call from a friend, telling me he knew of a company that needed a sales person. They offered no basic salary and no car, but the commissions were great and I was quick to work out how many freezers I would have to sell in order to reach my goal. It was a lot!

The freezers were designed to be run for only an hour a day and still keep their contents frozen. The main market consisted of the farmers all over the country who ran generators for electricity. I put a freezer on a trailer, hitched it to my camper van and set off to sell.

Dancing on Raindrops

I had wanted a sales job, simply because I knew that a regular monthly salary, was not the way to accumulate enough money in a short period. For a while it seemed as though I had not made a good choice.

The first towns I visited were an absolute disaster; no one wanted to buy my new and expensive freezers. Most times, I was not even able to get the manager out of his air-conditioned office, to come outside and look at my amazing product. Something was going to have to change, if I was ever to get enough money together to build my yacht and go sailing.

I drove into the more desolate parts of the country, but I still had not sold a single thing. Rejection after rejection was almost getting to be too much for me. The endless miles of empty roads gave me plenty of time to think. What I needed was to somehow get the managers out of their cool offices and into the hot sun to come and look at my wares. Most of them were content to simply state that they did not need any more stock and leave the meeting at that. For days the question rattled through my brain, as I drove from one town to the next, as if in a daze.

The dry African countryside went by with scarcely a glance, my mind was so filled with trying to find an answer to my question. At the rate I was going, it was about to take me a lifetime to get enough money together and live my dream.

I remember it clearly. I stopped for gas in an almost deserted town and as the attendant was filling my car, I went inside the store to buy a cold drink and some snacks for the next part of my journey. Five young teenagers were in front of the ice cream freezer trying to figure out the best way to spend their limited coins and after much discussion, they all decided on a frozen stick of flavored water, an ice-lolly. That was when I had an idea.

Most of the people in those outlying areas were extremely poor, and the offer of free lollies was sure to create some excitement in the mundane lives of the unemployed locals. That might just give me the leverage I had been looking for to get the buyers out of their offices.

I went into a supermarket and bought two hundred frozen ice-lollies, then put them into my freezer, which I had kept cold by running it from wherever I stayed at night; using an electrical extension from my room to the trailer.

Ready to put my plan into action, I drove down the main street of some nameless rural town and stopped outside the front of a shop that sold kitchen appliances. Again I got the same negative answer. As usual they did not even want to come outside and have a look at my fantastic, amazing, incredible freezer. It was time to see what was going to happen.

I left the manager's office and went out into the heat, took my cover off the freezer and started to give away frozen treats to anyone who walked by. A most welcome gift in the heat of the day and in no time at all dozens of kids were around me, all clamoring to get a free treat. With all the commotion going on outside, the manager came out of his office. Now at last I had his attention and as I offered him a lolly, he had to have a look at my product.

Every time I opened the lid to get another treat, the cold air would condense and smoke seemed to pour from the lip of the cold freezer. I had his interest and we both stood on the sidewalk sucking on a frozen lolly, chatting about this and that. At the same time I was still handing out treats, but once he had finished his, he invited me back into the office and it was not long before I had an order for twenty freezers.

I was ecstatic, I had found a key to get the attention of the buyers and it became much easier to see my goals being realized before me, the instant that first order was signed.

On and on I went selling my wares in most of the towns I stopped in. In fact business was so good, that I decided to try another country and headed up into the desert lands of Namibia. There too, I used the same tactic and sales poured in. I was unswayed in my belief that I could do it and as long as I kept on trying, I was bound to succeed. So I was

Dancing on Raindrops

not surprised at the idea of giving out free ice-sticks to the children; it was one of a thousand ideas I had come up with, as I constantly tried to improve my pitch.

The sales began to pour in and three months later I arrived back in Cape Town with a full order book and enough commissions to build my yacht. My plan was coming together.

The big day soon arrived and I placed an order for a 37-foot fiberglass hull and deck. Tapestry was to be her name – 'a Tapestry to feel and see, impossible to hold'. I rented an inexpensive house in a run down part of town, put the hull in the back yard and began fitting her out.

I started with a bare white shell that had the deck attached, but down below there was nothing but a large empty cavern, into which I intended to build my home.

For the first two weeks, I did nothing but draw and measure. Not a single piece of wood was cut. I wanted to be sure of my design before I started and as it turned out the time was well spent, as I changed some of my ideas to make life aboard that much easier and more comfortable. In the early days, when the inside was bare, I would often take a foam mattress and sleep in the empty hull, trying to get a feel for the shapes that I had begun creating within.

The nine months of building the yacht was a period of dedication. I had met too many other aspiring yachties, who after taking years and years to build their boats, had lost interest and given up. I did not want to fall into that trap, so I threw myself into the construction. It became my passion. Every day was a day to work and the sooner I was finished, the sooner I could go sailing. There were of course the complaints from friends that they never saw me anymore.

"Take some time off, it will be good for you," they said, but I did not listen. I had seen what people who had given up had done. They took their eyes off their dreams and before they knew it, they were justifying their decision.

I decided to have two cabins down below. The forward cabin, with a hatch right above it was the coolest of all, but at sea it would also have the most movement. A double cabin aft was where I would sleep in rough weather and it would be a guest cabin when friends came to visit. All the bulkheads I painted in a very light blue, almost indistinguishable from white. The varnished wooden trim, a dark hardwood known as imbuia, gave the saloon a rich look as the reflected light shone from its surface.

On the floor I opted for both comfort and speed, so I declined to use the traditional effect of teak and holly planks. I went instead with varnished plywood and then covered it all in a thick, mottled blue and white carpet. An oak table on the port side with an inlaid chessboard, doubled as a chart table and it was there that I knew I would be spending countless hours navigating.

The starboard side of the saloon was a settee and not only was it designed to be a comfortable place to relax, but it also made some large storage lockers that were soon to be filled with food.

In the galley, I created a masterpiece. It was small, but totally functional. The standing space was limited to an area of six feet by two feet, but the narrowness meant that I would be able to brace myself against the sides of the counters, while cooking in rough weather.

To the outboard side, the top of the freezer was a solid oak chopping board and next to it was a gimbaled gas oven, complete with two rings and a grill. The opposite side had a deep stainless steel sink, the top edges of which were countersunk below the surface, to allow any water on the top to flow directly into the sink. All the plates and bowls were stored in specially made compartments, to stop them from sliding about. Even the coffee mugs had a custom made rack that would keep them secure in any sea. I decided to use a light colored wood to offset the dark trim of the main saloon, so I chose yellow wood, one of Africa's exotic hard woods with a fine grain and light yellowish cream color. It was bright below, as the light shone through the tinted windows. On the floor I laid squares of cork, sealed them with varnish and the effect was startling.

The shower and bathroom in front of the saloon were covered in light colored Formica, easy to keep clean and dry after a shower. The toilet (known as a head in nautical speak) used salt water to flush and I positioned it in such a way that no matter which side the boat heeled, it was easy to lean against a bulkhead and brace yourself - while still sitting on the head.

I installed a twenty horsepower diesel engine and besides being used for motoring, it would also power the 220V generator, from which I charged the batteries and kept the freezer frozen. By by-passing the voltage regulator and putting a rheostat in the line, I was able to fast charge the batteries at forty amps. That was usually enough to replenish all the electricity used the previous night. One of the perks of having learned about the freezers I sold, was that I got to install the exact same concept aboard. With only one hour of running per day, I would be able to keep my provisions frozen. The freezer was insulated with six inches of polyurethane foam and the shape of the hull formed the back. The thought of eating ice cream in the middle of the ocean seemed like absolute decadence.

Besides fitting out the interior, an enormous amount of work was needed outside. Hatches were cut into the fiberglass deck and every bolt hole had to be carefully sealed to prevent any leaks. By the time I began installing the sailing equipment: winches, cleats, toe rails and blocks, I had already ordered my mast and sails, the two most expensive items on the shopping list.

I spent hours and hours trying to find the best position on deck for a winch, or pondering if a block should go here or there. My sailing experience was limited to say the least, so I used books as references, spoke to as many sailors as I could, then added a little common sense. The result turned out to be extremely functional and made sail handling easy for one person.

Finally my task was complete and the great launch day arrived, so in celebration I had a party, a tin party. I supplied three sheep that were cooked over an open pit and all my guests had to bring were cans, lots and lots of canned foods. It was a huge success and cases upon cases of canned delights were stacked into the garage, ready to be loaded aboard.

Things took longer than I had expected and cost more than I had budgeted. Winter was coming and the South Atlantic gales had begun. The frontal systems start way down in the Southern Ocean and follow a northeasterly course, bringing rain and high winds to the Cape. I had wanted to leave at the end of summer - but that was well gone. Also, I had hoped to have at least one thousand dollars left over, but my cruising kitty was down to only one hundred dollars. My options were simple.

I could postpone the voyage for a year.

Leave the following summer.

Make some more money for the kitty.

Learn to sail and navigate.

Get to test all my new equipment.

They were perhaps the sensible choices, but I chose none of them. My original plan was to leave as soon as I was ready and I intended to stick to it.

Tapestry was launched at the Royal Cape Yacht Club in Cape Town. Situated at the foot of Table Mountain and on the edge of a busy harbor, it seemed the perfect place from which to begin. Dozens of friends gathered for the big moment and many times I was asked if there was a spare bunk aboard.

The sun shone brightly and my new home glistened as she was picked up by a large dockyard crane. I had heard, but have never verified, that the tradition of breaking a bottle of champagne over the bow to wish the vessel good luck, was a carryover from the Egyptian days. When a ship was launched, slaves would be tied to the ground between the wooden logs that rolled the ship into the water. As the logs rolled, the slaves were crushed and the more blood that spurted onto the hull, the luckier the ship was supposed to be. I opted not to partake in that ceremony.

She touched the water and in that instant, I felt as though my voyage had begun. I went below to check for leaks, but I could find none, so the straps were released and we tied alongside the dock. I readied the motor for its first running and hit the starter. With a cough and a splutter, it came to life and purred - to my ears anyway.

Moored safely in her berth at the yacht club, Tapestry was the center of attraction and I was in heaven. Everything had come together so well, through the ups and the downs I had stuck to my goal and right before me it was happening.

As the evening arrived only a few friends were left and we sat in the cockpit and watched as darkness covered the mountain, the city and harbor transforming into a sea of light. The night was calm, but still I could hear the gentle lapping of waves against the hull and the crackle of life below. I lay in my bunk that night, with perhaps the most contented feeling I had ever had in my life. That was what I had dreamed of; that was the result of the thoughts I had held in my mind.

Sea trials were supposed to be thorough, but because of the lack of time and wind, consisted only of motoring to a nearby beach with a group of friends on board. I set the sails anyway to make sure they fitted and they flogged gently in the light breeze. Bright and clean, a mainsail, storm jib and yankee - a genoa that is cut high off the deck - and it was a shape that I could put a reef into, thereby giving me two sizes of sail in one. I raised them all and they fitted perfectly. The headsails were 'hank on', meaning I had to go to the bow every time I wanted to raise or lower the sail, but it would have to do as the expensive roller furling systems were well beyond my budget.

On returning from our short cruise, I noticed that the water in the tanks had become tainted and smelt foul. The tanks were in the keel and I had epoxy coated them but I must have missed a spot. When water comes into prolonged contact with polyester resin, the resin used in the construction of fiberglass boats, it becomes tainted and smells like marzipan - undrinkable. So the rest of that night was spent emptying the tanks, drying and sanding them, then reapplying a new epoxy lining. Hopefully that would solve the problem.

Dancing on Raindrops

...It did.

Sometimes I would go to the yacht club in the evenings and try to pick up a bit of advice from the local sailors, all of whom thought me to be quite mad leaving at that time of year. One piece of advice that I was given, was that in the event I should hit a big storm, I should heave to. Well it all sounded simple enough.

Two weeks after launching, Tapestry was ready for sea. I did not sleep much that night. My mind was filled with all the things that still had to be checked and of course I had the nagging feeling that I had forgotten something, perhaps something important.

Up before the dawn, I checked and rechecked everything I could possibly think of. Walking the deck, I made sure that nothing was left unsecured. Below decks, all the canned foods had been stowed into the lockers and nothing was amiss. That was the day I had looked forward to and I must have been the most excited person on earth.

At eight o'clock my friends started to arrive to see me off. Zak, a close friend of many years, who saved my life by telling me that if I should ever find myself in an airless situation while diving, I should drink water before being overcome by the need to take a breath. He walked down the dock carrying a case of whisky on his shoulder as a farewell gift, and although I did not know it at the time, that case was to be my savior for but a brief period.

"Hey, what are you still doing here," he said. "I thought you were supposed to go sailing?" and with that he passed me the case of whisky. "You might need a drink or two on your way across the Atlantic, so here is a little gift for you." We sat in the cockpit and chatted for a while and made the usual promises to write and keep in touch.

"Phone me any time you want," he said, looking me in the eye. "Because if you can't phone your friends at any time of the night or day, then they are not your friends." Such true words.

My mother arrived with a large dish of freshly baked lasagna and baskets filled with goodies that would save me from having to cook for the next few days. We chatted for a while and soon it was ten o'clock and the chosen hour had arrived, so I started the motor and let go the mooring lines amidst the hugs and tears.

Emotions were high, so it was with some relief when Tapestry slowly moved from the dock and headed towards the entrance of Cape Town harbor. The air was chilly and the sky clear. The weather forecast for the next few days was good and thereafter terrible, but it was the best weather window for the foreseeable future.

Out of the harbor we went and into the icy waters of a Cape winter. Table Mountain in all its glory stood high and flat topped and seemed to wish us farewell. The winds were light from the south, so once clear of the entrance I set the sails and stopped the motor. The sudden silence seemed to make the parting of friends and family that much harder.

Beyond Robben Island, where Nelson Mandela was incarcerated at the time, my favorite mountain began to melt into the horizon behind. Nothing but ocean lay ahead for over seventeen hundred miles and then hopefully I would be able to find a tiny dot on the chart, the island of St Helena.

My plan was to head northwest as fast as I possibly could. Up beyond the cold frontal systems and into the warm trade winds. From then on I was out of contact with humanity and my only means of communication was a small VHF radio, with which I could call other ships that were in the vicinity. But I had no need to talk to anyone. Goodbyes were said and I was off to sail around the world.

That was the first time I had Tapestry sailing and it seemed as though she had been doing it forever. At five knots in a calm sea the boat was very comfortable and the autopilot seemed to work well enough to allow me to begin the task of learning to navigate. I sat outside and began to read Mary Blewitt's Celestial Navigation. Azimuths, declination, geographic positions and so on, it made no sense whatsoever.

Night soon came and the loom of Cape Town rapidly diminished astern. A fiery sunset seemed to bode well for the weather to come, but as darkness arrived, so the temperature plummeted and it was not long before I had on layers and layers of clothing.

For dinner I heated a portion of mother's lasagna in the gimbaled oven and as the boat rolled, so the oven swung and kept the surface horizontal. Eureka, it worked.

That night seemed lonelier than any I could remember and the adrenaline still coursed through my veins, as I sat out in the cockpit with only the stars for company. I had shortened sail before the sunset to make for a relaxing first night and then I bided my time in the cockpit, as I did not wish to go below to sleep. There were too many ships about and I did not want to miss a moment of the first night, as Tapestry sailed over the horizon to a different world.

Adrenaline and coffee kept me awake, and as Orion's Belt moved overhead, I pondered the enormity of the task that lay ahead. I'm sure someone at some time, has said that a good student is one who has to learn. That was my predicament, I guess I had jumped off in the deep end and would quickly have to learn to swim.

By the time the dawn came the horizon was nothing but sky and water and as soon as it was light, I shook the reefs out of the sails and our speed increased. I was still trying to get away from the cold front that was supposed to be on its way. I spent most of the morning making sure that nothing on deck had chafed during the night and it looked as though everything was fine. So far, so good.

Much of the day was consumed by my mission to learn to navigate. Slowly I came to understand the language of celestial navigation and by the end of the day, although I was a long way from actually being able to use the information, I felt that I was slowly beginning to grasp a basic understanding.

On the second evening, dark clouds began arriving in the sky from the west and I knew it would not be long before the wind picked up and changed direction, so I shortened sail and prepared the storm jib ready for use. Within an hour it was blowing a full gale out of the northwest and the seas had picked up to over ten feet. Ice-cold spray was continuously blowing over the deck and the motion of the boat had changed to that of an obsessed maniac, as we slammed into each successive wave - heeling over so that the gunwales were sometimes well below the surface of the water. The front had arrived sooner than anticipated.

As the seas rose, my stomach took a turn for the worse. I began to feel terrible as seasickness took a hold and it was not long before I was vomiting overboard - being sure to do it on the leeward side.

Seasickness comes in three different emotions. First you are scared you are going to be sick. Second you are scared you are going to die. Third, after a few hours, you wish you had died.

The wind increased and so too did the size of the waves, and before midnight it was blowing well into the fifties and the seas were huge. The tops of the waves broke and slammed into the hull, then covered the decks in solid 'green water'.

By then I had wrestled down the main sail, tied it to the boom and lashed the yankee on the foredeck. My new storm jib was the only sail flying and sometimes I had the feeling that even that was too large for the wind and the boat.

Hove to they had told me in the bar before leaving and these surely seemed like the conditions they had described. That was all very well in theory, but in practice, I did not have the faintest idea what to do. I clipped my safety harness onto the jackstay, a strong line that ran from the bow to the stern on either side. It would hold me if I fell overboard and at the same time allowed me to move about the deck.

Cautiously I made my way to the base of the mast to let down the storm jib, holding on for dear life, as the boat was moving so violently. One hand for the boat and one for me. Down came the sail and all of a sudden Tapestry took on a new motion, it was far more erratic and pronounced than before. A wave hit us on the side and we rolled over until the spreaders almost touched the water. I clung to bottom of the mast, soaking wet and scared. That was not what I had envisaged and it did not feel right to be totally at the mercy of the waves, so I hauled the storm jib back up, crawled to the cockpit and sat there in the freezing cold, vomiting over the side.

The wind vane wanted nothing to do with those conditions and I cursed it. Before leaving, I had lots of sailors tell me that that wind vane autopilot was the finest you could buy, but so far I was not impressed. I tied the tiller hard over to the leeward side and that seemed to ease the awful motion, as the jib would blow us off the wind and the rudder would bring us back into it.

Little did I know I was then hove to and as the waves slammed into the hull they were glanced off the side and Tapestry shook the water from her decks. Then she sailed down the back of the wave, only to reach the trough as the next one broke in front.

For three days the storm raged and for three days I lived in the cockpit, hanging on for dear life and dry retching almost continuously. I felt so sick and exhausted that many a moment I was ready to toss in the towel and head down wind, back to Cape Town. Back to a warm shower and no seasickness. Not once did I ever think it would be that hard, or that seasickness would affect me to such an extent. I had tried going below to get dry and warm but I felt so violently ill, that I could not stand it for more than a few moments.

By the time the weather had abated I was exhausted and frozen. Everything I had drunk for the last few days had been brought up within moments, and I was so cold and wet that my body was an opaque white; covered in wrinkles from being saturated in cold salt water for so long. The wind had died enough for me to set a little bit of mainsail and that helped enormously with both the uncomfortable motion and the sickness. For the first time in three days, I went below, put on some dry clothes and collapsed into my bunk like a dead man. For eight straight hours I slept and it was good, for when I woke I had an unquenchable thirst and began to consume huge amounts of water. The sea had calmed and the remaining swell was rounded and comfortable, so I set more sail and continued on my way.

It was time to start taking some sun sights and see if that stuff really worked, for I had no idea where I was. I stood in the hatchway to brace myself and while looking into the eyepiece of the sextant, I slowly swung the bottom in a small arc. Through the eyepiece I could see a vertically split screen, one half was the horizon and the other the sun. As the sextant rocked from side to side, the sun would follow the same arc and the idea was to get the base of the sun to touch the horizon, then note the exact time and the angle.

I took three readings and went below to work out the numbers. For each step of the process I had to refer to my book and two hours later, with a page full of calculations, I arrived at an answer. Then I plotted that position line on my chart. Woops, something was wrong. My sight put me in Johannesburg, over a thousand miles away and nowhere near any coast. I was glad at the time that the harbormaster could not see my first attempt, but it did not take long to realize that somewhere along the way, I had added a number instead of subtracting it. I took more sights, reworked the calculations and sure enough, that was my position, two hundred miles offshore. Ouch, two hundred miles, that was a long way, a very long way.

Day six and the ocean turned color. It changed in the space of a few hours from a cold and inhospitable gray, to a beautiful crystal blue and the temperature of both the water and the air rose. Flying fish were all about, leaping to get out of the way, then gliding across the surface on their silver-blue wings. A small bird landed on the deck and I wondered where he might be headed, so far from land.

I was in the trades and winter was behind me. From there on, with a bit of luck I would be sailing downwind all the way and as long as we went downwind, the seasickness stayed away. It is said that gentlemen only sail downwind, I understood why.

Life was close to perfect, twenty-two years old and there I was living my dream, slap-bang in the middle of my paradise. A routine seemed to come naturally. I would have to be on deck mid-morning, noon and mid-afternoon to take my sights, but beyond that everything went with the rhythm of the ocean. I spent a lot of time reading, reading about navigation and I was getting the hang of things. Daily I plotted my position on a large chart of the Atlantic and it was thrilling to see the little crosses slowly progress towards St Helena.

If I needed some fish for the pot, I would put the lines out early in the morning and usually by noon I brought them in again, having caught what I needed. Tuna and dorado (mahi-mahi), those were my two staples, but sometimes I was lucky and a wahoo would find itself on the dinner table. Early afternoon became shower time, before the sun lost its heat. I had a bucket with a length of rope attached to the handle and standing at the side of the boat I would toss the bucket forward. As soon as it hit the water it would begin to sink, all the while coming back towards me. When it was directly below, I hauled on the line and there it was, one bucket of sparkling clear ocean water. The bath of the gods!

Most shampoos do not lather in salt water, so I would spray myself with fresh water first, lather and then rinse the soap off with a few buckets of salt water, finishing the process with a bit more fresh. I had a shower down below, but it certainly could not compare with showering outside in the middle of the ocean.

Beginning to hate my wind vane intensely, I gave it a name to make cussing it more face-to-face and personal,

George Philemon Kanga. Strange perhaps, but it fitted and he became known as George. George was the other crewmember and at lunchtime every day he was fed with a drop of oil. Sometimes for hours on end he would steer perfectly, then all of a sudden he would go belly up and start keeping an erratic course. For no discernable reason, the tiller would be pushed over from one side to the other. Tapestry reacted instantly to the input of the rudder and changed course, which caused the sails to flog and made me run to the cockpit to sort things out. George you dumb ass!

When the wind picked up, day or night, I would have to stay alert for George's antics and I was getting annoyed with him. Hours upon hours were then spent trying to figure the ins and outs of George the beast. Unfortunately he had arrived without instructions but it seemed an easy enough installation, as he hung over the stern attached by two large aluminum pipes. A light piece of plywood acted as a wind vane that pointed directly into the wind and would flop to one side or the other, as the boat changed course. That in turn moved a paddle in the water and that moved the tiller. Simple enough, or so it seemed.

Since the first few days out of Cape Town, I had seen no ships so I took to sleeping at night but still I would be woken often, as George went off course and needed attention. Sailing downwind is far more gentle a motion than going into the weather. I carried a full main out to one side and on the other, the yankee was attached to the spinnaker pole, which kept the sail in the correct position so the wind from behind could fill it.

As the days molded into one another, the island came closer on the chart. Beyond the halfway mark, then only five hundred miles to go, then two hundred and it was with bated breath that I scanned the ocean on the last day looking for land. I had not put my navigation to the test and had heard of a few stories where people could not find the island, forcing them to go and look for the South American continent instead.

Eighteen days after leaving Cape Town, there it was and it looked magnificent. A brown peak protruding up through the vastness of the ocean. The island belongs to Britain and it was here that Napoleon Bonaparte was exiled after his defeat at Waterloo. Prior to his capture by the allies, in a coup d'etait, he became one of three consuls who ruled France. Only four years later, he was Emperor of France and shortly after, also became king of Italy. He built a huge army that captured Moscow but lost it to the winter. That lonely and barren rock was a place from which there would be no escape. Or so we are told.

The island slowly grew larger and soon I could make out the vegetation but there were no houses to be seen. Much of it was lush and green, however one part in particular looked barren and devoid of any life. It looked almost as if it were from a scene on the moon. The trade winds are constantly battering that section of the island and because the volcanic soil is so erosive, nothing ever gets the chance to grow there.

I dropped the sails as I rounded the corner of the island, into the lee and motored along the coast to the village of Jamestown. It was small and nestled in a steep sided valley, surrounded by lush vegetation. One of Jamestown's most notable features, Jacob's ladder, was clearly visible against the contrast of green. Six hundred and ninety-nine steps and nine hundred feet long, it looked fit to 'break your heart going up and break your neck coming down.' It was constructed in 1829 to connect Jamestown to the garrison on Ladder Hill and was used to haul ammunition to the gun battery.

The anchorage was filled with a dozen small fishing boats and two other cruising yachts, both of which I had seen in Cape Town. The customs boat came out to greet me and showed me where he wanted me to drop my anchor. Because it is such a small and deep anchorage, boats had to anchor both the bow and the stern, as there was not enough room to swing on a single anchor line. My first port of call, there it was and it was real. The customs official was

Dancing on Raindrops

a very pleasant old gentleman and he came aboard after helping me get both anchors out and set. He had a cup of tea as I filled out the necessary paperwork and he welcomed me to his island with such genuine pleasure, that I knew I was going to like that place.

Once he had left, Aussie Dave came over in his dinghy to say hello. He had sailed thousands of miles since leaving Australia and I could surely use some of his knowledge. We were sitting in the cockpit talking, when all of a sudden he exclaimed, "Bloody hell mate, what's up with your bloody wind vane?"

"That piece of shit! George the terrible I call it," I replied.

"Oath mate, it's no bloody wonder, you got your bloody lines wrong haven't you."

"What do you mean?"

"Bloody hell mate yours is set up for a wheel steering, with a tiller you got to cross the bloody steering lines!"

I spent a month on that remote island. Most of my time was taken up by trying to finish some of the things aboard that still needed attention, and of course changing George's steering lines so that they crossed - that was my first priority.

The town was a single street and included the courthouse, hotel, bank and police station. All the buildings were made of stone and an aura of the islands colonial past permeated everywhere. To get out of the town there were two roads, one on either side of the steep cliff and the countryside beyond was beautiful. Hills surrounded green valleys and the island was dotted with mansions, one for the Governor, one for Napoleon and so on.

The only way on or off St. Helena has always been by boat. Once a month the mail ship arrived and brought with it not only mail, but also the many other things needed to sustain the small and isolated population. In fact the isolation and thus the lack of jobs, forced many of the young men to move to the island of Ascension, the nearest neighbor some eight hundred miles to the northwest. The American military kept a base on the island and that provided the nearest source of work. Unfortunately it did nothing to stem the huge problem of interbreeding, as all the girls remained behind.

Sometimes getting ashore was a mission in itself, for when the swells picked up, so the waves would crash into and sometimes over the pier. One day I needed to go ashore for something and the swells were large. I waited just off the wave line for a while to get a feel for the rhythm of the ocean. Judging the moment, I hit the throttle and the little outboard sprang to life and headed straight for the concrete wall. At that moment I was thirty feet away from the pier and the top of it was ten feet above me. As I raced closer, so the swell behind overtook me and an instant before we struck, the water rose up and swamped the dock, carrying with it my little dinghy and me.

Getting out again was not so easy. That time I had to ask the local lads for help, as they held the dinghy with me in it on the edge of the pier, waiting for a wave that was big enough to carry me out.

One of the most disturbing sights I had ever seen sometimes greeted me when I went ashore. There, the local people ate dolphins and occasionally there were three or four of my friends lying dead on the dock - a sight that always touched a chord in my heart.

Tapestry was ready to go and it was time to leave. The second half of the crossing was much the same distance as the first, but I did not have to take on the gales of the South Atlantic. I motored out passed the lee of the island, hoisted the sails and set my course to 270 degrees.

No longer was I the novice, the inexperienced beginner who did not even know how to heave to. I had confidence in my abilities and had proven to myself that I could navigate. My seamanship, although it was improving daily, was good enough to sail the first leg and by comparison, the second half of the crossing was a walk in the park.

George worked like a charm, his steering was perfect and so was the weather; it was ten days before I had to adjust George or the sails. Life was about rolling down the gentle swells, as the warm and constant trade winds pushed us onwards.

Dancing on Raindrops

BAY OF THE DOLPHINS

Two hundred miles east of Forteleza, a large town off the east coast of Brazil, lies paradise. A small volcanic island of such unspoiled pristine beauty that the spinner dolphins chose to make it their home, Fernando de Noronha.

I anchored in Santo Antonio bay amidst a multitude of small fishing boats and set off ashore to clear customs. The water was crystal clear and the seashore was covered in white beaches, all under the shadow of Morro do Pico, a phallic like rock that rose almost vertically over a thousand feet above the sea.

Pulling my dinghy high onto the deserted beach, I tossed the anchor out to prevent it from floating away, then set off to find customs. On the hill above were a few buildings and I stopped at the largest to inquire as to the whereabouts of the customs office.

Well, I did not speak any Portuguese and no one seemed to speak any English, but I understood that that was the right place and customs would soon be here to clear me in.

An old man sat behind a broken desk shuffling papers and he motioned to an empty chair for me to take a seat. No sooner had I sat down, an elderly woman came into the room. The two of them chatted for a moment and then she looked at me and asked if I would like a beer while waiting. I made out that that was a great idea, so she left and returned with two cold beers. The man behind the desk and I saluted one another and began to drink.

What friendly people. The customs official seemed to be taking his time and every once in a while the old woman would return with more beer. Eventually when the customs man arrived, he too ordered a beer. We proceeded to fill in the necessary paperwork, all the while the cold beers kept arriving and the three of us kept on drinking.

Well it turned out that the building was not only the customs office but also the bar. Tapestry was the only yacht in the bay and I guess that was a reason for an occasion, so it was late that night when I finally made my way back to the dinghy on unsteady legs. After all that the official did not clear me in, I was told I would have to wait until the mainland.

Close to where I anchored was a bay called Baia dos Golfinhos (bay of the dolphins). Home of perhaps the world's largest resident pod; sometimes there would be literally hundreds of dolphins. The group is reckoned to be six hundred strong and they would leave in the evenings to hunt, returning every morning to spend the day in that gorgeous bay.

Soon I became acquainted with a few of them, as most mornings I would ride over in the dinghy and go for a swim. Sometimes they were there to greet me, splashing and jumping in excitement and as I dived into the water they would come over and say hello. One young female was so friendly that she allowed me to stroke her and together we would swim across the bay and back. As I left the water, she would put her head above the surface and squeak, like a child wanting to play some more.

One afternoon I was walking along the beach with a local boy and he looked up into the sky where hundreds of seagulls were flying. He began to call something in the sky.

"Come on baby, come on, come on," or words to that effect.

I was starting to think that he was a little crazy, I mean who calls to a flock of seagulls? Then I noticed a bird leave the flock and dive down towards the beach. My young friend put out his hand and the seagull flew along the beach and landed on it.

"Oh my baby, how good to see you," he cooed as he kissed the bird and stroked it. He explained to me that he had raised this bird from the nest - had seen her flying in the sky and she had come to say hello.

Such were the natural wonders of that paradise.

Dancing on Raindrops

THE RED WAX SEAL

Arriving in any new country, the first thing you have to do is clear in with customs and immigration. Arrival by yacht is no different, except for the amount of paperwork required. A clearance certificate from your previous port of call and registration papers for the vessel, are two items that are most usually needed. I had the clearance certificate from St Helena. That form stated that I was good to go and that my next port of call would be Forteleza in Brazil. It was the registration papers that I did not have.

On leaving Cape Town, I had not had the time or the inclination to formally register my yacht, so I had a friend, a lawyer, draft a letter for me. It stated that I was the sole owner of the yacht Tapestry and thus owned 64 shares in the vessel. (Maritime law has only 64 shares available for 100 percent ownership.)

The document by itself was unremarkable in any way, anyone could have written it, so I decided to make it official. I placed a large red wax seal at the bottom right corner with a piece of red cloth imbedded into it. When it was still soft, I used a coin to make an impression on the surface of the wax. The result was a very official looking piece of paper.

Thus far I had not needed the paper, as the customs in both St Helena and Fernando had not asked for it. So, armed with passport, clearance certificate and my registration paper, I set off to clear customs and immigration in Fortaleza.

After asking directions in 'mime language', I found myself in the immigration office with a surly looking official on the other side of a gray steel desk. The room was empty, except for large files stacked on a single bookshelf. Paint was peeling on the walls and a bare light bulb hung from a wire on the ceiling. I handed over my passport and clearance certificate but kept the registration paper, hoping I would not have to use it.

"Blah, blah, blah, papéis do registo?" he looked at me questioningly.

"Non, no registo," I replied, thinking that the matter would then be overlooked.

"Whaat, no papéis do registo! Blah, blah, blah," he replied in a loud incredulous voice, which I took to mean that I if did not have registration papers, then I was not welcome in the country and would have to leave immediately. That was not a course of action I wished to pursue.

"Aaaah, registo," I said, trying to sound as though of course I had such a document and had simply not understood what it was that he wanted. My heart began to beat faster.

Oh boy, here goes, I thought as I shuffled in my briefcase looking for the emergency piece of paper. The idea of being told to leave and head back to sea was not one I was looking forward to, so it was with great anticipation that I handed over my home made document.

He took the piece of paper and I could not help but notice that it was up side down in his hands; the red wax seal in the top left-hand corner, as he seemed to read every word.

"Aah, papéis do registo," he said, nodding his head and continuing to try and read the inverted document. Placing the paper on the desk, he reached for my passport, opened it and gave me the much-needed official stamp.

"Three months," he said smiling, as he handed all the paperwork back to me. Oh yea!

WHISKY FOR SALE

The one hundred dollars I left Cape Town with was history and I was almost flat broke. Here was a country whose currency was almost worthless. One cruzeiro was worth less than a piece of single-ply toilet paper and those with dollars were able to live well - that however was not me. But I did have whisky, Johnny Walker red label.

My friend Zak had given me the case before I left and it was to come in very handy, especially as I had found out that it was selling on the black market for about $100 per bottle. If I could sell the case, my financial uncertainties would be over.

The Red Lion was a small local bar down one of the back alleys in town. It was there I was told that I would be able to sell my wares. So the night before, I calculated how many cruzeiros I would accept for the case. Twelve times one hundred. Wow, then that times however many thousand cruzeiros to the dollar was bla bla bla million cruzeiros. I would be rich.

Knowing hardly any Portuguese, I made a mental note of the amount and set off the next afternoon with a dozen bottles carefully wrapped in a shoulder bag. Through the seedy parts of town I walked, trying to look as inconspicuous as possible. White skin, blue eyes, long blond hair and there I was trying to be inconspicuous. What a joke, I must have stood out like a sore thumb.

There it was, The Red Lion, a run down old building in perhaps the nastiest part of town. The paint on the walls was cracked and dry. Litter covered the sidewalk but to me it was beautiful. There was my fortune - if I could only get the owner to buy my wares.

I entered and walked over to the bar where a big burly man stood behind the counter. Half a dozen elderly men sat about the room drinking Pitu, an alcohol that is made from sugar cane and I had been told by other yachties that it could run a stove as well as any cooking alcohol. They would mix it with lime juice and sugar, then its name would change to caipirinha. Same rotgut stuff but it sure tasted better.

I ordered a beer, lit up a local cigarette and smiled at the barman, wondering if he was the man to speak to. He brought my drink and I took a few sips, waiting for everyone to stop focusing in my direction, for I certainly was the center of attraction. "What is this gringo doing in our bar?" I could read the minds of the locals. A few minutes went by and soon they ignored my presence.

It was my moment. I leaned over the counter and quietly whispered to the barman, "Johnny Walker" and motioned to the bag on the floor beside me. There, it was done and I waited with bated breath to see the result of my two words. A huge grin covered his face, as he stood upright and motioned for me to follow him into a back room. *Well here goes*, I thought.

The small room was dim and musty, in the center an old kitchen table. A bare light bulb glowed in the corner, covered in cobwebs and dirt. My man tapped on the table. Here, put it here. I placed the bag on the table and unzipped it. The smile on his face could not have been any bigger, as he picked up the bottles one by one and placed them upright on the table. Yep, twelve bottles, there they were.

"How much?" he asked.

"Bla bla bla million cruzeiros," I replied.

"Non non non, bla bla bla million cruzeiros" he countered, as the smile disappeared off his face.

Oh boy, what was that all about, I wondered? *Whatever, keep going.*

"No, bla bla bla million cruzeiros," I said once again, shaking my head, hoping that I had remembered the correct set of words from the night before.

"Non non non, bla bla bla million cruzeiros," he countered once again, deadly serious.

Whatever amount he was coming up with, I had not the faintest idea. All I was sure of was that I had no money, but I needed to buy provisions and to pay for my clearance in order to leave. I felt my back was to the wall.

What to do? To say no, meant I would have to find another buyer and go through the whole thing again. What would be their reaction to the words 'Johnny Walker?' I wondered.

"Okay" I said and the smile returned to the barman's face in an instant. Wait; he motioned as he went out the door.

My heart was pounding. There was nothing to stop him coming back with a couple of friends and kicking me out, while the whisky still stood on the table. I waited and waited, each moment taking longer. I listened to the sounds that came from the other side of the door, to try and get a heads up on what was going on, but they told me nothing.

Then he came back into the room, a large pile of dirty brown notes in his hands. Oh yea, payday. He started counting the notes on the table and I counted along. One thousand, two thousand, ten thousand, one hundred thousand; as the pile grew taller and taller.

Bla bla bla million cruzeiros. That was my number, but he carried on adding notes to the table. Once my magic number was reached, I stopped counting. Not intentionally, I was just so amazed that my brain went dead, so I stood there and watched as the pile grew and grew. The big man was concentrating and as the last note in his hand was placed on the top of the pile, he looked up at me.

"Okay?" he said questioningly, raising his eyebrows.

"Okay, obrigado," I smiled and nodded my head.

Yea baby I'm rich, now to get the hell out of here.

"Bla bla bla," he was speaking so fast that I did not understand a word. However, thanks for a good deal and if your friends have any whisky to sell then please send them here, was what I took his words to mean.

I scooped up the pile of notes off the table, split it in half and put one wad in each of my pockets.

"Obrigado," I said once again, nodded and headed for the door - I wanted out. No one in the bar seemed to notice my passing, but I guess I wasn't really looking at them. My eyes were fixed on the doorway and a moment later I was out in the street.

A small dark alleyway appeared to my right and I stepped into it. Deserted, excellent. I dug into my pocket, pulled out one of the wads of notes and slipped it into the front of my underwear. Then, with the second wad I did the same, except that time I left a few notes in the pocket. If I were to get mugged, they may be happy with what was left in my pocket and not notice my bulging crotch. All done in four or five seconds, I went back out onto the street feeling much more secure.

I walked quickly, like someone in a hurry, keeping a watchful eye all around. Occasionally I would stop abruptly and look behind to see if someone was following me. No one was, of that I was sure.

Back to the boat I headed. There and only there, would I feel totally secure. I launched the dinghy, started the outboard and a few minutes later was safely below decks in Tapestry's main saloon. I reached down into my underwear to retrieve my wad of freedom notes and I must have jumped as though there was a scorpion in my pants.

Nothing there. Not a single note remained in my pants. The small bundle of mugging money was still in my pocket, but my pants were empty. It was a disaster, but fortunately there was enough cash left in my pocket to pay for my clearance out of the country.

What happened to all that cash? I had no idea but I chose to believe that someone needed it more than I. After all, I still had enough to get by and it seemed as though lady luck was with me in everything I did. Good luck or bad luck, it's still luck and I was glad to be associated with it.

In Cape Town I had bought a new Seagull outboard motor, but I found it so temperamental and so hard to start, that often I would have to row ashore anyway. It was first on the list of things that could be turned into cash for provisions; so I put a notice on the yacht club board and to my surprise, the very next day three people came to see me. They all wanted that fantastic motor. It seemed the Brazilian sailors regarded it to be the best and because of the high rate of exchange to the pound, they were very expensive and highly sought after.

"Yes, British Seagull, that's the best motor you can buy," said the highest bidder as he handed me a wad of notes.

I wished him luck, readied Tapestry for sea once again, provisioned and headed for the Caribbean. No longer would I have the frustration of trying to start that outboard.

Dancing on Raindrops

WAKEY WAKEY -
YOU ARE ABOUT TO DIE

I left Forteleza on Friday the 13th, with a stiff breeze blowing from the southeast. Never leave on a Friday. Any old sea salt can tell you that. For me however, that was simply superstitious nonsense and a good time to throw fate to the wind, for I was about to embark on a voyage to a tropical paradise.

In days of old, when sail was the only means of sea transport, finding a crew willing to undertake the long sea time and dangers of the ocean, was often not possible. Payday was on a Thursday, so come that night the bars and taverns were packed with revelers partying to the full. Some were so fall down damn drunk, that they were easy pickings for the groups of henchmen who would knock them over the head if necessary and carry the poor hapless and unconscious drunks back to a ship. Before dawn, the vessel would be far out to sea as the new crew started to awake.

Surprised faces? One of the major drawbacks to that method of finding crew, was that should the boat experience any foul weather, the new crew did not have the seamanship necessary to control the vessel. Therefore a good many ships went to the bottom of the ocean, or were smashed to pieces on some foreign coast because they had Friday crew.

Tapestry's white hull shone in the sunlight reflected off the choppy water. I pushed the engine into gear and began to move forward as André, a yachtsman from another boat who was helping me out on the foredeck, shouted that the anchor was up.

Soon the sails were set, and it was only once we were pointing out to sea and everything on the deck ship shape, that I slowed down and the excitement of the voyage seemed to be strong upon my heart. With a little less than 1500 miles to go, once again there was only my boat, the ocean and me.

My choice, if it were possible, was to head out to the 100 fathom line (600 feet) and there, hopefully catch some of the current that moves northwards towards the Caribbean islands. Along that depth, there is a huge mountain range below the sea and it rises quickly from the ocean floor, some 3000 fathoms below. Then, from there to the shore, it is a gentle gradient that takes one or two hundred miles for the mountain to rise up as beach. The ocean currents converge on the undersea mountain and are pushed off to the north, as they cannot cross that huge ridge.

On the surface and if you were heading north, that was great news. It meant that in addition to the five knots Tapestry was able to average, I should have an extra two or three knots of current to help me on my way. That meant an additional thirty miles per day. I would be there in no time at all.

The first night was filled with action. The land had slowly disappeared behind and once again, water was everywhere. I had shortened sail before dark and although we were then about a knot slower, she was easier to manage. The thick clouds that were last seen pouring across the sky around the time of sunset, had removed all the stars from the heavens; the only light to be seen was an occasional small fishing boat, a white hue far in the distance. It was so dark that combined with the new motion of the boat and the lingering effects of excitement, it was very disorienting sitting out in the cockpit, trying to hone in on where the horizon should be. Up, down and all of every which ways she moved, as we reached to the northeast in twenty knots of wind. The seas were choppy and every once in a while a wave would come from nowhere and slam into the side of the boat, covering me in spray.

Every hour or so, I would go below and make some coffee or a snack and then spend some time looking at the chart. I would estimate how fast we had been sailing and in what direction, then add in a compensation for what I felt the current was doing and plotted the result on the chart.

A DR position (dead reckoning) was where I reckoned myself to be. I still don't know what the dead part means, but I did know that in that environment, you either had to be dead good or dead lucky for that type of navigation to be worth much.

On the chart, I had seen an oil rig about ten miles ahead and I wanted to stay well clear of it, so I changed course, a little more north and kept as good a lookout as I was able. Beginning to weary, I was startled by the sight of a small fishing boat suddenly appearing in front of me, as they shone a light to be seen. Aye, seen them, that I surely had.

In an instant I grabbed the tiller, fumbled to disengage the autopilot and turned Tapestry enough to miss them. The boat was only about twenty feet long and known as a Jancada. It was made of wood with open decks and had six or seven fishermen aboard, all waving as one of them lifted the lantern. Then, the crest of a wave would come between us and they would be gone again, reappearing only when both them and I were on the crest of another wave. A couple more sightings and they were gone, leaving me to breathe a sigh of relief and once again hook up the autopilot and try to get comfortable. That is as comfortable as I could be sitting outside in the dead of night, the boat heeling and jerking below me, as she rode the short and uncomfortable seas. There was twenty to thirty knots of wind blowing over the deck and every once in a while I got a bucket of salt water thrown at me.

That first dawn made my spirit soar. Slowly the sky began to change and faster and faster the light came. Once again I had a horizon and soon it was as bright as it was going to get, as the clouds had not gone away. The motion of the boat then had a visual sense, as I could see the waves coming. As beautiful as it was to have the light back, it was the time I needed to go to sleep. Only an hour, then back up to check on things. Who says you can't sleep while holding on with both your hands and your feet at the same time?

I kept up that routine for most of the day. In my wake times, I would plot my lucky position on the chart. That was the only means I had of keeping track of roughly where I was. Besides a compass and a sextant, it was all I had to navigate with and that day I was not going to be seeing the sun, so I could not take a sight and thereby give myself a position line.

A position line is a line on the chart, calculated from a sextant sight, along which I am somewhere. I wouldn't know where on the line until several hours later. That is if I could take another sun sight, do the calculations that require numbers to be looked up from two different volumes of books, then added, subtracted and whatever else. The new line will be at an angle to the old line, because the sun has moved position in the sky, so the two will cross each other.

There, on the intersection, is not where I was. The old line had to be moved, because that was the line along which I was several hours ago. So I would figure out how far I had traveled and in what direction, then move the old line in the direction and the distance traveled. Where the two lines intersected, was my position, give or take a few miles and only made possible if I could see the sun.

Added to the complexities of celestial navigation is time. The sun moves across our planet at a rate of four seconds per mile. That meant to me that for every four seconds my watch was off, I would have a mile of error, regardless of how good the sight was. Oh for a quartz watch.

By late afternoon the water began to change color and the wave motion changed, as if on cue. Almost imperceptible at first, but within a few hours the water had turned to a deep blue; that color of blue that you can see into - down and down - crystal clear water, with a comfortable rounded swell. Gone was the brown, shallow section and here once again was ocean sailing.

After the first three days at sea, I developed a routine. To begin with, my bowels began to work again and the terrible feeling of seasickness slowly went away. There I was, out on the ocean all by myself once again. What a fantastic feeling. The weather was clearing, so I was able to get a position fix. Only fifteen miles out in three days of DR. Beginners luck?

Normally I would take short naps during the day, as other ships were more likely to have people out and about and therefore I reckoned there to be less of a chance of collision. All the vessels I had so far encountered were traveling in the same direction as me, making the most of the northbound current.

One day soon became the next and the only passing of time, were the crosses on the chart that kept making their way north, one hundred and fifty miles per day - screaming along.

Five days out, two hundred miles offshore and the ocean turned to mud. Literally, in the space of a few miles, the sea changed from that crystal blue to an ugly shade of brown. Oil slicks and logs covered the surface. I checked the chart to make sure I was still in deep water and sure enough, that is exactly where I was. The mud and muck was coming from the Amazon River, two hundred miles to my west.

Fresh water is lighter than salt, so as the river flows into the sea, the fresh water tends to stay on top. It was a crazy feeling, being far out to sea and sailing in fresh water. For two days the water remained muddy and its dissipation was a lot slower, due to the fact that it then had time to mix with the current and flow north like everything else in that environment.

Bequia, pronounced Bequi, is a small island in the southern part of the Caribbean chain and is one of a group of islands called the Grenadines. Other islands include such beautiful names as Mustique, Baliceaux and Mayreau - small slices of heaven tucked away in a special part of paradise.

My intended route was to leave all the islands to port (left), then, when I approached Bequia, I would turn and sail through one of the channels between the islands and into the Caribbean Sea. However, even the best of plans are sometimes forced to change.

Studying the chart one day, I noticed that the channel between Trinidad and Tobago was called The Galleon's Passage. It was too much; it had to be done. I don't know if it was the seclusion or what, but the idea of sailing through a passage by that name was too much to resist. I would sail the passage and enter the Caribbean Sea south of Grenada, the most southerly island in the chain, then approach Bequia from the southwest. It seemed like a great plan.

It was about twenty-four hours to landfall and I had not seen the sun or the stars for three days. The chart was a mass of lines rubbed out and redrawn, only to be rubbed out once again and replaced with a new and improved version. Somewhere in front of me were two islands but exactly where I did not know. Hours upon hours I poured over the charts, trying to get an estimate on my position, for after so long without a fix, the possibility for error grows exponentially.

On the night of the 4th day I knew that I must be close and by then I was allowing an error of fifty miles from my DR position. Not exactly what I needed to make an accurate approach on a body of water only a few miles wide, with a low sandy island on either side.

Many a moment I was tempted to abandon my plan and head back out to the safety of the open ocean. I had hardly slept for the last four days and it was not a good time to go down for a nap. With such exhaustion, I might have slept too long and ended the voyage on some shore ahead.

A pharmacist in Forteleza had given me some pills, in the event that for some reason or another I did not wish to sleep. I felt that right then was a good time to try them out, as I was dozing in the cockpit doing my best to stay awake. The pills sure worked and I spent the rest of the night walking the decks.

Dawn on the eleventh day after leaving Forteleza and there directly in front of me were two small islands,

Dancing on Raindrops

Trinidad and Tobago. Between them - The Galleon's Passage. Oh wow. Yes, yes, yes!

I had done what I had set out to do, even though the sun had not been seen for five days and I was ecstatic, ecstatic and exhausted. It seemed to take forever to sail the passage, but by evening the islands had receded into the horizon astern and it was time to change course to the northwest; south of Grenada and up into the Caribbean Sea.

Almost there, but I could stay awake no longer, so I shortened sail and checked that my course was away from land, turned on my navigation lights and collapsed onto my bunk. I am sure I was fast asleep in seconds.

The next thing I knew, I was standing in the hatchway looking at the bow of a ship about to run me over. Two hundred feet to go, then crunch. The dark shape with red and green navigation lights visible high in the sky above, was seconds from impact. I dived for the tiller and unhooked the autopilot - no fumbling that time - as I pulled the tiller as far over as it would go. Tapestry reacted instantly and not a moment later the large ship passed close by. Oh so close. The sound of her engines overcame all other sounds, as a wall of steel filled the night. On she came, only feet away. Then the lights of the bridge shone directly overhead and the stern went by, leaving only a white light and the smell of combustion to tell of her passing.

Sleep was not forthcoming for the rest of the night and I could see a loom of light on the northeastern horizon, so I changed course and headed for it. Sitting in the cockpit with a cup of hot coffee, I thought about the close encounter and tried to comprehend how I had woken in the hatchway looking at the ship; because prior to that my only recollection was of how nice the pillow felt, as my face slumped into it and I fell asleep.

Why and how had I woken after only an hour?
How come I woke in the hatchway and not in my bunk?

Only five more seconds... how come the timing was so perfect?

I felt humble, thankful and very very lucky.

Daybreak and there it was, an oasis in the ocean, slowly taking shape as the light increased. To the north, the neighboring island of St Vincent was clearly visible, with its high volcanic peak towering above anything else in sight. Lying below the mountain and separated by only a few miles of water, was Bequia.

The day seemed to fly by as I rinsed the cockpit and the decks, making Tapestry shipshape for our arrival. Below, I vacuumed the carpets and wiped down all the bulkheads and counter tops, and of course washed the dishes that always seemed to accumulate by themselves. It was mid-afternoon before we finally sailed into Admiralty Bay and I dropped anchor outside the town of Port Elizabeth. It was beautiful.

I AM JIMMY

I was working as a carpenter in Charlotte Amalie, on the island of St Thomas, when I met Brian. He had a forty foot wooden boat, but didn't know the first thing about wood. He did know however that he wanted certain changes down below. His cabin was too small he told me, so all that needed doing was to remove a bulkhead and put another one in some three feet further aft.

Well it all sounded simple enough, but I knew the amount of work involved without even looking at the boat. For sure, it was a couple of weeks worth of solid work. Brian was unfazed, he wanted the job done and he wanted it started immediately. There was however a catch.

He did not wish to stay another minute in Charlotte Amalie, 'the world's largest open-air loony bin,' as he called it. He suggested that I bring whatever tools and wood I may need, and we each take our boats somewhere secluded, away from the craziness of the town.

I had arrived on the island penniless and within a day had found work in the local carpentry shop. That was six months ago and the cruising kitty was growing slowly. Soon I would have enough to set off for the South Pacific and the money Brian was offering to pay me was well in excess of what I normally charged. Seeing as I was quiet for the next two weeks anyway, it was not a hard decision to make. I too was feeling claustrophobic in the loony bin and some clean water would do me the world of good. We decided on Hurricane Hole, a secluded cove on the nearby island of St John.

On Friday afternoon we set off in convoy. Once there, we would spend the weekend relaxing and then I would start work on Monday morning. I had aboard Tapestry all the tools and wood I would need for the job, plus an electric generator to run the power tools. It was good to set the sails again.

It was a perfect Caribbean day, flat blue seas and a gentle trade wind blowing out of the northeast. I set a full main and yankee and Tapestry heeled over as the sails bit into the wind and we powered forward. That was more like it, that was the reason I was there. We headed along the south coast of St John, the island clean and green, most of it a national park. Rounding the corner of the reef, we both took down our sails and motored into the bay.

What a pleasure it was to be amongst nature once again. The shore was covered in white sand and palm trees lined the beaches, the scrub on the hills above, green from the recent rains. We dropped anchor on the western side of the bay and rafted alongside one another, both with anchors out. I needed Brian's boat close to the generator aboard Tapestry.

That night we went ashore to the local shack. It was literally a shack, a shack that sold ice-cold Heineken. Sitting right at the water's edge, it consisted of nothing more than a couple of wooden tables and an iron roof. Brian and I started discussing the what's and how's of altering his boat, when some guy arrived carrying a guitar case.

Oh yea, live music coming up, I thought to myself and it was not long before we were asking the stranger to play us a song or two. His first song was Jimmy Buffett's Cheeseburger in Paradise. - I think every yachtie in the world knows that one, - so before the end everyone in the bar was singing along. Then the next song came, again a Jimmy Buffett number and then the next and the next, all Jimmy songs. He was good, but I had been listening to Jimmy songs all day while sailing over here, so something else would have been nice. As he finished a song I leaned over and said, "Great song, thank you, but can't you play anything else besides Jimmy Buffett?"

"But I am Jimmy Buffett," he replied!

BETWEEN THE SEAS

Eight months after arriving in the Caribbean, my cruising kitty was full enough and it was time to take on the next part of my voyage - the Pacific Ocean.

It was late at night when the first lights became visible over the horizon. The city of Colon on the eastern side of Panama looked huge, the foreshore covered in a mass of condominiums.

How strange, I wondered to myself, *the chart showed it as a small town, all concentrated in one area.* I had been at sea for four days and the islands of the Caribbean were well behind me, the lure of the Pacific foremost in my mind.

As I neared the coast, I found out that what I had believed to be condos, were in fact ships at anchor. Dozens of them were all waiting for their turn to use the canal. The dawn was dull and gray, much like the first impression of the town. Oil covered the surface of the water and many of the buildings were in a state of disrepair.

I dropped anchor near the yacht club and was preparing to go ashore, when the customs boat pulled alongside. The officials were friendly and once the paperwork was completed, they warned me about walking in the town.

"Always travel in a group, never alone," they said.

I made an appointment for the next day, for the measurer to come aboard and measure my yacht, as you pay according to the volume of the vessel. Then I headed ashore to see what was going on at the yacht club and to find out if I knew anyone in port. Travel around for long enough and there is always someone you know from some other port somewhere. Colon was no exception.

The town was of no interest to me, so I set about getting the necessary paperwork to pass through the canal. A fee of

$50 was levied to measure the vessel and after all the calculations, I was to pay $16 for the use of the canal. What a bargain, as opposed to sailing around Cape Horn. The fee even included the pilot, who would have to be aboard for the entire journey. I had the four mooring lines of one hundred feet each and needed only the three additional crewmembers. Where to find three willing and able crew?

As so many of the cruising yachts had only one or two people aboard, there was a system set up, whereby you had to go through on two other boats before your own. So when my turn came, I had already transited the canal twice. The scariest part of each crossing was the bus ride back. Late at night and full speed ahead over the mountain passes, I was sure at times that I would never get to see the Pacific Ocean aboard Tapestry.

By four o'clock in the morning, the pilot and crew for the day were aboard. We headed to the first set of locks, the Gatun locks. A set of three locks in a row, each one thousand feet long and one hundred and ten feet wide. We came in behind a large bulk carrier and set our four mooring lines to each 'mule'. The mule is a locomotive on the side of the lock and as you move from one lock to the other, it pulls you along.

Ready to go and the gates closed behind, then the water started to boil as millions of gallons of fresh water from the Gatun Lake above, began to flow into the lock.

In 1878, Count Ferdinand de Lesseps, fresh from his success with building the Suez Canal, began work on the Panama Canal, then a part of Colombia. The project proved to be bigger than he or the French government could handle and it soon ended in bankruptcy.

The Americans then took over the dream and in 1914, the SS Ancon was the first official vessel to pass through the canal. The cost of life and money was horrendous. The combined French and American monetary costs were a staggering $640 million. An estimated 30,000 people were lost in construction, mostly from disease, as Malaria at the time was still believed to come from breathing bad air.

Up we went, rising eighty feet with each lock and soon we had traveled through all three and were spilled out into the Gatun Lake, once the largest man-made lake in the world. The water in that lake is what feeds the canal and is piped to each lock by gravity only. Not a single pump is used to transfer all that water.

It was mid-morning by the time we were motoring away from the first locks. The canal is fifty-one miles from ocean to ocean, so we were full speed ahead, fascinated to motor past mountains that had been moved to create a path between the seas. The Gillard and Culebra cuts, were two such spectacular examples of the tenacity of humankind. Once through the Gatun Lake, we went down one lock, Pedro Miguel and into a smaller lake, the Miafores Lake. Then two Miafores locks to go and the Pacific Ocean would be in sight.

What a feeling it was, as the last lock began to open. The salt water mixed with the fresh and Tapestry strained at her mooring lines. As the gates parted, so a welcoming committee of dolphins came into the lock and accompanied us into the great Pacific Ocean. I deposited my pilot and crew on the dock in Panama City, then sailed under the Trans-continental bridge of the Americas and into the sunset; bound for a small island some four hundred miles to my west, Isla del Coco.

4. SECRETS TO YOUR SUCCESS

LOVE

I love my life. It was a phrase that came easily and often found its way to my lips. At times I would shout it out, for deep within me I was happy. I was living the life that I had dreamed about and all the obstacles and hardships I had overcome thus far, were diminished by the anticipation of what lay ahead.

Tapestry was in perfect shape and ready for sea in every way. It had been sixteen months since I had left Cape Town and that time my departure was way less scary. By then I knew how to navigate and sailing came as naturally as driving a car. My home was tried and tested, money was in my cruising kitty and every locker on board was stuffed to capacity. My life was truly abundant and I was grateful for it.

- Love takes on so many faces. It is a word that we use to describe all levels of an incredible emotion, but its essence is hugely powerful.

- Say thank you for the things you have received and for the things you are yet to receive, because love is a force that is in close harmony with gratitude and it is part of an essential principle - that action and reaction are always in equal and opposite directions.

- Give and you will get in return, for sharing through love, always creates more, it is a grand emotion, far more magnificent than receiving.

- Without love your world would be awfully gray, for it is the color in life's picture. It is a sweet sound that can fill your senses and it certainly has the ability to change your perception, or attitude.

This next section of my adventures, was the part to which I looked forward the most. The Pacific Ocean, it was here that I had envisaged the pictures in my mind to be and somewhere amongst the thousands of islands ahead, lay paradise. I had enough money saved to last me until I reached Australia, or so I thought but I had not counted on the passage taking two years.

BE AWARE OF THE POWER OF LOVE.

* For more information visit:
  www.dancingonraindrops.com

" Love yourself first."

TO PARADISE

SURROUNDED BY SHARKS

For the last three hours and with only fifty miles to go, I had been avoiding waterspouts. (Tornadoes over water.) Three of them had formed in the space of an hour and had stayed about half a mile behind me. The surface of the water was lifted six feet into the air and the swirling spray rose up into a dark cloud several thousand feet above. The largest spout was about thirty or forty feet in diameter and I could hear the hum of the wind behind.

Between them, they had taken all my wind away, so I lowered the sails and lashed them down, just in case. I started the motor and no matter in which direction the waterspouts traveled, I was sure to keep them behind and off to one side of me.

On one occasion, the nearest spout to me seemed to be catching up, so there were a good few minutes of apprehension. I tried to ascertain its direction and turned Tapestry away from the course in which I assumed it was traveling. With smoke pouring out of the exhaust as I pushed the throttle full ahead, the water filled twister passed only a hundred yards away, far too close for my liking. It was with no regrets, that I watched the three menaces blow themselves into the distance and as they went, so the wind returned and once again I was able to pull my sails up and continue on my way.

The little bay reminded me of some fantasy movie. Seven waterfalls cascaded into the ocean from the green cliffs above. The sea was a turquoise color and the coral strewn bottom, clearly visible below. Tapestry was the only boat in the bay and once the anchor was set and the boat shipshape, I sat in the cockpit and rewarded myself with an ice-cold drink.

Costa Rica owns the islands of Isla del Coco and a couple of local soldiers were the only inhabitants. These were the customs and immigration delegates, who were shouting from the beach, so I launched the dinghy and motored over to pick them up. They were happy to see a new face and we all returned to the boat to do the paperwork. They spend a month there as part of their military service they told me. Clad in fatigues and armed with old Lee Enfield rifles, antiques from world war two, their paperwork was as minimalistic as I have ever seen.

They wrote down the number of my passport on a scrap of paper and then were only interested in a cold beer.

The morning was bright and clear and I was on top of the world. Here was my first Pacific island and it surely was beautiful. Almost surrounding the bay, the mountainsides were covered in a vine that grew on the treetops, making them seem like a giant tent.

The first mission of the day was to go for a dive and get some fresh fish for lunch, so I loaded up the dinghy with my spear guns, mask and fins then headed off to a nearby reef. I dropped anchor in about forty feet of water, grabbed my kit and hopped over the side.

The water was warm and felt refreshing. I lay motionless, slowly sinking and enjoying the feeling. The little bubbles dissipated and I began to look around. Yikes, there was a hammerhead shark, not twenty feet away. Shit, another and another, I was surrounded by them!

In a second or two I saw more sharks in the water than I had ever seen in all my years of diving. Time to get out and with the help of a spurt of adrenaline, I found myself floundering on the floor of the dinghy. So much for diving for lunch, there was no way I was going back into the water, not with that many sharks about - yet I still felt like eating some fresh fish. It was time to make a plan.

I had two spear guns with me, one a small 'James Bond' like thing and the other my large regular gun. I put on my mask and lowered my head over the side. Yea, the sharks were then clearly visible. Dozens of them and below on the reef were enough fish to feed an army. I grabbed the small gun and fired it into the water to see if it had an affect on anything and to my surprise, a mass of fish came up off the bottom to look at the spear. Then, I took my large gun and chose lunch. No too big, wrong flavor, aha there you are and zap, lunch. That soon became my regular way of spear fishing in those shark-infested waters.

Life was about as peaceful as you can imagine. During the day I would get some fresh fish and the rest of the time was spent exploring the island, maintaining Tapestry, or simply doing nothing. One afternoon found me at the top of the mast checking for chafe and wear, when out on the horizon I noticed what at first seemed like a wave heading towards me. I watched in fascination and as it came closer, it was apparent that it was not a wave at all, but a huge school of dolphin and giant tuna. Together they were hunting and they herded a large shoal of fish into the bay below me. They kept a perfect formation until all of a sudden, as if on command, they broke into a feeding frenzy. Literally hundreds of dolphin and the same again in large tuna, raced around the small bay. My view from the top of the mast was spectacular, for I could see clearly into the water as that spectacle of nature took place far below.

As wonderful as that little island was, it was soon time to be heading on. My next landfall was to be the Galapagos Islands, the land of Darwin, about four hundred miles to the southwest.

Dancing on Raindrops

THE LAND OF DARWIN

Wolf Island is one of the northern most islands in the Galapagos chain and was therefore the first to cross my path. A small volcanic island, eroded on one side, made the crater accessible to the sea. I was hoping to spend the night there and at least catch up on some sleep, but it was not to be.

On entering the crater, the depth was two hundred feet and as I slowly motored around inside, it did not change. Even close to the cliff face, the wall of rock was still vertical to two hundred feet, so unfortunately I was not able to anchor.

Oh well, you win some and lose some, I thought as I headed out to sea towards my next destination, the main island of Santa Cruz.

The wind was light and there was a small current working its way north. As Murphy's Law would have it, I wanted to go south, against the current. The next afternoon, I had finished taking a sun sight that put my position only ten miles from the island of Isabella, a towering peak of five and a half thousand feet but I could not see it. The sky was hazy and I was beginning to doubt my position, when in the distance, shortly before sunset, I could just make out the shape of land.

That night the wind died completely and I was carried back north with the current. Only ten miles to go and I did not have the diesel to motor there. The next morning the island was nowhere to be seen and it was a long three days of light winds and flat seas before I finally arrived. Such are the joys of a small boat and not much fuel.

Academy Bay was home for but a few days. I explored the island and saw the iguanas and tortoises but my mind was on the long voyage to come. Three thousand two hundred miles from here to the Marquesas and nothing, absolutely nothing but ocean in between. I tried to restock what provisions I could, but the store had meager supplies of food. I managed to buy diesel, enough to fill my little tank and a few extra jerry cans.

Much of my time here was spent copying charts. I would borrow the charts from another yacht and copy them onto translucent paper. That was standard practice for many cruising yachts. Our destinations could change at the drop of a hat and a need to buy all the newly required charts would not only severely dent the budget, but often in a place like that, new chart selections were simply not available. So piles of charts would be handed from boat to boat and copied.

Fresh water was my main concern. The only available water was to be had out of an old drum, filled with rainwater and sitting under a broken gutter. No thanks; I did not wish to contaminate what little water I had left, especially at the beginning of such a long passage. Soon I realized that the water situation was hopeless and I would have to leave with only five gallons of fresh water. Fortunately, I had a plan.

After four days I was ready for the long haul and very soon the huge peak of Mount Isabella was out of sight and a vast stretch of water lay ahead. The winds were light out of the east and we settled into the quiet downwind rhythm of the trades, with the boat slowly rolling from one side to the other.

That was sailing at its best. I was outside any shipping lanes and at that time of year the weather should be perfect, the trade winds slowly increasing throughout the month I was to spend at sea.

Three days out and my lack of fresh water was becoming a problem. My plan would soon have to be put to the test. I spotted a squall on the horizon and it was precisely what I had been looking and hoping for. There was fresh water. I had rigged up a system to catch rainwater; lower the main halyard a little and that would then cause the mainsail to sag at the bottom near the boom. I would also lower the end of the boom, so as the rain fell onto the sail, it would collect and run into the cockpit.

On the cockpit floor there were two drains that allowed water to flow back out to the sea and a third that I used to fill my water tanks; so I would simply rinse the cockpit, block off the two drains and open the water fill. All I had to do was catch the squall.

This way, that way, I adjusted course trying to intersect it at some future point and soon it was raining cats and dogs. Hardly any wind, only a constant deluge of fresh water. It did not take long before the tanks were overflowing, so I shut off the inlet pipe, opened the drains and proceeded to have a shower. A rain shower is the best. My hair was long and curly, so always after a normal shower, I would use conditioner, but after a rainwater shower, I needed no conditioners. The ultimate conditioner for soft and silky hair comes right out of the sky!

Thirty minutes later I sailed out of the storm and back into the world of blue skies, only that time I had plenty of water to see me through. It always seemed so amazing that you can make the boldest or craziest of wishes and if you believe in them enough, they come true. How foolish to leave on a thirty day passage with only enough water for three, but I believed I would find water; so much so that I left and knew that it would be taken care of.

Days began to mould into one another and once my familiar routine was established, time meant nothing. It was five days into the passage when I took my first sight and lo and behold, that's where I thought I was. Occasionally during the day and the night I would fill in my log, writing down what I felt my speed and direction to be, then at noon I would plot my position on the chart. With a couple of thousand miles still to go, it would not have mattered if I were a few hundred miles out.

Day ten - becalmed. Not a breath of wind and the sea was like a moving pane of glass. Unlike any other ocean I had sailed in, there the swells were miles apart and even though the surface of the water was flat, the swell created some movement and Tapestry would slowly rise and fall to its rhythm. I was stuck in the doldrums, so the only thing to do was to move outside.

I had made up a couple of pieces of plywood to fit between the two long seats in the cockpit, thereby forming a large flat surface, so I transferred my mattress and bedding and slept under the stars. So far from any other light, they seemed to fill every inch of the sky. With no sails up and going nowhere, I would lie awake and gaze at the heavens for hours on end.

During the day I removed my bed and put up the large awning that went all the way from the mast to the backstay. That helped to keep the deck and the inside cool, as well as giving me shade in the cockpit. There was nothing to do but wait it out.

I had only enough diesel to motor about one hundred miles, so if the wind didn't blow, this ship didn't go. It was so calm, that once I threw a match into the water and I could see the concentric rings, as the ripples spread outward on the shiny surface.

After five days I was starting to long for a breeze, that and I was going a little crazy I think. Day after day, moving nowhere, just sitting in the heat. A few times I ran up to the mast and hoisted the sails as a zephyr came by, only to have it go away and leave the still air behind.

Despite these hardships, the fishing was good. The Dorado would come by and with a light rod I could sometimes snag supper.

The doldrums had moved further south than I had anticipated and often I contemplated motoring for a while, to try and find some wind to the south, but my range was too limited. Also I did not wish to have a repeat of arriving in the Galapagos - that of not having enough fuel to motor the final stretch.

It was when I was playing Ping-Pong in the cockpit, that I was sure I was going mad. The frustration of being becalmed was starting to show. Reality took on a different feeling and my mind filled with strange images of wind.

The next morning I woke and the sea had lost its shine. The zephyrs were closer together, so I put up both sails and slowly Tapestry began to move. Most of the time the sails hung lifeless, but occasionally they would fill and move us slowly forward; always south, south out of the doldrums. Two more days and I was back in the trade winds, rolling once again to the down wind boogie and with the memory of six days of calm still fresh in my mind.

One day the ocean was literally covered in fish. Tuna were everywhere, as far as the eye could see. At any time there were perhaps thirty around the boat and they would surf the waves with us. It had been a while since I had had some tuna and I waited eagerly for one to take the lure that was trailing behind, but for some reason they did not. I changed lures often, but still nothing. It was so frustrating having an ocean full of fish and not being able to catch even one. One, that was all I wanted.

By mid-afternoon the frustration was too much and I pulled out my spear gun. What I was supposed to do with it, I was not sure; but I was sure that I wanted tuna for dinner. I went up to the bow and tied a piece of line between the handle of the gun and the handrail. I loaded the gun and looked into the water.

As we surfed down a wave, the water off to the sides of the bow was clear and the fish could be seen swimming alongside. I waited for the right moment and fired. It was a good shot and the spear went deep into the back of a twelve pound tuna. The fish stopped and the boat kept on moving. The line from the spear to the gun took off rapidly and in an instant it pulled taught. The stationary tuna shot high out of the water and flew in an arc that had it land right in the cockpit. Supper!

One thousand six hundred miles from the nearest land was the half way mark and once again I was becalmed. A

Dancing on Raindrops

light breeze would occasionally come over the deck, so I had the mainsail up, pulled tight to stop it from flapping. That was until I decided to go for a swim. It seemed a fitting thing to do, in the point of my travels where I was the most distant from land that I would ever be; it was a milestone, or so I made it seem. I took down the main and lashed the tiller hard over to one side, for I certainly did not want the boat to start sailing away as I jumped into the water.

With mask and fins on, I surveyed the scene. There was still a little swell left over from the wind of the past few days. The surface sparkled from the sun's reflection and I swept a wary eye for sharks. My heart began to pump when I realized I was about to do a silly deed, but the water was too inviting and the idea of actually swimming in that particular spot, all too alluring.

I jumped in as cleanly as I could, the bubbles began to dissipate and the sight that emerged took my breath away. The hull seemed so huge, but it was the only solid thing visible under the water, besides the two small fish swimming at the bow - the same ones that had been with me for a few days. Looking around, my eyes were greeted by a most wonderful sight, as shafts of sunlight penetrated deep into the crystal-blue water. It was awesome and the different colors of blue danced about, going deeper and becoming darker, as the light tried to penetrate the murky blackness far below.

Swimming a little distance away from the boat, to get a better perspective of what she looked like, out there all alone in the middle of nowhere, I felt a surge of emotion. How lucky I was to be there and to be able to experience such a thing. I thought that it would be nice to see the hull from underneath, so I took a few deep breaths and began to dive.

The shafts of dancing light seemed to beckon me on, as I dived deeper and deeper, mesmerized by the sheer beauty of it all and oblivious to my depth or the call of my lungs. I was in another world, far from reality and I kept on kicking. Slow powerful strokes were taking me deeper and deeper into the blue, to which I was somehow attracted. I had no notion of stopping, or heading back to the surface - not until I heard the voice. Somewhere far away, it was so far that I could not hear what it said, but it slowly started to bring me back to reality.

There was a moment when I could easily have kept on swimming, chasing the shafts of light - if only to find out where they went to. But the voice returned and my lungs began shouting for air, my brain finally conscious of how deep I was. I looked up and was startled to see that the hull was a small dot above, so far, and I wondered for a moment if I would ever reach it.

My kicking took on a sense of urgency when the hull did not seem to be getting any closer. My heart was pounding in my chest. How had I allowed that to happen, why did I go so deep? Lots of silly things went through my brain, but the one overriding thought was that of air, air on the surface that still seemed so far away. The last twenty feet were the worst. My body became frantic.

Exerting every bit of energy, I literally clawed my way up, consciously reminding myself not to breathe, as the natural instinct to fill my lungs almost overcame me. There was no sweetness in that first breath. It was simply needed to sustain life and my mind was able to distinguish neither taste nor fragrance. The compelling thought in my head was to get back aboard, and as my chest heaved I made my way to the steps on the transom and climbed up. At the top, I tripped on the edge of the cockpit and fell to the deck, drained and relieved to be there.

Thirty-three days after leaving the Galapagos, the island of Motane in the Marquesas group, was visible on the horizon. Of my time at sea, nine days had been spent becalmed and the rest was perfect downwind sailing. I had done it; the longest passage was over.

MOTANE AND THE HUNTER

The anchor slid through the water and came to rest on the bottom. Baaaa, the air filled with the sweet sound of sheep, wild sheep on the mountain. I readied the dinghy and in no time at all I was heading ashore, the image of a roast mutton dinner in the making made my mouth water. It had been over a month since I had eaten red meat. Tapestry's freezer had long since been emptied and for a while my diet had consisted of fresh fish and canned foods.

The only weapon I had aboard was a .357 magnum revolver and it was loaded with hollow point shells. Standing on the water's edge I looked up at the mountain above. It was covered in a thick bush and rose to a height of three thousand feet. A long way up, I could see little white specks moving – sheep.

The going was tough because my legs were still weak from so long at sea and it seemed that wherever I went the sheep were always that little bit ahead of me. Up and up I climbed, hour after hour, around this hill then around that one. I tried going into a ravine and working my way around to the other side of them, but once I got to the top and slowly peeked my head over the ridge, all the sheep had moved over to the other side of the hill. It was hot and I was tired.

At about two thousand feet the view was spectacular, so I stopped to take a rest. Perhaps the roast for dinner was not to be. The sea was a deep blue and little white horses blinked every once in a while. Far in the distance the island of Hiva-oa, barely visible on the horizon, looked like a flattened brown volcano. Below, Tapestry rode at anchor in the crystal clear waters of the bay.

A story crossed my mind. A solo sailor stopped off on a deserted island and went to climb the mountain. Half way up he looked back and saw his boat dragging anchor, slowly heading out to sea. He hurried down to the beach, but by the time he arrived, his home had drifted far away. After an extremely depressing three days, he awoke one morning to find two boats heading into the bay. A yacht happened to be passing by the island and late the previous evening the crew noticed the drifting boat. They went aboard, saw that she was deserted and took her in tow to the nearest island – the one on which the hapless sailor was stranded.

A noise startled me from my daydream, a rustling in the bushes about thirty yards up the hill. Sheep! I made ready my revolver and kept dead still. Out of the thick undergrowth they came, over a rocky outcrop and disappeared around the ridge of the hill. One by one they walked by, about a dozen in all, none seeming to pay me any mind.

An old male was far behind the rest of the group and as he came into view, I decided that he was to be my dinner. As he stepped onto the exposed rocky outcrop, I shot him right through the heart; or at least that was where I had aimed.

The sheep, still standing, stopped and looked at me. So I shot him again and with that he started to run away, so I shot him a third time before he disappeared behind the ridge. I couldn't believe it, three shots from that hand cannon and it looked as though I had missed with every one. *Surely I wasn't that bad a shot?*

I climbed up to where the sheep had been for my first two shots and there on the ground were specks of blood. Shit, he had been hit, so I would have to follow him. I rushed to the edge of the rocky outcrop and as I walked over the ridge, there at my feet, was one very dead sheep. There were two holes on either side of his heart and a third where the bullet had exited his chest from my last shot.

Dancing on Raindrops

Once the heat of the kill had subsided, I began to focus on my predicament. There I was, almost two thousand feet up a deserted mountain, with one hundred pounds of dead sheep that had to be taken to the beach. First I contemplated dressing it right there, as that would certainly reduce the weight but I would be a bloody mess by the time I reached the dinghy, so I looked for another option.

I tied together the front legs and the back legs, hauled the heavy carcass over my shoulders and began to head down the hill. It was not long before I realized that that was not going to work. As I walked, his pubic hairs rubbed against my ear and with every step his balls would swing up into my face. I kept going until I came upon a steep cliff. There was no way I could carry that weight down. I had two choices. Walk back and try to find an easier route, or... as I tossed the sheep over the edge.

Down it fell, bouncing off rocks. Three hundred, four hundred feet and then it came to rest far below. Climbing down was easy not having the extra weight, and when I reached the sheep he looked rather distorted but all in one piece, so I put him back over my shoulders and set off to find the next cliff.

By the time we eventually arrived at the beach, the poor sheep looked like the most mangled trophy I have ever seen. I dressed the carcass up from the water's edge and rinsed the meat in the sea, before carefully packing it into the bags that I had brought with me.

As I chopped away, I noticed that the sharks began to arrive. First one fin broke the surface and within minutes there were dozens of them, all trying to hone in on the source of the blood. It was late in the afternoon before I was done. All the meat was in freezer bags and the offal I put into a large black garbage bag, to be emptied overboard only once I was safely on deck.

The dinghy was too heavy to move further down the beach and this area was shark infested, so I made sure not to put my feet too deep into the water. It was a strange feeling slowly motoring through shark alley in a little dinghy, as fins darted back and forth around me. I crouched low and some of the fins were as far out of the water as I was.

When I reached the boat, I quickly climbed aboard and left the meat in the dinghy. I was simply glad to be back home and I wanted to wait for the sharks to lose a bit of interest before I began passing up the bags of mutton, so I showered and prepared the galley for cooking. Some of the meat I would cook immediately and some I would freeze.

My first cooking priority was to fry the fillet in butter and prepare some brown rice. Home was the hunter, home and hungry. I lifted the meat from the dinghy up onto the deck and then packed it into the empty freezer. It was good that I had one, as there was a huge quantity of meat and I would be eating mutton for weeks. It had been a long passage and I was tired of fish, so I was looking forward to dinner.

I took the bag of offal and emptied it over the side and as soon as it hit the water, a dozen or more sharks devoured it, as they turned the still water into a foaming and splashing frenzy. Within minutes it was all over and the calm returned, leaving no trace of the sheep.

Soon it was time for dinner, so I sat at the main saloon table and ate like a hungry man. It was excellent and the meat was so tender that I did not even need a knife to cut it. Two thousand feet of cliff - that's what I call tenderizing!

TAHITI

Ninety miles away the volcano of Tahiti was clearly visible, although in the light winds it would be at least twenty hours before I arrived. I had skirted the western edge of the Tuamoto chain during the night and my star sights before the dawn put me seven miles clear of the reefs.

The entire island of Tahiti is almost completely surrounded by a barrier of coral reef and its emerald green vegetation became more distinct the closer I sailed. I picked out the entrance markers in the early morning light and motored through the reef into the town of Papeete on the western side, a small picturesque village at the foot of the volcano.

Dropping anchor in the calm, clear water, my first task once again, was to go ashore and clear customs and immigration. I had been told that I might have a problem, for I had heard that in order to stay in Tahiti, I would have to deposit with the government, enough money to cover a return ticket to my country of origin. That meant a ticket to Cape Town, South Africa - almost halfway around the world. I did not have the money, so it was with some trepidation that I walked into the customs office, telling myself that somehow everything was going to be fine.

People were standing about, waiting to be served by the only available agent. The line moved slowly, but soon the man in front of me was having his turn. There was a sailor who did not believe in smartening up before visiting foreign officials. His long hair was dirty and his clothes were in need of a fresh water wash.

"I have the money, but the bank has not yet transferred it," I could hear him saying in a harsh manner.

It seemed as though the official was having none of it and a lot of shouting was going back and forth. His turn ended when the immigration man said that he had twenty-four hours to come up with the money, or he would have to leave the island.

Oh boy, why did he have to go in front of me, I asked myself. *Now I have an irate official to deal with.* My turn.

"Bonjour," I said with a huge smile on my face. The tension seemed to fall from the air and after a few moments, he smiled back.

Well, here we go and it's going to be all right.

"You seem to be having a day of it," I said, "but my bank has not sent me any money either." I did not want to lie, but it was true, the bank had not sent me any money. I waited for his reply, all the while smiling and trying to give off good vibes.

He asked me how long I would be staying and I replied two weeks. I only needed one but felt I should ask for the other, just in case.

Smile, keep on smiling. His answer almost blew me down.

"No problem; when your money comes in, come and see me."

I spent the week doing maintenance and topping up my provisions for the voyage ahead. My final destination for that ocean was to be Australia, but I had no plans in between. I would go where the winds blew or my heart lead.

The town of Papeete was immaculately clean and all the cars and scooters were new and well cared for. Here there were signs of wealth that seemed unimaginable on some of the other islands. Almost everyone I met worked for the French government in some way or another and the standard of living seemed good.

It was however very expensive for my budget, so my shopping list grew shorter as I became acquainted with the inflated prices. Rice, flour and beans still stayed at the top of the list however. With these staples, I could eat for months, as I would supplement them with fresh fish and whatever else Mother Nature sent my way.

At night I sometimes took in the sights of the city and I was quite astounded once when I found out that a beautiful woman with whom I had spent the last half an hour talking, was in fact a man. Such are the ways of their custom and culture. I wish I had thought about Crocodile Dundee's method to find out if it's a boy or a girl!

Getting about on the island was easy enough, as a shuttle service, known as 'le truck,' covered most parts. Exotic hotels and houses lined the shore, some so far out over the water that they were built on stilts above the lagoon, where its water colors ranged from the palest turquoise to a light blue, the deepest blues found only in the water well beyond the reef.

Several hundred yards away, the surrounding reef was clearly visible and the views, as I stood high on a rocky ledge, were spectacular. To the west, Morea looked magnificent, the perfect image to my perception of a Pacific paradise. The warm water sparkled and a fresh breeze, clean from the ocean and laced with the smells of the tropics, gently blew over the island.

Beyond Morea, the other islands of the Society group, Huahine and Raiatea, then far in the distance, although I could not see them, were the twin peaks of Bora Bora, where the basalt obelisk of Mount Otemanu stands godlike, often draped in white clouds.

One week later, I was back in the immigration office to clear out, having finished my provisioning and maintenance.

"You don't have to go, you have only just arrived," the same man said.

"Well the bank still hasn't sent any money and doesn't seem likely to, so I feel bad staying longer without the bond," I replied.

He tried to convince me that the bond did not matter in this case and I would be free to stay as long as I wished, so long as when the money came through, I would inform him.

I had done what I wanted to do in Tahiti and it was time to leave, but getting him to accept the fact took some persuasion.

From Tahiti, my next stop was to be the twin peaks of Bora Bora, but having spent that week looking across at the spectacular neighboring island, I decided to make a stop at Morea.

Only ten miles from Tahiti, it was perhaps the most beautiful island I had ever seen. Also protected by a barrier reef, the vegetation was lush and continued all the way up the steep mountainsides. I made my way into a deserted bay and dropped anchor close to the beach in ten feet of water. I did not bother to launch the dinghy and whenever I wanted to go ashore, I simply swam there.

Few people lived in that area of the island and most of the homes were private holiday cottages of the rich and famous, all locked and deserted. Fresh fruits grew wild and in abundance. Coconuts, bananas and mangoes, all grew amongst the thick vegetation. Everywhere there was breadfruit. About the size of a melon, it has a mottled green and brown skin that is almost smooth to the touch. Inside, the white flesh once cooked tastes much like a potato. It is the food that Captain Bligh was commissioned to take from Tahiti to the West Indies.

The goal of the voyage was to take a large number of breadfruit plantings to the Caribbean, where they would be transplanted to provide food for the slaves in those colonies. His ship, the Bounty, was overtaken by a mutiny and Bligh, along with a few of his men were cast adrift in a small rowing boat. Through enormous tenacity he and his crew survived, but once back in England, Bligh refused to take responsibility for the mutiny; blaming the impact of the Tahitian culture and its women, on his men.

He was given the same assignment again and that time he was successful, hence the breadfruit is now common amongst the West Indian islands.

For a week I languished there. Tapestry was ready for sea so I set up my hammock between two palm trees, whose branches leaned out over the water and read a few books.

On my wanderings ashore I would always return with a variety of fruits that I picked from the side of the path. Most days I dived for lunch and dinner on the surrounding reef and there was never a shortage of food on the table.

From Morea I made a short stop in Bora Bora, but the water in the anchorage was very deep, so it was not long before I was headed towards a deserted atoll in the middle of nowhere.

Paradise is really just a state of mind in a beautiful place.

Dancing on Raindrops

SUWARROW

The highest parts of the island were the tops of a few palm trees, scattered on a small stretch of sand about a hundred yards long and fifty wide. That vast expanse of untouched land that was no more than six feet above the water, became known as the main island. It was the largest throughout the entire atoll whose calm waters covered five miles by five miles.

The weather was fantastic and as the dawn broke, I put myself three miles from Suwarrow, a small dot in the Cook chain of Islands. My next task was to find the needle in the haystack, namely finding a palm tree that may well be over two miles away. My star sights gave me a fairly accurate position and as the sun rose in the sky, I was able to get a few more sights, one of which put me directly on top of the island. I was close.

All morning I searched the horizon, for a clue as to the whereabouts of the tiny spit of land and a few palm trees. Eventually something in front did not look right; a bump on the horizon, sometimes noticeable, sometimes not. I headed towards it and within half a mile it took on the shape of trees.

Only a single narrow channel fed that huge atoll, so I suspected that the currents could be strong. The channel was about fifty yards wide and I approached slowly, for I had only a hand drawn sketch of the atoll that gave its latitude and longitude; plus an arrow showing which side the entrance was on. The water was clear and the bottom could be seen clearly at one hundred feet below. All of a sudden, I noticed a rock in the water that seemed to come very close to the surface, right in the middle of the channel. I quickly put the motor into astern and slowed down.

As I came closer, it was apparent that the rock was still well under water, but the water was so clear that as it rose off the bottom to fifteen feet, it gave the effect of being just under the surface. Luckily, I had timed the slack tide perfectly and there was not a ripple as I entered the lagoon. Coral heads were dotted about on the sandy bottom, often causing alarm, as they too looked so close to the surface. I motored around in a few circles to be sure that there were no hidden surprises and let go the anchor.

The chain rumbled out and I could see the anchor touch the bottom, a small cloud of sand rising from the seabed thirty feet below. *Surely this must be paradise?* The white sandy beaches shimmered in the noon sun. The skies so clear with only a few puffy clouds about - their presence only for the poet's eye. A few dozen large palm trees on the main island and thousands, if not tens of thousands of small ones covered the edge of the atoll, giving a little bit of green to a landscape otherwise made up of only sky, water and sand. The effect of such pristine beauty was awe-inspiring.

After squaring away the boat and launching the dinghy, I headed ashore to the main island. Pulling the dinghy up onto the beach, I tossed its small anchor onto the hot sand and made my way to the shade of the palm trees. A hermit by the name of Tom Neil had lived on that small island for a number of years, and the undergrowth was overtaking the remains of his wooden house. A metal water container still stood high upon its steel tower, but besides that, there were no signs of humans having been here. No gum wrappers or plastic containers and certainly no footprints in the sand. I walked to the seaward side of the island and the ocean sparkled. Hundreds of terns were in the sky and as I walked, it became evident that they used the island as a nesting ground; dozens of eggs were lying on the sandy beach, well above the high water mark.

For two heavenly months I lived there and the tern's eggs became a breakfast favorite. Somewhat smaller than a chickens egg and with a bright red yolk, they were so rich that one was enough.

Most days I spent in the water, either shooting fish or prying lobster from their holes in the rocks. For greens, I had an abundance of heart of palm, a delight so hard to come by fresh off the tree. Cut a small palm tree off at the base and inside the core, is the heart.

Sharks were not much of a problem once I had figured out their pattern. When the tide was coming in, they would be at the entrance and would spend the next hour or two inside the lagoon, but as soon as the tide began to change, they would head back to the open water. Sometimes, I took the dinghy well out to sea beyond the entrance and floated next to it as the current swept me back into the lagoon. The ocean was alive with fish at these times and floating on the surface, none of the sea creatures paid me any mind.

After a week or so another cruising boat stopped by but they were in a hurry to get to American Samoa, the next large island some three hundred miles to the west, so they stayed only a couple of days. Besides that brief visit, the island was all mine, my own deserted tropical slice of heaven.

One tends to think of daiquiris on the beach as the sun sets and long lazy days with nothing to do, but in reality it was quite different. I did not have much food on board, so many of my meals had to come from what nature could provide and that usually took most of the day to acquire. Even simple tasks, like shooting a grouper for lunch could take a few hours, if for some reason the fish had moved elsewhere for a while.

Some dream of lying in the sun all day but I found that when the sun was always there, I tended to seek the shade wherever possible. A large awning over the decks kept the boat cool and at night I used a wind scoop to funnel what little breeze there was, down through the front hatch and over my bunk - bringing with it the sounds and smells of the ocean and the reef.

When I felt the need for a new adventure, it was time to leave my paradise and head on to the next islands; those with people and garbage, supermarkets and fresh water. The price of civilization.

Dancing on Raindrops

THE GREAT BARRIER REEF

For two days I had been eating dried fish, for I had heard that when you cleared into Australia, all foods were taken off the boat and destroyed. I made sure that I left Fiji with the bare minimum to see me through, but I had not taken into account the light winds.

Brisbane lies at the southern end of the Great Barrier Reef, a huge uncharted expanse of ever changing coral. I skirted the tip of the reef and dropped anchor in Morton bay on a Friday afternoon. Friday is only significant because I was broke.

There they charged yachts to clear in over the weekend, so I had no choice but to sit out my time at anchor and clear in on Monday morning. It was going to be a long wait, as I was not permitted to go ashore and I had run out of cigarettes and food. Sitting below, I heard the knock on the hull and a muted voice calling, so I stuck my head out of the hatch to see what was going on.

"Howzit, where did you just come from?" Someone in the dinghy asked in a strong South African accent. We got to chat and Joe was with a group of South Africans who had come out to Australia on business and were taking a few days off before returning home. They had rented a large yacht with crew and were being chauffeured about the different sights.

During our conversation, I mentioned my plight of sitting at anchor for the weekend and that I was out of cigarettes and food. With that he went off to his boat and returned with a carton of cigarettes and an invitation for dinner. One moment hungry and in need of a smoke and in the next, both were satisfied.

The food and hospitality were fine and we partied into the wee hours of the morning. As I was leaving, one of the blokes came over to me and speaking in hushed tones said, "Hey Mike, I don't know if it means anything, but I heard the captain mention the name of your boat whilst he was talking on the radio. Tapestry isn't it?"

I nodded.

"Well I didn't catch all of what he was saying, but I think he also mentioned the word, drugs; thought you should know."

I thanked him, but could not think why the captain would be talking about Tapestry and drugs, so I tossed the idea aside and headed back to my boat.

By the time I woke in the morning, the big boat had gone. I busied myself the next two days cleaning Tapestry and getting her ready for a lengthy stay in port. It had been two full years since I had had any income and I was flat broke; well I did have twenty-three cents. My plan was to find work as soon as possible and then start to save for the next leg of my voyage; up the barrier reef and across the Indian Ocean.

On the Monday morning I weighed anchor and headed up the river to the customs wharf. I had called them on the VHF as a courtesy to inform them that I was coming, but little did I know what an event it must have been; for waiting on the dock were a dozen customs officials - some from every department.

Three divers were in full kit and ready to search under the water. The canine folk were there too with a dog and as I came alongside, I handed my mooring lines to the waiting officials. They tied me up and swarmed aboard.

First the dog was shown around, but after it came up with nothing and the divers came up with nothing, the tool kits were opened and four men came below armed with screwdrivers and wrenches.

Exactly what they were looking for they would not say, but the words of a few nights ago came back to me and I realized that the captain of the charter boat must have been

Dancing on Raindrops

speaking to the coast guard, perhaps telling them that I was running drugs.

I filled out pages and pages of paperwork. No, I was not permitted to keep my revolver and the morphine that was in my medical kit, was also not allowed to remain on board. These would be held and when I left Australia, they would be returned to me.

They searched inside every nook and cranny and three hours later, just as they were finishing, they found something. In the back of a locker, they found a small packet of dried beans and a whole clove of garlic. Those were not allowed to be brought in, so they were taken and burnt. That was all there was aboard.

It was early afternoon by the time I had been given a clean slate and permission to stay, so I cast off my lines and headed up the river in search of somewhere to dock. I had heard that right next to the city, was a set of pile moorings that were available to international yachts. The river was wide and brown, and the current made my progress slow, so I had time to take in the sights and ponder once again, where I could start looking for work.

I needed a job immediately. I had no money and no food.

Quite a predicament, I thought to myself and smiled. *It will be interesting to see how this unfolds.*

Sandy Goanna, said the name on the transom of a small yacht. She was tied alongside a pier, next to a caravan park. Dave and Suzie, I knew them well. We had spent much of the last year together, as we sailed the islands of the South Pacific. I hailed, a head popped out of the hatch and five minutes later I was rafted alongside.

It was good to see old friends. We sat in their cockpit, under a large awning and reminisced of the islands and the times we had spent together. They had been back only a couple of months, after having completed their circumnavigation and were still trying to adjust to their new lifestyles. Dave had gone back to his original profession as a mechanic and Suzie was once again an air hostess.

Dinner was mentioned and I realized how hungry I was. I had not eaten a meal since the night Joe had invited me to his boat. During the weekend, I lived on the remains of my dried fish, so as Dave threw the steaks onto the barbie, my tummy began to rumble.

As the evening wore on I explained my predicament - I needed a job and fast. They racked their brains but it did not look promising. A maybe here and a maybe there, but a good piece of news was that there were moorings available at the city marina, about five miles up the river.

It was late when I went to take a shower in the caravan park. Oh yea, a never-ending supply of hot water, something I had only dreamed about for months and months. There were two shower cubicles and one was occupied. We talked as we showered, that person on the other side of the wall and me. He seemed an amiable sort and he laughed a lot. Oh, the hot water was heavenly.

That was where I met Guy and he said he was a house builder, so immediately I asked if he needed any help.

"Yes" he said, "be at my caravan at four-thirty tomorrow morning and you can help me build some houses." I think I was speechless for a while. That was it, I had work and I was ecstatic. Within twelve hours of clearing customs, I had a full belly, a hot shower, work and a place to dock my boat. Welcome to Australia.

Well, I was at his caravan at the appointed hour and began learning about building houses. On the second evening, I moved the boat from the caravan park to the marina in the center of town, a half an hour ride in the dinghy. That meant that I would leave home at four in the morning and commute down the river. No traffic jams, only the peace of the calm water and myself flying along on the surface.

For the next nine months I worked with Guy and in that time he and I built four houses, each from a bare plot of land. First the excavations were dug, then the concrete poured and within days we had the wooden frames in place and it started to look like a house. Guy had a large personality, even larger than his six foot four muscular body and his tools were his most important possessions.

One day we had a young man helping us and he was up in the rafters using the circular saw, when all of a sudden, he let out a whopping scream. Before I could move, Guy was on his way. The kid was standing on a roofing beam two stories up, holding the saw with his good hand, while the other poured blood.

"Hang on I'm coming. Don't move," said Guy as he worked his way along a beam. He reached the distressed young man, put out his free hand and grabbed the saw.

"There we go mate, seemed like you were going to drop the bloody thing," Guy said in a matter of fact voice. I reckon the young bloke nearly fainted, but Guy grabbed him and helped him climb to safety.

Every day we worked long, hard hours in the baking sun, but every night we would sit on the banks of the Brisbane River in the caravan park and drink a few beers together. Fosters or XXXX (four X) the local Queensland beer, there was always an abundant supply. When the night was done, I would commute back in my dinghy, shower, eat, then go to bed; to be up at three-thirty and do the same thing all over again.

It was time to move on. Tapestry was fully provisioned and there was cash in the bank. Definitely enough reason to take a few years off and go sailing once again. I spent the next six months traveling up the Great Barrier Reef, enjoying the incredible diving and fishing.

GIANT CLAMS

The water was two hundred feet deep and five hundred feet across. On either side, the coral reef came above the surface and the sea was a gorgeous light blue. The bottom was flat until the base of the reef, where it rose vertically to the surface.

I was looking for a place to spend the night, but anchoring here would be impossible, as it was too deep. The afternoon was marching on and there were only a few hours of light left. In addition, the charts I had of the area were sketches at best and over most of the region I was in, were the bold words, **Uncharted.**

In amongst the vast corals of the Great Barrier Reef, was not a place I wanted to be drifting aimlessly as night came. Most of my navigation for the previous three days had been by eye and by always keeping the sun behind me, it was easy to see into the water ahead and avoid any obstacles.

Slowly motoring up the channel, with the autopilot steering for me, I stood by the mast and searched ahead for an area that looked as if it might be shallower. It was then that I noticed the small shack, raised above the water on stilts in the center of an atoll, about two miles ahead. I could even make out that there was a dinghy tied off and floating nearby.

Signs of life. However, they were in the shallow water inside the reef and I was on the other side with no way to get into the lagoon. Anyhow, the water only looked to be a couple of feet deep in most places. My options were getting slim, until I noticed a wooden structure on the edge of the reef. A small dock about ten feet long, protruded into the deeper water. Tying a forty foot boat to a ten foot dock was hardly a secure berth, but it might do for the night. I approached slowly in the calm water and by the time my bow touched the top edge of the reef, my depth sounder was still reading two hundred feet, meaning that it was almost vertical.

The dock was a flimsy affair, a few pieces of wood nailed together and as I tied alongside I noticed the dinghy that had been next to the house was motoring in my direction. Two young guys were aboard and their progress over the coral infested lagoon was slow, as they had to lift the propeller almost out of the water to avoid hitting the 'bommies'; the coral heads that made their way up to the surface.

Eventually they arrived and after greetings, they informed me that they worked for a dive company and had decided to spend the night in the shack, as their boat was coming back the next day with new divers. They did not use the dock and I was welcome to stay. What a relief, I did not have to continue looking for an anchorage at that late hour. They invited me to the shack for a beer and I was disinclined to accept the offer, but they persisted and soon I relented, on the condition that they bring me back before darkness.

There was no wind and the sea was flat, so although the dock was small, Tapestry seemed secure enough to be left alone for an hour or two. I climbed into their dinghy and slowly we headed for the shack. The bommies were everywhere, so it was a slow journey, but the guys said they did it all the time and they knew the route. It still took half an hour to travel the few hundred yards to their dwelling.

The shack was a real Robinson Crusoe type, roughly put together. Normally the dive boat would motor around to the other side of the reef, where there was an opening wide and deep enough for it to fit through and a channel up to the shack. We drank a couple of beers together sitting on the front verandah, surrounded by water. The solitude and remoteness reminded me of the time I spent on Suwarrow Island, only here there were a lot more people. I asked if there was an anchorage further up the reef, but they did not know as their dive sites were elsewhere.

Quickly the sun moved across the sky and it was time to head home, but first they had to put some more gas in the dinghy. Then they had to find the oil to mix with the gas and by the time we were ready to cast off the sun was low on the horizon, but as it was only a couple of hundred yards to go, so I was not worried.

That was when the propeller struck a bommie. The force of impact sheared the pin between the shaft and the propeller and we were dead in the water. The light breeze slowly started blowing us away from both the boat and the shack. It was then that I found out that the dinghy did not have any oars, but I was assured that there was a spare pin. Somewhere, there was a spare pin.

The spare it turned out was at the bottom of the toolbox, amongst a pile of rust. By the time the motor was removed from the transom bracket and laid in the dinghy, not only was the light fading fast, but we were also near the far edge of the reef, half a mile from home.

Next came the problem of having a tool to remove the propeller nut. A rusty pair of pliers was all they had, but after much perseverance the nut came off and it was only a few minutes thereafter that we were ready to go again.

By then it was dark and everything blended into the night. The propeller was mostly out of the water, but we were making progress. That was until we rammed into another unseen bommie and as the dinghy turned from the impact, the propeller caught a piece of coral and once again the pin sheared. I was beginning to worry, with no motor and no oars, the only alternative was to swim and walk home.

A few days prior, I had been snorkeling and came across a giant clam. At first it looked more like a piece of reef, with large bits of fan coral growing around it and I almost missed its true identity - until I noticed that the center of that 'reef' was bare, just a smooth white surface.

Only then did I recognize it for what it truly was. It was perhaps eight feet across and was fully open below me. While hovering above, I saw two holes in the flesh of the clam and inside the larger hole, was what looked like a ball of gold about the size of my fist.

How long had that clam been there? Slowly filtering the water and with that water, I presumed had come minute particles of gold. Over the years the gold had settled in one place, right inside the clam. I was fascinated and after returning to the surface for air, I went down time and time again to stare at the incredible sight. By mistake, I happened to touch the outer edge of the clam with my fin and the nearby reef started to move, as it began to close. Ferns ten feet tall were attached to its edges, so I stayed well out of the way of the vice-like jaws below, knowing that if any part of me was caught inside, it would stay there until long after I had drowned.

Faced with the predicament of getting back home, I put on my sandals and slid over the side of the dinghy, into the warm dark waters of the atoll. It was not deep and I went in to my stomach and started to pull the dinghy along; all the while my mind replayed pictures of the giant clam I had seen.

There in the shallow water, the clams were not as large, but even a small one that was only two feet across would probably do much damage to a shin or an ankle. Each step forward was like walking in a minefield - not knowing what the next would bring. One step was in shallow water and the next would drop me almost totally below the surface; then my shin would be the first to know of another lump of coral and I would have to climb up and over it. Because of that, my legs were bruised and bloodied by the time we reached Tapestry, some two hours after dark. She was right where I had left her and that was a very welcome sight.

IN THE SHADOW OF THE DEVILS

As I was having breakfast, a dive boat pulled alongside and the guys returned my oars. Leaving the small wooden dock, I decided to continue my quest to try and find an anchorage further inside the reef. I had to wait until almost noon to leave, as I was to be heading east and I did not want the sun to obscure my vision into the water. Somewhere out beyond the deep channel had to be a nice shallow anchorage.

The weather report for the next few days was good, so I made up my mind to take a chance. Two hours was all I could give it and if I were not able to find a place to anchor, then I would have to return to the wooden dock. The return journey would be in a westerly direction and I did not want the sun in my eyes, so I had only a small window of time in which to find what I was looking for.

After one hour and thirty minutes into my eastbound trip, just as I was beginning to think of having to turn around, I noticed that the bottom started to rise. Bommies were randomly dotted about below the surface, so progress was very slow, but I found it. Twenty feet of water and I was in an area clear of coral with a nice clean, sandy bottom. After dropping the anchor I surveyed the view, but there was nothing out there, save the water and the reef. In the distance I could see the white water and spray, as waves broke against the outer reef but the surface was calm and the air clean, with the slightest aroma of both reef and ocean.

It was good to be out of the city and the first thing I wanted to do was to dive and check the anchor. Here was not a place I wished to start dragging in the middle of the night, so I jumped into the water with my mask and fins.

Too many times sharks had surprised me in the past, so I was in the habit of checking what was below as soon as I hit the water. It was all clear, not even a fish to be seen. In fact the bottom looked like a desert - white sand as far as the eye could see. I swam to the anchor chain and then followed it on the surface towards the anchor. I had let out about one hundred feet of chain in twenty feet of water. More than my basic three-to-one scope; that is if the water is twenty feet deep, then the normal amount of chain would be sixty feet.

Diving down, I took the sharp end of the plough and dug it into the sand as far as I was able. By doing so, I knew that as long as long as the wind did not change direction, I would be safe. It took several attempts to get it buried as much as I wanted and on one of my descents to the bottom, I noticed a shadow come over me. My heart skipped a few beats.

There I was over a hundred feet from the boat and something was in the water with me. Of course, the first thing my mind went to was shark. Holding onto the anchor, I lifted my head to see what was above me, hoping to myself that it was simply a cloud passing under the sun.

Whatever it was, it was large. I turned and directly above me, were two manta rays swimming side by side. My heart raced even though it was not a shark, I had never seen one of these magnificent creatures in the wild. As they glided over me, I slowly surfaced behind, trying not to scare them. The fresh air in my lungs felt good and I started to follow.

They were swimming about ten feet below the surface, their wide wings moving in slow motion. On top they were black and in front of their heads were the 'horns' that gave them the nickname of devil rays. As I neared, I half expected them to move off, not wanting the company of a human, but to my surprise they were unaffected by my presence.

That was my chance to see how unaffected they really were, as I took a deep breath and dived down. Closer I went and still they did not mind. I was about a foot above one of them, when I put out my hands and gently grabbed its horns. I expected it to speed off, but there was no reaction, only the gentle rhythm of the giant's wings.

They were both the same size, about eight feet across and there I was being pulled through the water. I did not want to let go, even though my lungs were bursting for air, for I reckoned that I might never have a chance like that ever again - so I held on. The skin on the horns was hard and slightly coarse to the touch and its face was only a foot away from mine. Eyes glassy and staring ahead.

My lungs could take no more and so I was forced to let go and head for the surface. Carefully I released my hands and tried to point my body up, but as I did so, I touched the end of his tail. That was it. That must have spooked him, for in the next moment they had disappeared from sight. Coming to the surface, I breathed hard and looked about as to where I was. The boat was two hundred yards away, bobbing gently on top of the flat water, but at that moment it seemed a whole lot further, I was out in the middle of nowhere without even a spear gun for protection.

Once safely back aboard, I had a chance to relive my encounter. Never in my wildest dreams had I ever thought of swimming with a manta ray. In fact, the only rays I had ever seen were the small eagle and stingrays. Yet, out there in the middle of nowhere, our paths had crossed and I was elated.

BABY SHARKS

I was about a hundred miles north of the Whitsunday islands, anchored in forty feet of water behind a reef. All morning I had been working on fixing a leak in the hatch above my bunk. In a squall the previous night, it had started to drip and so it became my priority for the day.

To start, I had to remove the head lining in the cabin and then remove the dozens of bolts that secured the hatch to the deck. Once the hatch was off and all the old sealant removed and cleaned, I lay a new bead of silicone on the deck and carefully placed the hatch on top. It was hard to imagine how such a small job could take six hours and by the time I was done, I had lost the motivation to start anything new on my list, so I decided to take the rest of the afternoon off and do some fishing.

First I looked in the fridge for a piece of meat, but I was out of luck. I found what I was looking for in the freezer, a chicken leg. Taking the skin off the leg, I threaded it onto the hook and threw it in the water. This was not for sport, I was trying to catch dinner, so I used a hand line. Monofilament line with a two hundred pound test and a hefty weight on the end. The hook quickly sank to the bottom, so I tied off the line to the guardrail and settled down to read my book. I would be able to see if I had a fish when the line pulled taut.

I think I had read perhaps one paragraph, when the line suddenly started to move. I threw down my book and hauled in my catch, a small golden trevally. Great eating, but it was a little on the small side, so I decided to use it for bait. I put some fish onto the hook, tossed it into the water and went back to my book. Once again, it was moments before I had another strike. That time however, as I pulled the line up, it suddenly went slack.

I've lost it, I thought and continued to bring in the slack line to at least check on the bait. Everything was gone, the hook and the sinker. The line looked as though it had been sliced by a carving knife. Whatever was down there stealing my dinner had sharp teeth. Time and time again that same scenario played itself out and I was getting tired of it. All I wanted was one fish for dinner, but everything I hooked was stolen before I could get it half way to the surface.

It was time to try a new tactic, so I put a steel trace between the swivel and the hook, threaded one of my last remaining pieces of fish and stood by the line waiting for something to happen. Again it was only seconds before the bait was taken and I could feel the fish on the other end, as I started to pull in the line as quickly as I could. Once more, half way to the surface, I felt a tug and the line went slack.

The steel trace had been cut clean through, so I searched about for something heavier and came across a short length of chain and dug deep into my fishing box for the largest hook I could find. I put the last pieces of fish onto the big hook and then took a fender, a large inflated rubber ball used to keep the boat away from the dock and tied the fender to the line about twenty feet above the hook. I threw it all into the water and secured the end of the line to a winch in the cockpit. I waited and was beginning to think that the thief below was only interested in stealing my dinner, when the line pulled. The fender tried to go below the surface, but the buoyancy was too much and each time it would pop back out.

Meanwhile, Tapestry was being towed sideways through the water and at times the line stretched so much, I was sure it would snap. Judging by the strain, I would never be able to pull it in by hand, so I had no option but to wait. Wait until it tired itself out.

Ten minutes later, my prey was losing its steam, so I put on a pair of gloves and began to pull in the line. It did not want to come, but the fight was over and slowly, foot by foot up it came, until the dorsal fin breached the surface and I could see what I had. It was a bronze whaler and she was about six feet long. My intention at that point was to get it alongside and try to remove or cut the hook, for I had no wish to kill it. The shark was then twenty feet from the boat and up on the surface.

A monster's head came out of the water. It had to have been a monster, as I had never seen a shark so large. A hammerhead of perhaps fifteen feet or more, came up from below, bit off the end of my shark's tail, flew out of the water and then disappeared back under the surface. *So much for wanting to keep the shark alive,* I thought, because that wish was pointless, as she thrashed about in the water with only half a tail, so I had to put the poor thing out of its misery.

When I entered Australia they were sure to take away my revolver, but I soon found out that I could purchase a rifle in almost any convenience store, so I had bought myself a little .22 magnum. It was not much in the way of firepower, but I felt that I needed some sort of weapon out here in the vast expanse of the reef.

I pulled the shark alongside, tied the line to the winch and raced below to get my rifle. With perhaps a dozen holes in her head, the thrashing had long since stopped and I reckoned it was safe to bring her aboard. Unfortunately she was too large for me to eat, as the meat in larger sharks often has a high mercury content. The smaller ones however have fine tasting flesh and anything less than three feet was fair game for my table.

I released the main halyard from the mast, tied a loop in it and managed to get the loop around the body of the very dead shark. Then using the winch on the mast, I hauled her out of the water and set her down on the deck.

She was fat, my was she fat. Then it dawned on me that she might be pregnant. I took a sharp knife and carefully slit open her belly; sure enough she was pregnant and five baby sharks lay inside her.

At that point I was feeling wretched. I had not intended to kill the shark, let alone her babies too, so I had to do something to give back a little. I grabbed a bucket and filled it with seawater, then one by one I removed the babies from her womb and gently slid them out of the sacks that surrounded them. It was fortunate that they were ready for birth and as I put them into the bucket they came alive.

With five baby sharks getting their first taste of salt water, I lowered the bucket into the sea. They seemed a little dazed and unsure of what to do, but one by one, with their heads still above the surface, they headed to the shallow water on the edge of the reef. My heart soared with joy, for I had given back a little of what I had taken.

TWO CANOES TO NOWHERE

Thursday Island is on the northeastern tip of Australia. A small island with a population of about four thousand people. I had arrived three days prior and was getting ready for the long trip to Darwin on the northwest coast.

Tapestry's engine had broken a valve spring and because of the remoteness of the island, a new part would take forever to be shipped out. I had spent the last four hours plundering an old scrap yard on the edge of the town, looking for something I might use as a spare spring. Diesel engines normally require a stiffer spring than gas engines, but there was not an old diesel in sight. I broke apart several motors until I found what I was looking for. The spring was way too long and certainly not as stiff as the original, but it would have to do. I cut the spring to the correct length and ground a flat surface on the bottom. Time to try it out.

I returned to my dinghy and was about to launch it, when I heard two young guys shouting and trying to catch my attention. They were about a hundred yards down the beach, so I waited for them to arrive to see what it was they wanted.

"Sorry to bother you mate, my name is Chris and this is my friend Rob. We have a bit of a problem and hoped you might be able to help," said the more vocal of the two.

Chris went on to explain their plight. They had spent the last two months paddling up the reef by canoe, all the way from Brisbane. From here, they wanted to go over to Papua New Guinea (PNG) but they had run into a problem. Australian immigration would not clear them out unless they were to leave Australia and not touch land before arriving in PNG.

For them that was impossible, they would have to stop at a couple of the deserted islands in the Torres Straits, the small strip of water between Australia and Southeast Asia, if only to spend the night on some beach and continue in the morning. Immigration was having none of it; their vessels were not capable of doing the trip non-stop. That was the law and that was that.

I felt sorry for them; they had spent years planning the trip and had made it so far, only to run into a bureaucratic technicality. My mind at that moment though, was more concerned with whether or not my valve spring would work, so we agreed to meet in the bar later and I promised to give the matter some thought.

Back aboard, I made some fine adjustments to the spring, put the motor back together and pushed the starter button - while holding my breath. Perfect, it sounded as good as new, so I was able to continue on my way into the Indian Ocean.

That evening I met Chris and Rob in the bar and they had a plan. If they were to put their canoes on deck, then I could take them up to PNG. That way they would not have to set foot on Australia again. I tried to put myself in their position as a fellow traveler and thus I had no option but to help in any way I was able. For me, I did not intend to clear immigration here in Thursday Island, for my next port of call was still in Australia. For them to clear out meant that I would have to clear out, but I did not want to go to PNG. I would take them yes, but they would have to deal with the problem of having no clearance, once they met the immigration officials on the other side.

We left the bar and I took the dinghy back to Tapestry. The guys paddled out and soon we began the task of putting two large canoes onto the deck and securing them for the passage to come. These were not regular canoes as they had been specially built for their adventure. They were about eighteen feet long and contained inside was everything that they might need. A small mast and sail could be raised to help them when going down wind.

A shotgun was strapped outside each, as they had had quite a problem with sharks along the way. On one occasion they were forced to shoot them; that, or be capsized and turned into lunch.

We were all up early the next morning, but it was late in the day before we were ready to depart. What with one thing and another, time seemed to slip away. By then there was no way we could make it beyond the small islands and reefs that lay ahead, while still in daylight - but I decided to go anyway. We could always anchor behind some island for the night.

That was exactly what we ended up doing. It was a beautiful night as we lay at anchor behind a tiny little spit, on the edge of the Torres straits. They had many a tale to tell and it warmed my heart that I was able to help them continue their voyage. It takes more than a little officialdom to derail an adventure.

We were only about fifty miles from the PNG coast, so I decided to make a late start in the day. At five knots that was ten hours of sailing and I planned to drop them off before dawn. I did not intend to spend the next part of my life in a foreign jail for importing people.

The seas were short and choppy as the wind blew out of the east, but we made good time on a powerful reach. There was no moon as we neared the coast and clouds were scattered across the sky. Without radar, I had no idea as to exactly how far offshore we were, or if there were any other vessels in the vicinity. A few lights were visible on the coast, but besides that, the landmass could have been nothing but a figment of the imagination. The depth sounder started to show a rising bottom, and then I was able to estimate our position as a little over one mile out.

That was it, it was three in the morning and the bus ride was over. I took down the yankee and reefed the main, then headed the boat onto a broad reach to make for a more gentle motion, as we all set about the task of getting the two huge canoes into the water without an incident. I put a couple of fenders against the side of the hull and we lifted the canoes by a rope tied to each end, then lowered them into the water on the leeward side. Quickly we said our good-byes and then Chris and Rob tried to get into their canoes without capsizing. It was not easy as we were moving forward slowly, and the motion of the sea and the boat never stopped for an instant.

As soon as they were safely in their canoes, I turned Tapestry up into the wind and hoisted some more main sail. She bucked and jumped heading into the seas. One hand for the boat and one for me. Then when it was done, I turned back onto a broad reach, set the yankee and headed for Darwin. The night was so dark, that it was not a minute later that my passengers were out of sight, slowly paddling their way towards a foreign shore.

I headed west-southwest and skirted the Gulf of Carpentaria to the south. The Arafura Sea was shallow, only a couple of hundred feet, so whenever the wind blew the swell would pick up and the sea turned into a short, uncomfortable chop. It was a far cry from the long swells of the Pacific. There was a lot of shipping about, so I stayed awake in the cockpit. Besides the sharp motion, it was a beautiful night to be out and sailing in unknown waters.

I spent only five days in Darwin, a dry and remote town. The tides were so great that I had to anchor about half a mile from the shore. When the tide was out, a huge expanse of mud lay between the shore and the boat, which meant that I had to stage my excursions to coincide with the tide. Customs were as good as their word and when I cleared out, my revolver and morphine were returned to me.

My next stop was a group of islands on the other side of the Indian Ocean - the Seychelles. The run across that ocean was unremarkable, except for the amount and size of the fish I caught. Everything seemed fifty percent larger than in the Pacific. One day I caught a barracuda and once aboard, I lifted its head above mine and two feet of its tail was still lying on the deck.

It had been five years since I had seen any of my family and every time I looked at a chart, I could see South Africa;

I was beginning to miss them terribly and my mind was set on going home.

The Seychelles were somewhat north of my direct passage to Durban, but I was sailing with the trade winds; and also I had a desire to see the Coco de Mer, a species of coconut native to the island of Praslin and the Vallée de Mai.

The Coco de Mer palm has a history filled with myth and legends. This is partly because the bi-lobed nuts were discovered before the palm itself, and partly because the shape of the nut holds an uncanny resemblance to a woman's hips and pelvis - complete with pubic hair. The male plant on the other hand, resembles a huge penis. The palms grow to about one hundred feet tall and the female produces the largest seed in the world, that can weigh as much as fifty pounds; a truly magnificent palm.

Dancing on Raindrops

FOLLOW THE DOLPHINS

It had been a long day, or rather a long ten days. The storms coming off the African coast had slowed my progress and made for some difficult and uncomfortable sailing. One night I was hit by an electrical storm of such magnitude, that the night really was turned into day. Non-stop, for two hours, I could have read a book outside without once losing my place due to the lack of light. The lightning was everywhere, such a magnificent display, but of course with it came the wind and the rain.

The more it blew, the angrier the ocean became. The more the ocean lost its temper, the more we were tossed about on that vast expanse of water, always seemingly endless.

The first eight hours out of Mayotte, a small French island in the Comoros group off the East African coast, were idyllic with gentle breezes and flat seas. From there on, we had to fight for every mile. Foot by foot, we had made our way forward, slamming into wave upon wave, until I was sure the boat could take no more. Really I think the boat could have taken much more, it was me who was tiring.

Two hundred miles offshore, I carefully plotted my position on the chart and smiled to myself, as a strange sensation overcame me. Five years previously I had left Cape Town and the first usable navigation sight I had ever taken, had put me two hundred miles offshore. That was a long way out I had felt at the time. Now, I was the same distance offshore, only this time it meant that land was so close. Only two hundred miles of sea room, only two hundred miles between some rocky shore and me. It was time to start seriously navigating.

The following day I made contact with a passing freighter and asked them to please relay a message to a friend in Durban, my next port of call. "I shall be in at around ten tomorrow night," was the message. Slapper and I had known each other for many years and I figured he would want to be there to greet me.

Time dragged that final day at sea. The coast became visible in the early morning light and once I had ascertained my position from the land, there was no need for me to keep taking sun sights, so I busied myself by cleaning the boat and getting ready for port.

It was to be a night approach, so I dug deep into my lockers and found a list of lights. This is a book that defines navigation lights for the area; some are red, some green, some white and each has a distinct characteristic of flashes. Fl 2 12s 15m 20M. Flashing twice every twelve seconds, fifteen meters high and visible for twenty miles; was the first light I could see as the day gave way to darkness. A large lighthouse.

I was down below making notes on what lights to expect in the approach and entrance of the harbor, when I noticed that the publication was seven years old.

Oh well, fine time to worry about that now, I thought as the loom of the city started to turn into individual lights. Over the VHF radio, I had managed to place a call to Slapper on his cell phone and he assured me that he would be waiting for me - with about fifty others.

The weather calmed and the air was thick and heavy. The sea had flattened and a sheen began to form on its surface. I started the motor and took down the sails, ready for the entrance. About a mile away, the city was barely visible and I could not find the lights for the harbor entrance. Everything had changed in the last seven years.

Once I saw a red flashing light. *That's it, that's the light I'm looking for,* only to get closer and find it was a flashing Coca-Cola sign. Another certainty was a steady green light, only when it turned to yellow, then red, I felt hopelessly lost. All those people waiting ashore to welcome me and there I was not knowing which way to turn. What a hopeless situation.

It was then that the dolphins arrived, twenty, maybe thirty of them. Normally they would take a quick look and be on their way, but tonight was different; they all stayed around the boat, going nowhere. One put its head out of the water and started squeaking at me.

"Yea, so you say," I retorted, "but that doesn't help me none." With that they all moved to the bow of the boat and some were slapping the water with their tails.

Am I missing something? I wondered to myself, wanting to believe that this was some sort of a sign; a sign that I seemed incapable of understanding.

Why not, give it a go? It was a crazy idea, but somehow I found myself following through with action. I put the motor into gear, heard the usual clunk as the gearbox engaged and slowly started to head for the brightly lit shore.

The dolphins were off to my right, so I changed course and followed them. Always staying the same distance in front of me, they led me into the glare. At times I heard the sound of waves breaking onto the shore and I knew I must be really close to the beach, but between the fog and the glare of the city it was impossible to make out any land in-between.

I followed and concentrated on the group ahead, hoping that they wouldn't disappear and leave me all alone out there. Then they slowed and I slowed too.

"Okay, so what now?" I asked, not really expecting an answer.

The dolphins had encircled the boat, so I put the motor into neutral and looked around. Off to my left was a red flashing light and to my right, a green. That was it; I was in the middle of the channel. Shaking my head, as if to wake myself out of my dream, if indeed it was one, I put the motor back into gear and headed between the two lights.

The dolphins stayed at my side as I came into the outer harbor, then in an instant, they were gone. Just like that, one moment there and the next, I was all by myself again.

As I approached the international jetty to tie up, I could see dozens of people waiting on the dock. Festivities were well underway it seemed and I glanced at my watch - exactly midnight. *What's a couple of hours between friends?*

"So what took you so bloody long, I've been waiting for five years," Slapper said as he gave me a huge bear hug and placed an ice cold Castle beer in my hand.

He was a tall man and at six foot six was easy to pick out in a crowd. His hair had grayed a little with the passing of the years, but he had not lost his smile and his unbreakable positive attitude. Champagne and beer flowed as if from an endless supply and it was good to see old friends once again.

Slapper had commissioned his chef to make enough food for an army and anyone who walked by was invited to join in, as sumptuous snacks were continually being brought to the tables. Even the customs and immigration officials, who had arrived at that late hour to clear me in, joined in the festivities.

We slept on Tapestry that night and the next morning we drove to his house in the country. I didn't give it a thought as I climbed into the passenger seat, but it had been a long time since I'd been in a car. It was only when we were traveling at sixty kilometers per hour on the main road, approaching a stop light, that I realized that it was going to be a huge transition to readapt to a normal life. I was convinced we would not be able to stop in time and that we were about to crash!

Arriving at Slapper's house, I was glad to have survived the journey on the freeway. One hundred and twenty kilometers per hour (75mph.) was almost the speed of light as far as I was concerned, but in reality, it was only the speed limit. Before going into the house I savored the smell of the freshly cut lawns, and my eyes feasted on the abundant colors of the flowers in his garden and the view out over the ocean.

Inside, I went to the fridge to get a couple of beers and as I opened the door, the light came on. It was so unexpected and altogether too much for me at that moment, as I dropped to the floor holding my sides in hysterics of laughter. Slapper believed I had finally lost it.

That night I lay in a bath for the first time in many years. It was not something I had missed, as living in the tropics a cold shower was always welcome, but it certainly was good to relax in full tub of steaming hot water.

It was not my intention to stay in Durban more than a couple of days. My family was waiting in Cape Town and I wanted to get home, but I awoke the next morning and felt terrible. By noon I had the sweats and knew something was wrong, so Slapper drove me to the hospital and after a few tests, I found out that I had hepatitis.

For the next two weeks I felt like hell and I lay in my bunk too weak to do much. A kind doctor from the local hospital paid me a visit everyday to check up on me and give me injections or pills, but I do not remember much of what happened that first week, except my refusal to go to the hospital. I wanted to stay aboard. Once I was healed, that generous man would not accept a penny for his services.

It was tragic, there I was in one of the finest centers of Indian cuisine, comparable to the best in the world and my diet was restricted to bland and tasteless foods. No spices and no alcohol my doctor had warned. Nothing for six months!

"A bottle of the Cape's finest wine and a plate of lamb curry for my friend - and I'll have a glass of water and a bowl of plain white rice please." It was not easy.

A month later, I felt strong enough to make the final passage of my circumnavigation. The treacherous seas on that coast are well known for their huge waves. As the strong warm Mozambique current flows to the southwest, it is often met by a weather front coming up from the southeast. The South Easter or Cape Doctor, as it is affectionately known, helps in keeping down the smog levels in Cape Town. But, when it attains winds of over one hundred knots, blowing in the opposite direction to the current, it causes the most horrendous seas and freak waves.

I remembered seeing a tanker tied up in Cape Town docks, with a hole in the hull large enough to drive a double-decker bus through. They had been hit by a freak wave and it had punched clean through the empty vessel. The thought of it took me back to that first raging storm I had survived at the beginning of my voyage. It was perhaps the most powerful and violent conditions I had experienced up until then, so I kept a watchful eye on the weather reports.

When the forces of mind and nature come together, the result is spectacular.

Dancing on Raindrops

COMING HOME

It felt strange to be leaving Durban. Of all the countless times in the previous five years that I had cast off the dock lines or raised the anchor, I knew that would be one of the last. The time was coming when I wished to take a break from the ocean and try to live on land for a while. For the past year, I had been wondering what it would be like, for I had become so accustomed to a life at sea.

It can't be that bad, I thought to myself. *Millions and millions of people around the world do it every day and surely they must love it; or else why would they continue to do it?* I had much to learn.

I left before lunch on a Friday and motored out of the harbor. The entrance buoys seemed so well marked and so obvious, that I wondered how I had managed to have a problem finding them when I arrived. The weatherman had given me a five-day window before the next front was due to come up from the southwest. It was not enough time to get to Cape Town, but if things turned nasty, there were a couple of ports en route where I could find shelter from the storm. I set the sails and the last leg of my voyage was underway.

Seasickness was still an issue for the first few days, especially if the water was rough, but thereafter my body became acclimatized to the motion. The warm wind was from the north, which made for a pleasant broad reach, my most comfortable point of sail. I kept close to the coast for the afternoon, but once I had passed Slapper's house on the beach and had seen him waving, I changed course away from land to give me some sea room and also to take advantage of the southbound current.

As darkness came, Haley's comet seemed to fill the sky, as there were no other lights about besides the stars to detract from its brightness. It felt like a good omen, having such a unique event on my final passage, a mark to the beginning of a new era. It was time for a change, time to experience new things and I looked forward to it with anticipation and excitement.

Life aboard was second nature by then and with every movement the boat made, I would know exactly what was happening. Even lying in my bunk, I was able to tell if we were on course or not, simply by the feel and the sound of the motion. George was still in charge of the steering and since being reset in St Helena, he had taken me around the world perfectly. Most of the time his course was within a few degrees and when he started to have a problem, it was usually time for an adjustment in the sails. Tapestry was well provisioned for the short passage of about a thousand miles and I ate like a king, enjoying some of the foods that I had missed for so long.

Biltong was perhaps the food that I missed the most. A stick of dried meat, similar to Jerky but worlds apart in taste. It is made in strips of about eighteen inches long, three inches wide and a little under an inch thick. There is usually a thin band of fat on one edge to add to the flavor. Thinly sliced, it was all too easy to eat a half a pound of meat without realizing it. Samosas too were in abundance aboard. A three-cornered delight filled with curried meat and covered in thin pastry, then deep-fried. Two or three bites and it was time for another.

As the days passed, I kept a wary ear on the weather reports. The front was moving faster than anticipated, but it was expected to reduce in strength by the time it would reach me the following evening. Because of that, I decided to stay out at sea and not run for the shelter of a bay, or harbor on the coast. I even headed further offshore to give myself a little more sea room.

Sea room, or the lack of it, has changed the course of naval history; let alone the lives of countless seamen, whose ships piled onto the rocks of some distant shore. An English naval toast, is 'give me a willing foe and sea room.'

The front was stronger than I had anticipated and by midnight, I was down to carrying only a storm jib. Close hauled, we pounded into the steep seas, the bow often burying itself into the face of an oncoming wave. The wind was not the problem - it was the sea. As the wind and current were traveling in opposite directions, they created those famous vertical waves.

At three in the morning, there was a moment when it seemed as though my voyage might well come to an end. Standing in the galley and trying to make a cup of tea and a sandwich, I felt the boat rise up the front of the swell. It was the same feeling I had felt thousands of times before and I braced myself for the impact of the oncoming wave. Sure enough, the white water slammed into the side of the bow and Tapestry jumped and shuddered from the force of it, but in the next moment I knew something was wrong. There was no sound and the boat felt as though she was falling - as if over a waterfall. As she fell, she turned sideways and instinctively I dropped to the floor.

Time compresses in such moments, for it seemed as though we were falling forever, but as we hit the water below, it was with such force that I was aware that she could well break apart. My body slammed into the side of the galley counter and it sounded as though there had been a thunderclap outside. I could feel the rigging vibrate, as it battled to keep the mast up. Slowly she came upright and by the time I had gathered my wits and begun to head for the companionway, the next wave struck and I dived back onto the floor.

Fortunately that one didn't have a vertical face behind it, so I made my way into the cockpit and clipped on my safety harness as I came out of the hatch. Tapestry was well off course and I could see the white water of the next wave approaching from the side, as the top was carried off in a spray that seemed to be everywhere. I reached for the tiller to point the bow into the wave, but it was not there.

Frantically I groped in the darkness and my hands came across a stump of torn wood. All that remained was the last foot of the tiller, the rest had snapped off.

Wave after wave crashed into us, as I dug into lockers looking for a piece of steel pipe and some rope. It was a dangerous task, as Tapestry was at the mercy of those enormous waves. Often I was forced to hold on for dear life, as a wave broke over the cockpit and instantly filled it with water. Then before I could open the locker lid again, I had to wait for the water to subside.

Sometimes we were hit broadside on and Tapestry would feel as though she was about to turn turtle; a frightening situation when a boat rolls all the way over and comes up the other side. My mind was crystal clear, and as the minutes passed by and the waves successively slammed into us, I knew that time was of the essence. In fact time was survival. I had to turn on the deck lights, before I was able to begin lashing a three foot length of aluminum pipe to the remaining stump. Every time a wave hit, I could feel the rudder taking huge strain.

I tried to remove the thought from my mind, that *it might give way at any moment and tear away from the hull;* as it smashed from one side to the other. An hour later, with bruised and bloodied hands, the pole was securely lashed to the remains of the tiller. It was a messy job, using whatever pieces of rope were at hand, but at least it gave us steering for the rest of the night.

As the dawn came, so the wind began to ease and I was able to make a proper repair to the broken tiller. I had not slept the previous night, so I made sure that my course was away from land before I went below to rest. Lying in my bunk, I pondered the incredible power of nature. That one wave felt powerful enough to tear Tapestry apart from the force of impact, and I was surprised to find that there was no structural damage. Breaking only the tiller seemed a small price to pay.

Rounding Cape Agulhas, the most southerly point of Africa, I could clearly see the large red and white lighthouse above the needle sharp rocks on the shore. (The name Agulhas means needle.) I experienced a feeling of joy that must have been felt by many a sailor before me, when rounding the horn of Africa; but it was not until the following morning that I passed Cape Point, the meeting place of the Atlantic and Indian oceans.

Dramatic cliffs rise vertically out of the sea, upon which are two lighthouses, one above and one below the fog line. As I neared Cape Town, so the Twelve Apostles came into view, a truly magnificent range of mountains that run off the back of Table Mountain. In the last few miles, the water had cooled noticeably and turned to an ice blue color. It was autumn and the chilly waters of the South Atlantic Ocean were making their presence known.

Cape Town harbor had also changed in my years away. A new breakwater and container terminal had been built, but it was midday when I arrived, so finding my way was easy. It warmed my heart to see Table Mountain once again and when I stepped ashore at the Royal Cape Yacht Club, my circumnavigation was complete. It was an incredible feeling of both sorrow for the end of an era, but joy and excitement for the beginning of a new one.

Unlike the huge party that Slapper had so generously provided in Durban, here I enjoyed a quiet reunion with my family. My mother, two sisters and of course my good friend Zak. It seemed as though it had been forever since we had last seen each other and I was overcome by emotion to be back amongst those that I love, as tears of joy flowed freely. We sat in the cockpit until the wee hours of the morning, trying to catch up on the five years that had passed so quickly. It was good to be home.

The transformation of moving off the boat and into a house in suburbia was awesome, but was made easier because I had a new goal. I had made the decision to sell Tapestry and embark for a period on land. I wanted to expand myself in two of my interests; the stock market and helping people to overcome their fears. Settling again into society, it did not take me long to see the fear that many people were living under.

Fear of losing something, fear of having something, or the fear of not getting anything - so much negative energy, it was not surprising that many of my friends were not happy with their lives or situations.

To sell Tapestry, I wrote an advertisement and pasted a photograph of the boat to it, then pinned it to the notice board in the yacht club. Twenty-four hours later, I received a phone call and three days later she was sold. I was not surprised, awed perhaps, but not surprised. For once again the wheels of thought were in motion.

I moved off the boat and rented a house in Cape Town for a couple of months, then from there I went to Johannesburg, South Africa's financial center. I rented a huge house, too big for my personal needs, but it had rooms for offices and seminars. Carefully I outlined my new plan, then set it into action. It was fantastic, the more I taught, the more I learned and the more I learned, the more I was able to teach and show people that there is another way to live. In fact without fear, you can live the life you choose.

Sure there were stumbling blocks and things I had to overcome before I could continue. To get over my fear of public speaking, I invited fifty people to my first seminar and from that moment on, every seminar was easier. Giving up because of my own fear was not an option, it is simply like a hump in the road, something that either has to be gone around, or in some cases, surmounted before continuing.

PRESENT DAY

The sound of a ringing telephone startles me away from my thoughts.

"Hello, Lucky Mike here," I say as I answer.

"Hi Mike, it's Ed."

Ed is organizing tomorrow's event, it is his responsibility and for the past week he has thrown himself into the details of creating something special. I am only a guest speaker, speaking as a favor to him, as I managed to find a last minute space in my calendar.

"I want to let you know that we are all set for tomorrow at noon," he says, his voice resonates that same positive excitement for which I know him. It is always a pleasure to speak at his events, as things are always well organized and they simply seem to flow. I thank him for the courtesy of the call, assure him that I am looking forward to it and hang up.

My thoughts are now distracted, so I walk to the kitchen to get a glass of juice, trying to recollect my mind; to get back to the level I was on and at the same time trying to look at the big picture, the message as a whole. For this is not a concept where if you do nothing you will be punished; if you do nothing you will receive only the flotsam and jetsam that floats down the river called life, and that happens to pass your way.

I pour the orange juice into the glass, close the fridge and my mind begins to focus again. The juice is cold and that first sweet sip tastes like more and makes me smile.

5. SECRETS TO YOUR SUCCESS

ACTION

A thought can cause the wheels of creation to be set in motion, but action is required to make your dreams happen. As previously mentioned, it is by thought that the thing you want is brought to you, but it is only with action that you receive it. This is often the most difficult step on the road to your success, so just begin where you are, for you cannot act where you are not.

Take baby steps to your goals, for each positive accomplishment has a cumulative effect and the more times you achieve your objective, the more you will begin to use specific action to get the things you want out of life.

Johannesburg was booming and I started a stock management company, called 'The Insider.' A great bull market was happening at the time and making money for my clients and myself seemed easy, so I started another company.

'Attitudes – Development Specialists.' Attitudes was all about the thoughts you hold in your head and although I did not know it then, the principles of these **7** secrets. I knew that almost anyone who wanted to could do what I had just done, but most people thought only of the barriers and obstacles. They never gave themselves a chance to create the life that they would choose to live.

Business was good, but I was missing my old lifestyle. One morning, while I was studying the stock prices on my computer I noticed that a stock that I had been watching looked perfectly positioned for a buy. I bought a lot.

By noon the price had soared and I sold with a tidy profit. After placing the sell order with my broker, I put down the telephone and sat back in my chair. When I looked out of the window and saw the city outside, I realized just how much I missed the sea. I should have been elated, or at least content at having made such a successful transaction, but I was not. After less than two years in the city, I decided there and then to follow my heart, for I was not yet ready to live apart from the ocean.

Two months later I bought a yacht in Durban, sailed her down to Cape Town and then spent the next year doing a total refit. Chandelle was her name, she was forty-seven feet long, made of steel and she took me on a beautiful adventure. I returned to St. Helena and although it had been almost ten years since my last visit, the old gentleman who ran the customs recognized me immediately. It was great to be back.

Fernando had changed little, but one was no longer allowed to swim with the dolphins, or anchor for free. I explored the coast of Brazil, from the uncharted rivers to the Illes du Salut, located off the coast of French Guiana, the islands made famous by the movie Papillon. French convicts were sent to the islands of St Josef, Royale and Diable, (the notorious devil's island). That time I was able to see the Caribbean at a leisurely pace and after visiting almost all of the islands, I headed to the Mediterranean.

Almost six years after leaving Johannesburg, Chandelle was sold and I returned to the Caribbean to spend the next five years building a bar and restaurant business. I thought my life quite settled at last, but nature had other plans – for along came a hurricane and blew it all away.

Then my friend Mark needed help to deliver a ninety-eight foot yacht, from Antigua to Palm Beach, Florida. I obliged and for the next five and a half years we sailed the north Atlantic together aboard Jabula, an African word meaning happy.

That too was the time I became acquainted with the sky. During the yacht's refit in Savannah Georgia, I went to the airport to find a flying school. Jabula was to be out of the water for two weeks, so I had a little time off, but the instructor insisted that it normally took about three months to get a license.

He did not know that I had been visualizing the event. I had seen it in my mind's eye in the greatest detail, so where he saw problems, I saw solutions. With a hefty deposit on the table he agreed to give it a go and two weeks later I received my Private Pilots License.

It was fun being able to rent an airplane and fly wherever I chose. A girlfriend to the Cays for lunch, or New Orleans for the weekend, but then Mark started speaking about skydiving. The thought of it reminded me of the nine jumps I had done while I was in the Navy. Static line jumps from a little Cessna at three thousand feet had filled me with fear, but seeing as my life at that stage was all about conquering my fears, it had to be done.

BE AWARE OF THE POWER OF YOUR ACTIONS.

* For more information visit:
  www.dancingonraindrops.com

*" Never give up.
Never, never give up.
Never, never ever give up."*

SKY TIME

FEARLESS PETE

Three of us hit the road early in the morning to make the drive to the nearest drop zone. We were filled with excitement and nervous apprehension. The three hour ride did not seem to take that long as we rambled on to one another, but soon there was the dirt landing strip, with a small Cessna parked off to the side.

We completed the paperwork formalities and began training immediately. One hour of classroom lectures, followed by three hours of jumping off a six foot platform and trying to perfect the PLF, (parachute landing fall). Both feet to strike the ground together, then you roll over to one side, transferring the force of the fall to the side of your leg, then hips and side of the body - as you roll over and end up as an unsightly pile in the dirt. Over and over we practiced, until fortunately it was lunchtime and we had a chance to rest our bruised and dusty bodies.

After the break, we went into the classroom to learn about emergency procedures. The plane would take us up to three thousand feet, where we would climb out onto the step and exit with a static line attached to open the chute. In the rare event of a malfunction, you simply lift the two release covers of the Capwell clips, located on each side of your shoulder straps and pulled down on the two metal rings. That with a bit of luck would release the main parachute and put you back into freefall.

Then, to deploy the reserve, roll over on your back and reach for the reserve parachute located on your belly. One hand pulls the ripcord, as the other keeps the bag closed. Take one hand and slide it into the bag behind the parachute, grab the cloth and toss it out into the wind. It sounded like an awful lot to remember.

"Oh and if the cutaway does not work, then take this knife and cut your lines," the instructor said, showing us a large bowie knife. I think I was sweating at that stage.

The plane fired up and the four of us boarded. I was the first in, so would be the last to exit. We taxied to the end of the dirt strip, the pilot making his final checks.

Full throttle and slowly we began to pick up speed, the plane bouncing on the dirt runway. The clubhouse came by and we were still bouncing along. At one point I was convinced that we were going to run out of runway, when the nose lifted ever so slightly and up we went - clearing the fence at the end of the runway by only a few feet. The load was heavy and we spent the first mile a little above the cornfields, and then slowly we rose into the sky.

Three thousand feet and on jump run. The instructor clipped on the first static line and opened the door. The wind rushed into the plane and instinctively I braced myself and tried to move away from the opening.

"You first," said the instructor pointing to my friend Pete. Pete was a man of steel, with whom I had done the Navy divers' course. He was fearless and felt no pain.

"Remember to count," our instructor yelled above the noise. We had been taught that upon exit, you start counting out as loud as you can. One thousand, two thousand, up to five thousand and then it was time to check that your parachute was open above you.

Pete made his way to the door and tried to put his foot on the outside step. Each time the wind would blow his foot back towards the tail, but after a few attempts he finally got it firmly planted on the step and then pulled his body out of the plane, as he held on to the wing strut.

"Remember, kick your legs up and then push off with your hands. Ready, set, go!"

I could see his body lift up, then his arms pushed against the strut and he was gone. Gone out of sight, but not completely gone. All I could hear, instead of the one thousand, two thousand - was one thouuuuuuuuuuuuuu, as his voice slowly faded below. Oh boy, that was fearless Pete. I was not instilled with confidence.

Next was Georgeo. Not quite in the fearless category, as he had enough brains to know when danger was about. The plane slowly circled and as it banked, I could see Pete floating to earth under a large round canopy.

Jump run again and Georgeo's static line was clipped on, the door opened and the instructor motioned for him to climb out. He was far more adept at getting his foot onto the step and was soon standing outside the plane, facing forward and looking over his left shoulder at the instructor, waiting for the call. The instructor put his head out the door to check the spot and looked up at Georgeo.

"Ready, set, go!"

I could see his body rise as he kicked up off the step, but the next instant the plane shuddered. The look on the instructor's face told me that something was wrong. The plane started to go into a shallow dive and out of the window I could see my friend floating to earth; he was totally unconscious and had blood pouring from his chin. He had jumped up off the step, but had failed to push himself far enough as he left and had therefore caught the edge of the step on his chin as he fell.

"Okay, take us back up, one more to go," the instructor shouted to the pilot and we began to climb once again. By that time my legs were knocking, my mouth was dry and my palms sweaty.

Jump run and he hooked up my static line and opened the door.

"Let's go and remember to push off," he shouted above the noise of the wind and the motor.

I simply wished that he would go away, him the plane and everyone. *How the hell had I gotten myself into this situation?* I was not even sure that my legs would work, let alone have the strength to jump.

I too had difficulty in getting my foot onto the step and only when I concentrated on applying forward pressure to counteract the wind, did my foot land squarely on the metal grate. I leaned forward and grabbed hold of the strut and swung myself outside. The wind was blowing by at about sixty miles an hour and it felt really scary out there.

"Ready, set, go!" I heard the familiar sounds. Right then it was so tempting to say NO; but before I had a chance to finish the thought, I felt an almighty slap against my leg and heard the words – "Go! Go! Go!"

I jumped up and pushed off with all my strength. As I exited, I was supposed to see the plane flying above, but I did not see it and I did not count. The next thing I knew, there was a sudden jerk and I was floating under a parachute. I looked up to make sure everything was okay.

Oh no, I had what looked like a line over. Two of the suspension lines were wrapped over the canopy, thereby giving me two little parachutes, both only half inflated.

Cut away! Screamed through my head.

The idea of doing the cut away procedure on my first jump, with only a partial malfunction, was about as frightening as they come. I looked up at the canopy and tried to find which lines were causing the problem, all the while the little pieces of cloth that were fluttering above me, were not slowing my descent rate much. Quickly I pulled on each of the line groups to see if it would have any effect, as time was running out on a decision to cut away or not.

I decided to count to three while trying to sort out the malfunction and if it was not solved by then – it was time to cut away.

One.

With the strength of Samson, I tugged at one of the line groups and noticed the parachute begin to change shape, as my tugging caused the affected lines to slide over the top of the canopy.

Two.

A few more pulls and the lines came loose, the parachute opening fully above me and as the adrenaline rushed through my body, I could feel the shaking effect in my hands.

Oh wow, there I was floating above the valley at about a thousand feet, the mountain peaks rising up on either side of me. People had stopped their car on the roadside of the mountain pass and I could clearly hear them shouting their greetings. It was so serene and peaceful, a moment that could have gone on forever, but I needed to think about landing.

A round parachute steers about as well as a brick and the best I could hope for was to land in a clearing and not up a tree, or on the roof of a house. Luck was with me as I floated down into a clearing in the orange groves. From one hundred feet up, it seemed as though I was floating so slowly towards the ground, but as it came closer, the faster I seemed to fall.

I hit the ground. Smashed into the ground was more like it. I think I tried to do the PLF, but who knows and who cares? I was alive!

As for unconscious Georgeo, he came to before hitting the ground. And by the time I made it back to the hangar, he was well on his way to the hospital to get himself stitched up.

Often, the less you know about something, the greater is your potential to fear it.

THE STUDENT

For twenty years I had said, "been there, done that." My last encounter with skydiving had been one of terror and the constant question of will I die or not - but Mark would not let up. He had made a number of jumps about a year before and felt it was time for us to try. I remembered only to well the round parachutes and the static line jumps from three thousand feet, where the ground seemed so close even before you started to fall.

Mark, Ian and I were working on Jabula. Summers in the south of France and winters in the Caribbean - it was a fantastic lifestyle. Occasionally we would sail the east coast of the States and when we found ourselves in Florida, Mark decided it was time.

We succumbed and the three of us were finally on our way to a drop zone. Combining two adventures, we stopped off at a small airport and rented a plane for the day. Mark had done his jumping at a drop zone about an hour's flight away, so we decided to head there first.

The little Warrior climbed into the morning sun, the hum of the engine, a constant noise - very comforting. Up over Lake Okeechobee and we settled into our journey at three thousand feet. We were all very excited and the vibe in the small cockpit was a tangible thing.

Ian and Mark, brothers who had fallen in love with the sea. Together we shared the delights that our lifestyle offered and in the name of friendship and love, it was only right that Ian and I try this skydiving lark. Circling the airport, it looked deserted below, but to be sure we landed and confirmed our suspicions. The drop zone was closed; a sign on the door said so, its faded ink and paper showing its age.

South Florida has no shortage of places to jump, so we looked through my aeronautical chart and found another nearby. A town called Sebastian, a short hop away to the coast. We flew out over the ocean and came back in above the town and as we neared the airport, the radio came to life.

"Skydivers over Sebastian in one minute at thirteen thousand five hundred feet." Keeping well clear, we watched as the canopies opened in the sky at the same altitude we were flying at and then once they had landed, we came in to land ourselves.

The airport was alive with people, most dressed in bright colored jump suits. I parked the plane amongst the other small aircraft and as we opened the doors - the smell of burnt jet fuel was in the air to greet us. Those jump aircraft were a far cry from the little piston driven Cessna I had jumped out of before. They were large turbine aircraft, a De Haviland Otter and a Sky Van.

Walking over to the office, we began the process of signing wavers. Pages and pages of lawyer speak that needed signing at every paragraph. A swipe of the magic credit card and we were ready to begin. They had us watch a video first. In the presentation they explained the process of the tandem skydive, the do's and don'ts and of course, the inclusion of possible injury or death. Whatever, we were there to jump.

Soon we had our harnesses on and were heading for the plane, my adrenaline level started to rise. The Otter had both engines running and we boarded via a small metal ladder. Inside, the plane was stripped of seats, only carpeting on the floor and everyone sat facing the rear of the aircraft.

Twenty people boarded and we taxied to the end of the runway. The pilot gave full throttle and within moments we were airborne, climbing at an incredible rate of well over a thousand feet per minute. Yes, the fear started to show itself once again. I tried to breathe slow deep breaths and it helped a little, but still my palms were becoming sweaty and my heart pumped.

At ten thousand feet, my instructor began to clip the back of my harness onto the front of his. I noticed that the other jumpers aboard seemed unaffected by any fear, as they too readied themselves. Donning their helmets and goggles, checking their gear and waiting in anticipation for the door to open.

Why, I asked myself, *did I feel afraid when others in the plane, about to do the same thing, showed no fear at all?* Of course I knew the answer. They had overcome their fears and mine were still only being acknowledged.

Thirteen thousand five hundred feet and the pilot throttled back the mighty engines and set the flaps to reduce our airspeed. The door was opened and the cold wind rushed into the body of the plane. Instinctively I took in a short, sharp breath.

The light turned green and groups of people disappeared out of the door and into the sky, all the while we were shuffling closer and closer. Ian and his instructor were the first of the tandems to exit and his eyes looked as wide as mine felt. Standing there at the edge of the door one instant and gone the next. We moved to the opening, part of my mind saying no - no don't do it.

Mark was next and although wide-eyed, covering his face was a huge grin. Then I found myself at the edge looking down at the ground, far, far below. My heart was beating fast, as my instructor leaned over and put his hand under my chin to remind me to keep my head up, as my eyes were riveted to the ground. Making sure my arms were folded, somewhere in the swirling air, I heard a voice.

"Ready" - I think I nodded, unable to speak.

"Set" - and my heart beat even faster, if that were possible.

"Go!" - and we launched from the door, as my heart seemed to stop.

Wind, the wind was everywhere, or so it seemed. I felt a tap on my shoulder and remembered that that was the signal to put out my arms, to relax and enjoy the ride. My body felt stiff with fear and I am not sure if I was breathing or not.

The ground never seemed to get any closer, but the view was spectacular. The sandy beaches and the blue water of the Gulf Stream, speckled with white horses. The runway was visible far below. We flew a couple of circles and in the distance, Lake Okeechobee was shimmering in the afternoon sun. The land flat, flat as only Florida can be.

It seemed as though we had only just left the aircraft, when my instructor put his hand in front of my face and pointed to his altimeter. Six thousand feet the dial said and I remembered that we were supposed to pull at five thousand. For an instant we seemed to accelerate, then I felt the jerk as the canopy started to deploy. Relief flooded over me, as I looked up and saw that there was a square parachute above. It was okay; I was not going to die.

Floating high in the sky was the only aspect of the jump that I had experienced before and it was as magnificent as I

Dancing on Raindrops

remembered. Below I could see the other canopies landing on the green grass in-between the runways and all too soon, we were approaching the ground at an alarming rate. My instructor flared the canopy and my feet touched down for a perfect stand up landing - a far cry from my experiences with the round parachutes of yesteryear. That was it; I was hooked.

The adrenaline still flowed, but it seemed to have a calming influence and rather than inducing fear, it made me realize how awesome the experience actually was. Ian and Mark were both fired up, as we walked back to the hangar together. All three of us wanted to continue the experience and learn how to do that on our own. We could only imagine the feeling of jumping out of an aircraft and then being able to fly one's body.

The course consisted of eight jumps and the first three were with two instructors, but from then on with only one. Ian and I signed up immediately - it had to be done. We were going to take a week off work and learn to skydive, but Mark unfortunately couldn't spare the time.

Flying back that afternoon, it seemed as though my life had changed in some tiny way, a way to which I could not yet relate; but I did know I was ready to experience once again, the thrill and fear that I had felt that day.

One week later, Ian and I drove to Sebastian to begin our course. AFF it was called, accelerated freefall. We had arranged to stay with one of the instructors for the week, thereby giving us the opportunity to jump everyday. The first morning was taken up in the classroom, studying the basics of skydiving. I marveled at the new technology available in the sport since I had last embarked on a mission to skydive. The rigs were tiny in comparison and gone were the old cut away clips. Now only one handle was pulled to cut away and only one handle again for releasing the reserve, which was packed into the rig - not in a belly bag tied to your stomach!

Most impressive was a device called a Cypress. Should you become unconscious during freefall, this device measured your descent rate and if you were still falling close to terminal velocity at seven hundred and fifty feet, it would automatically deploy the reserve. We learnt about the different types of malfunctions and what to do with each of them, how to fly a pattern for landing and when to flare.

The course was broken up into small steps that the student had to complete on each jump, in order to move on to the next level. It was after lunch on the first day, when my two instructors and I boarded the plane for jump number one. As we climbed through five thousand feet, I was reminded that that was the altitude I would be pulling at on the way down.

Relax and breathe, I was told time and time again, but I knew it was going to be easier said than done. We stood at the doorway and my friend the fear monster was right there with me. Check left, check right. Both my instructors nodded that they were ready. The monster screamed.

To hell with you, I thought.

Dancing on Raindrops

Ready, set, go and there I was falling through the sky, as stiff as a board. I am not sure if it was the fear that made my body so unable to arch, or the back injury from long ago. I wished it were the latter, but knew it might well be the former.

I checked to the left and my instructor who was falling beside me gave me a huge grin and a thumbs up. To the right the same thing, I must have been doing OK. I checked my altimeter several times before the needle reached six thousand. Then, at that altitude I kept my eyes firmly fixed to the gauge and at five thousand feet, exactly as planned, I waved my hands above my head - the signal that I am about to pull. I then reached back with my right hand and pulled the ripcord.

Remember to keep the cord in your hand, I reminded myself. As the canopy started to deploy, my two instructors fell away below me and I watched as they turned head down for a moment and tracked off in opposite directions. With that, the parachute opened with a sudden jolt. It was there, it was square and it was steerable. My training came back to me. Phew!

Stuffing the ripcord into my jump suit, I released the toggles. These are two webbing handles on either side of the risers, (webbing at the base of the suspension lines) that are attached to the back tail of the canopy and are used to steer with. Pull down on the right toggle, to turn to the right.

Far below, I could see my instructors diving their canopies to land and I was the only one left in the sky. I was elated; I had done it. Under canopy I was more confident in my ability. Hundreds of landings in small planes gave me a bit of an edge, except that that time I was in for a dead-stick landing. Unlike a powered aircraft, that time there was no go-around, no second chance. It was uneventful; I flew the pattern and flared as the ground rushed up at me, my huge canopy giving me a soft, stand-up landing. Ooooh Yea!

Ian and I had both completed our first level and we were ecstatic. Talk that night revolved around one topic only - skydiving. There was so much to learn and we soaked up every bit of information we could. The image of my two instructors falling away on either side of me, then turning head down, was vivid in my mind. Such control - that was what I wanted to do, I wanted to be able to fly head down.

The next morning we both finished level two and after lunch, we were ready for level three. I was beginning to get a little more confidence in my ability, or lack thereof. Once I had passed that level, I would only need one instructor. I had to pass.

My exit felt good and I arched as hard as I was able. Check left and right, all okay. It was then that I started to spin - round and round like a runaway clock.

What the hell is happening?

I tried to turn my body to one side in order to stop the spin, but it made no difference, so I tried the other way. Again nothing. Time started to slow. Altitude awareness was gone from my mind and I felt powerless to stop the crazy spin.

What the hell is happening?

The next instant, I felt my canopy opening above me and as I looked up, I saw that I had several twists in my lines, so I began to kick my legs in order to get my body turning. One, two, three times around I kicked, my heart beating so fast I could almost feel it in my chest. Then the lines cleared and I turned and started to head for the drop zone.

Why had I gone into a spin?

How come turning my body had no effect whatsoever?

How did I forget my altitude and have my right side instructor pull my parachute?

My mind was a mess. Perhaps I was not cut out for this sport after all. I was scared. Even on the ground, my mind refused to clear. The fear monster was deep inside me.

During the debriefing, my instructor told me what had happened. My left side instructor had let go soon after exit, as I seemed to be flying well and with that, I started to power forward. The remaining instructor did not wish to let go, so he held on and that is what caused the spin. The more I kept that rigid body position trying to fly forward, the faster the spin became, until at seven thousand feet my instructor reached over and pulled my rip cord.

I was shaken and thoughts of giving up crept into my mind, along with all their usual justifications. Perhaps I was not meant to be a skydiver.

No! No! No! That would not do. I had set out to learn to jump and I would finish the course - even if it killed me.

The next two jumps I spent on level three. Each time I was doing something or another wrong. Forgetting to check my altitude, or not making a turn when I was supposed to. It was getting to me and despair was trying to creep into my resolve. Somehow, I was having difficulty remembering things during freefall. Sensory overload was the reason, but how do I overcome it?

When I discussed the problem with a fellow South African who was also an instructor at the drop zone, he suggested that we should do a fun jump together. Johan recommended that I did not concern myself with performing any of the maneuvers required for the course, but we would jump and take it from there.

The ride to altitude was without my usual apprehension and I was looking forward to the skydive. The pressure was off and the only thing I had to remember, was to pull before five thousand feet. As I jumped from the plane, Johan flew in front of me and smiled. There I was, without anyone holding on to me and my mind was as clear as can be. I was elated and began to do the required maneuvers anyway. A three hundred and sixty degree turn to the left, check my altitude, then the same to the right. It felt easy - as I turned my shoulders, so I begun to rotate in the direction that I leaned. To stop it, I simply leaned the other way for a moment. Precisely how it was supposed to be.

Sometimes I think that it was that single jump that committed me to becoming a skydiver. Until then, I was about as full of sensory overload as I could get and I was having difficulty with every part of the jump. From there on the next levels were a breeze, all the way up until level eight, a simulated emergency exit from five thousand feet.

For the first time, I was sitting by the door. A final gear check as the plane banked at three thousand feet and turned back over the drop zone. That was quite scary. I was used to the full altitude of thirteen thousand five hundred feet.

What if I cannot get stable quickly enough? What if, what if?

The red light came on to open the door and I knew my time had come. My heart was beating fast, as I peered out of the open door at the runway, so close below. At least there were no maneuvers to perform on that jump and all I had to do was to pull as soon as I was stable.

The light turned to green as we crossed the center of the runway. I took a deep breath, looked to my instructor for a confirming nod and jumped.

Get stable and pull, get stable and pull, I repeated to myself. The exit was good and I could see the plane rising in the sky above. I was stable, so I pulled my ripcord and within seconds I had an open canopy above me. Looking at my altimeter, I saw that I was at four thousand five hundred feet. Wow, I really had expected to be much lower, but I did not yet fully comprehend that it takes time to reach terminal velocity. I was still in that part of the skydive known as 'on the hill'; the seconds after exit when your body is still moving at the same speed as the plane. As you naturally fly in an arc, the friction of the air reduces your forward motion and soon you begin to fall vertically.

My course was over, but before I could get my A license I had to do solo jumps until my total was twenty. Ian and I were running out of time, as we had to be leaving for Europe in a few days, so we both jumped at every opportunity we could. Five jumps in one day and we were exhausted. At the same time we were both learning how to pack a parachute, as part of the requirement for the license. So many pieces of string and so much cloth that always seemed to have a mind of its own. As I had everything perfectly set, so the cloth would slip and slide, turning my whole pack job into an ugly mess and forcing me to start again. Over and over I packed and repacked, until finally it was beginning to make some sort of sense. The way the lines have to be stowed, the cloth folded and then how it all fits neatly into the container. I had done it, I had packed my own canopy and it was time to jump it.

Oh boy, I kept thinking to myself on the ride to altitude, *I hope it works.* Of course it opened, throw any piece of cloth into the wind at one hundred and twenty miles per hour and something is bound to happen. With twenty-one jumps in my logbook and a license to skydive in my pocket, it was time to sail to France.

THE DEATH OF A FEAR MONSTER

"Bonjour," I said to the woman behind the ticket counter in the bus station.

I had a few weeks of vacation, skydiving, ahead of me and my first stop was to be a small town called Gap. I had heard there was a drop zone there, so it seemed as good a place as any to start. It was not going to be as easy as it seemed, for she gave me the impression that she had never heard of a town called Gap. I kept trying, repeating the word with different accents, until finally the penny dropped.

"Ahaa, Gappa," she said with an enlightened look on her face.

It was a four-hour bus ride and apparently the small town was before the last bus stop, in a place called Tallard, at the foothills of the Alps - and yes, there was an airport there, before the town on the right. I was glad my French was better than my Spanish.

The south of France in the summer time, what a place to be. The bus was immaculately clean and the passing countryside so beautiful and oh so French. Small villages with cobbled streets, sunflowers swaying in unison to the breeze and the mountains, oh the mountains.

One of the things I really missed about a life on the ocean, were the mountains. Here I had towering snow-capped peaks, rugged and barren. My heart soared at the thought of the adventure that lay before me. My plan was to travel all over France, stopping at as many drop zones as I could find along the way.

Tallard 10 km said the sign, so I began to keep a lookout for an airport. Sure enough, the woman in the ticket office was correct. There was the airport, but the bus was not stopping. I jumped up and frantically asked the bus driver to stop. At first, I'm sure he thought I was crazy. I pleaded and begged in my best French, which probably meant that he did not understand a thing. As the airport was disappearing behind, he succumbed, stopped the bus and waited while I removed my belongings from the storage lockers underneath. I hauled out my rucksack, thanked the driver and he took off, leaving behind a moment of silence on the road.

I felt great on that mile walk back to the airport. The country air was full of the smells of summer and high above, the mountain peaks glistened in the afternoon sun. Stonewalls lined the road, giving an air of age and history. It was beautiful. I walked onto the airport and looked about for signs of skydiving. Sure enough I found them in a hangar. People packing parachutes upon a large carpet on the floor, a group of four practicing their moves for their next jump and about another dozen people milling about or soaking up the sun.

The sign said 'Office.' The young lady behind the desk spoke perfect English and informed me that they did have gear to rent and I would be welcome to jump the next day - as the last load was about to take off. There was a small hotel at the end of the runway and that was where she recommended I stay. I was elated, they accepted my U.S. license, had gear to rent and even a hotel nearby. I had yet to purchase a rig, actually my feet had hardly touched dry land since leaving Florida a month or so before. All I carried with me was my camping gear and a few sets of clothes. Therefore, my plan was to rent wherever I went.

The hotel Arizona, slap bang in the middle of the French countryside. I was not sure what to expect. It would have been reasonable enough to find it was owned by Americans - the name seemed to me to imply motel type accommodations and greasy food, but I was not there for the luxuries - I was there to skydive.

As I walked through the front gate of the hotel, I realized how often impressions can be wrong. It was beautiful. Outside on the green lawns were white umbrellas, under whose shade people sat eating and drinking. Everything was immaculately clean and the smells wafting out of the kitchen made my mouth water, reminding me of how hungry I was.

My room overlooked the lawns and the mountains. I could not have asked for more, so I showered and set off for an early dinner. The following day was going to be a big one and I wanted to be refreshed and well rested.

The restaurant was built of stone and wood, a fireplace in the corner awaited the return of winter. It was nothing fancy but rather had a feel of home, except for their wine list, which was something I could only dream of. Without hesitation I chose the snails for starters, a longtime favorite, followed by a piece of French boeuf, Filet Mignon. If I were to die the next day, at least I would have eaten well beforehand. Dinner was more than I expected. It was an experience - taste bud heaven. Even the glass of house wine seemed to taste like the nectar of the gods.

My belly was full as I climbed into bed and tried to get to sleep, but my mind kept focusing on the upcoming skydive and sleep would not come. I spent half the night practicing my exit, as I leapt from my doorway into the passage; arms and legs stretched out and spread apart, hips pushed forward, arching as hard as I could. Yea, I guess I was a little nervous.

By load four in the morning I was ready to go. All the paperwork signed and a rental rig on my back. It was not the prettiest rig in town and looked as though it had had a long hard life. The canopy was packed in a 'long bag' I was told, but I didn't have the faintest idea of what that was all about.

Six of us boarded the Pilatus Porter, a single engine turbine aircraft, a tail dragger. We climbed between the mountains, slowly rising above them and far in the distance, the snow-capped chain of peaks disappeared into nothing. Soon we were at altitude and before the door opened, I checked my rig once again. Three handles, three straps - I was good to go.

The door slid back and cold air swirled about. My heart was beating fast. All the practicing I had done during my sleepless hours last night, were for naught. I had visualized the doorway of a twin Otter, a large opening with room to almost stand at the doorway. That plane was different, not only was the door smaller and the ceiling lower, but outside in front of the door was the wing strut and below it, a wheel. I crouched in the door and counted to five, as the jumper before me left.

My fear level was high and my palms were sweaty. There was no thought in my mind that I would not jump, but nonetheless I could feel my blood pumping.

I dived out of the plane. It was not a pretty exit, but within a few seconds I was stable, belly to earth and the sheer beauty of my surroundings made me forget my fears. The air was cold, a clean crisp sort. I was high above the surrounding peaks, the valley a segmented yellow and green below. This was the adventure I had come for.

Soon I was at the same altitude as the peaks and it was a strange sensation to fall below them. At four thousand feet I pulled and my canopy opened with a snap. Whatever, it was open and my first jump in Europe was almost over. I floated over the countryside heading back towards the landing area and set myself up wind, ready to fly a left-hand pattern.

At one thousand feet I turned down wind and when I had flown a little beyond the landing area on my left-hand side, I turned crosswind at five hundred feet and flew my base leg until my spot was directly up wind of me. Once again I turned to the left, into the wind for final. The large student canopy flared easily above me and I touched down gently. Oh yea, it felt good to get rid of the cobwebs and after a jump like that I was ready for more.

It was time to learn how to freefly, flying in either a sitting position or head down. That was what I wanted to learn, because at last I was convinced in my own mind that I could, at any time, get stable and pull.

I went into the hangar and began packing my parachute and all went well until I tried to get the canopy into the bag. The bag was far too big and was unlike anything I had seen before. When I asked about how to pack it, it turned out that it had to be packed in a completely different way to which I was accustomed, so I hired the services of a packer and the problem went away. Aaah, so that's what the person was telling me when they gave me the rig and said it was packed in a long bag.

Time means different things in different countries. In the U.S., the drop zones stay open all day and take up as many loads as possible. In France, one o'clock was lunchtime and so everything stopped. Some went home for a bite to eat and a siesta, the others and I sat in the hangar and had a leisurely lunch. Warm summer breezes, French wines and cheeses; what a civilized way to live.

Jumping resumed at three o'clock and I managed two more loads, the last of which was the sunset load. I jumped out of the plane in the bright sunlight at altitude and then fell below the peaks and into the shadow of the mountain. Time seemed to leap forward into the twilight of evening and soon after everyone had landed, darkness covered the valley.

For four days I jumped as often as I was able to and on a couple of occasions I managed to get into a stable sitting position. Not for long, but it seemed as though I was getting a feel for the air. It was a fantastic sensation, sitting as though in an armchair, watching the world from thousands of feet above.

I had a date in Paris the next evening, so one of the skydivers gave me a lift into town and I boarded a night train bound for the city. Sally, my sister, wanted to try this skydiving stuff. She said it was all I ever seemed to speak about, so she flew from Cape Town to Paris. A long way to travel for a skydive.

We spent the night in a nondescript hotel in the city and over dinner, in a sidewalk café, we discussed where to go - for we knew what we wanted to do. Bordeaux was a place

Dancing on Raindrops

we had both heard about often enough. Many a bottle of wine from that town had sat on my table, so after spending the day seeing some of the sights of Paris, we caught the express train to the coast. Somewhere there, my little book said, was a drop zone and sure enough it was right.

The next morning we were in the airplane together, riding to altitude. Sally was doing her first tandem. She seemed so composed and relaxed in the plane, that I was glad she had not seen the look on my face when I did my first tandem. Once on the ground, she was hooked. She had an aura of energy radiating from her; something within had been touched.

We jumped on most days but also spent some time wandering the town and countryside, enjoying the ambiance of the surroundings. Time passes so quickly when you are having fun and all too soon we had to part, as Sally had to return to her business in Cape Town. At the airport she promised to come to Florida and learn to skydive, then we would be able to jump together; wishes that would soon come true.

I headed for a small town called Annemasse, located between Lake Geneva and Mont Blanc - the top of Europe. Arriving on the bus on a Sunday afternoon, I expected the drop zone to be alive with activity, but the place was deserted. A note on the door saying, 'Be back Monday.'

There was nothing to do but wait for Monday, so I pitched my tent off to one corner of the airport and relaxed with the sunset. On the way through town, I had figured I would need some provisions, so I had bought a fresh baguette and an assortment of cheeses and pâtés, plus of course a bottle of wine. After dinner, I lay in my tent with the flaps open, looking up at the stars and the mountains above. The airport was closed after dark, so the night was quiet, except for the distant hum of civilization and the local wild life.

In the morning, I was abruptly woken by the sound of the drop zone plane, as it returned home and came to a stop near my tent. It looked as if I would get to jump.

We exited at thirteen thousand feet and the summit of Mont Blanc still towered over two and a half thousand feet above. The peak was covered with snow and ice; dark vertical faces of rock were the only things not white. Down in the beautiful Chamonix valley, Lake Geneva, with its land mark 'Jet d'eau' fountain, shooting a solid jet of water over four hundred and fifty feet into the sky, was clearly visible in the frigid morning air.

My sit flying was coming on well and soon I was able to stay upright for most of the jump. Falling through the sky, I sat there enjoying the magnificence of the scenery as Mont Blanc towered above. I fell past the glacier and into the more temperate regions under the snow line and looking out over the valley it seemed to go on forever, green fields disappearing into the horizon.

The jet of water on the lake was getting noticeably larger, as I approached five thousand feet at about one hundred and fifty miles per hour. It was time to slow down and pull, so I turned onto my belly, waited for five seconds and deployed. I was open by three thousand feet and the drop zone was directly below, so I had plenty of time for a slower look at my surroundings. It was magnificent and I smiled to myself as I remembered the effort, the trains and buses I had taken to get there, but in that moment it all seemed so worthwhile.

By the time I had fifty jumps, I felt like a sky god - but even gods have to go back to work.

MOMMY MOMMY
THERE'S A MAN OUT THERE

"Load nine, five minutes," the loud speaker blared. Some people jumped up and began to get ready, myself included. The afternoon was hot and large cumulus clouds had been forming for the past hour or so, as the Florida sunshine helped in the creation of these magnificent formations.

Intense and isolated, they would pass overhead and the wind would pick up dramatically, followed by the rain. Then minutes later it was all over, and once again the sun was out and the remains of the storm would pass into the distance as a beautiful vision; a vertical column of cloud, moving and swirling, looking oh so serene and harmless.

I tightened the straps on my parachute rig, made sure I had my goggles and helmet and set out to board the plane. Nineteen of us sat inside the Super Otter, as she started to taxi towards the end of the runway. I was seated on the floor next to the door, one leg dangling outside the fuselage, enjoying the smell of the jet fuel and the prospect of the coming sky dive. As the plane turned onto the runway, I noticed a small cloud forming up wind of the airport. The base was at perhaps three thousand feet and the top could have been no more than five. The engines roared and we started to pick up speed. The air was filled with excitement as we accelerated.

Fly baby, fly, as the wings took the load and we began to rotate, my leg still dangled outside the door. At one thousand feet, Captain Chad our pilot raised the flaps and set the powerful engines for maximum climb. As we banked, I noticed that the little cloud I had been watching earlier had grown. We were then at five thousand feet and the top of the cloud was rising faster than we were, as it was still well above us. I started to take notice.

We were climbing at around one thousand feet per minute and the cloud was still beating us. If it kept on going, it would make a perfect cloud jump. Thirteen thousand five hundred feet, oh what a place to be. Captain Chad reduced the throttles, set the flaps and gave the red light to open the door for jump run. All the skydivers busied themselves, putting on their helmets, checking their gear and passing high fives all around. My cloud had grown in the past few minutes and was perfectly positioned about two miles from the drop zone.

Decision time. Yes, was my answer. I moved away from the door and headed towards the front of the plane, as the light turned green and people started to exit. I was going to do what is known as a hop and pop. Exit the aircraft and pull my parachute immediately. Then I wanted to fly beside that magnificent cloud, so I informed Chad of my intentions.

"No problem," he said, "wait until everyone has gone and I will drop you off near the cloud." The plane emptied quickly as groups left every few seconds and soon I was the only one aboard, as we banked steeply and headed for my cloud. Helmet on, goggles tight, straps and handles checked and I was ready to go. The huge thunderhead loomed in front and on the edge of it, Chad gave me the go signal and I jumped.

The air was cold as I looked up and saw the plane roll over into a steep dive. I deployed my parachute and seconds later, there I was on the top of the world - alone.

The cloud's edge was about one hundred yards away, so I steered towards it as I removed my goggles and loosened my chest strap to make for a more comfortable ride. The only sound was that of the passing wind.

Oh shit, as I noticed an aircraft heading directly towards me. The Boeing 727 was at the same altitude, but seemed as though it would pass slightly to my left, so I steered to the right. On it came, until it seemed to take up most of the sky and there it was opposite me. Close, oh so close.

I could clearly make out the windows and then a face suddenly caught my eye. In a window above the wing was the face of a small boy. Our eyes met and he waved, so I waved back. Then his head turned away and I imagined him with an excited voice saying, "Mommy Mommy, there is a man out there!"

Mommy I imagined as saying, "Yes sweetheart, I'm sure there is, now sit down as we are about to land," as she turns the page of her book. The little person looked back at me for an instant before he was gone and once again I was alone in the sky. I smiled to myself, as I relived the sight of the little boy trying to tell his story of what he had seen in the sky, but I was sure no one would believe him. Only he and I knew the truth.

I headed for the sunny side to play. From the ground, clouds seem almost motionless, but up close they are in constant motion; the white stuff swirling and moving, forming and dissipating right before my eyes. I flew up to the edge, the air suddenly became cooler and I could feel the moisture against my face.

Oh! I have slipped the surly bonds of earth
And danced the skies on laughter-silvered wings;
Sunward I've climbed, and joined the tumbling mirth
Of sun-split clouds - and done a hundred things
You have not dreamed of - wheeled and soared and swung
High in the sunlit silence. Hov'ring there,
I've chased the shouting wind along, and flung
My eager craft through footless halls of air.
Up, up the long, delirious, burning blue
I've topped the wind-swept heights with easy grace
Where never lark, or even eagle flew -
And, while with silent lifting mind I've trod
The high untrespassed sanctity of space,
Put out my hand and touched the face of God.
                    John Gillespie Magee, Jr.

Dancing on Raindrops

The words of that beautiful poem rang through my head. My heart was happy and in almost a spiritual sort of way, I felt at peace there amongst the sky and the clouds. Off to my left, I noticed a tunnel going into the cloud and without another thought, I steered into it.

About fifty feet across, it was a hole that went deep into the 'tumbling myth.' The air started to become turbulent and my canopy bucked and danced above my head. That was far enough, I did not want to become disoriented in the cloud, as I may never have found my way out again. The enormous updrafts of wind that keep the water suspended in the air, could well carry me upwards and there would not be much that I could do about it. As a last resort I would have to cut away my canopy, go back into freefall and then hope to come out of the base of the cloud before opening my reserve. That, or wait until the updrafts took me so high that I passed out from oxygen deprivation.

No thanks. I turned and went into a vertical dive before leveling off facing the opposite direction. The hole had closed around me and I was in thick cloud. As I expected to arrive back in the sunlight, I noticed a huge cave below me. The size of a cathedral, it was clean air with a wall of cloud all around. It was too much to resist and I dived down into it. The vast room was surrounded by cloud, every inch of it in motion. It was spectacular being suspended high in the sky, within a cavern; a place where no one had ever been before, nor ever would be again. The light was dim and it was impossible to see where it was coming from.

By then I was lost, which way was out? I did not know, so I spiraled down inside the cavern looking for some sort of clue. There below me was a shaft of light, what a relief. I put my canopy into a dive, my speed picking up instantly and leveled out heading into the beam of light. There was a small tunnel, only about ten feet in diameter and as I entered it, I could see blue skies ahead. Surrounded by the tube of cloud, my body was in clean air, but as I looked up, my canopy was barely visible in the dense cloud above.

Back in the brilliant sunshine and still at four thousand feet, I looked down and could see the airport below. The bottom of the cloud was black, heavy with water and it was fast approaching my landing area. I began to descend in a steep spiral, wanting to be on the ground before the winds picked up.

Positioning myself above my landing spot, at five hundred feet, I pulled down hard on my front riser and the canopy went into a vertical dive, while turning one hundred and eighty degrees. The ground rushed up to meet me at about sixty miles per hour and I planed out above the green surface, my feet skimming the tops of the grass as I bled off the excess speed. Slowly I increased my brakes and put down my feet for a tiptoe landing. No sooner was I on the ground, the wind began to pick up and light rain fell from the cloud above. Perfect timing.

Dancing on Raindrops

It was hard to tell if it was going to rain or not. The clouds were low, but there were still large patches of blue in the sky. It was one of those days that every time we boarded the airplane, we did not know what would happen to the weather by the time we reached altitude, at thirteen and a half thousand feet.

On the last load, we were forced to descend below the cloud layer at two thousand feet and those who wished to, did a 'hop and pop,' and deployed immediately - immediately if not sooner.

There is something incongruous about landing in an aircraft with a skydive rig on your back. It is however, infinitely better to be on the ground, wishing you were in the sky - than being in the sky, wishing you were on the ground.

We spent most of the afternoon on a weather hold, the most dangerous time at any drop zone. When the boredom sets in, out come the rainy day toys, bicycles, skateboards and all forms of dangerous items. Many a sprained wrist or a twisted ankle comes from weather holds. In fact for many, jumping out of an airplane is the safest part of their day; the drive to the drop zone being perhaps the most dangerous.

It was late in the afternoon when load five was called and the sky seemed to be clearing. Patches of blue, a mile or two up wind of the airport gave us hope. We took off and our pilot had to weave in between the massive cumulus clouds on the ride to altitude, and by the time we reached the top, things were not looking good.

A hole was still visible above the runway, but with each passing minute it was filling with cloud. Our pilot informed us over the plane's intercom that it was a go, but we would have to exit quickly after one another, in order to keep within the hole. I checked my gear, practiced once again my cut away procedures and was ready.

The red light came on - open the door and have a look. In front was a clear patch of sky, but at the end of the clearing, a large black cloud awaited.

The green light - exit, exit, exit. The first group left and the second group gathered in the door, taking their time like a bunch of old women at a tea party; all the while the dark cloud ahead loomed ever closer. When they had left, we were only a few hundred yards from the end of the road.

Decision time, to jump or not to jump? Actually it was not a hard decision. We were at full altitude, right on the edge of the cloud. Either jump, or ride the plane to the ground. Three of us gathered quickly at the door and as we started the exit count, so the first pieces of hail began bouncing in through the opening.

"Ready, set, go." We were committed.

Normally the first few seconds of a skydive are close to heavenly, a feeling of being set free - free to fly. That time however, every exposed part of flesh felt as though it was being ripped to shreds, as the hailstones tore at our soft skin. I put my hands over my face to try to give myself some protection, but it didn't help much.

At ten thousand feet, the hail turned to rain and the pain changed too. Instead of the impact of a solid piece of ice, we were then hitting the top of the raindrop, the sharp pointed end, at about one hundred and sixty miles per hour and it felt as though I was falling into a bed of needles. Looking over at my companions, I could see that they too were suffering.

Enough, I thought as I rolled over from a head down position to a stand. I hoped that the soles of my shoes would take the brunt of the rain. The others decided that

that looked like a good idea and they too rolled over into a stand.

At times the cloud was thick and visibility limited to only a few feet, so we kept close in order not to lose sight of one another. That was much better, I could feel the drops of rain striking my soles in a continuous barrage and it took most of the pain away from my face. I smiled to myself at the idea of *Dancing on Raindrops* and began to fool around, as though I was dancing and my friends did the same. A sky time boogie at six thousand feet.

Four seconds later we fell through five thousand feet and it was time to break up the party. We nodded and waved to one another, making sure everyone knew it was time to separate. I rolled over onto my back and began to track away from the others. Then, only my hands could feel the piercing raindrops, but that was only for a few seconds and it was time to pull. I rolled over onto my belly, reached back for my pilot chute and threw it out to my side.

Less than a second later my canopy started to inflate above me and as I slowed, I could see the raindrops slowing too. There was a moment in time when I was falling at the same speed as the rain and it looked as though we were suspended motionless in the sky together.

My canopy inflated and the rain started to come from above, as my descent slowed. That was normal rain, the rounded bottom part of the raindrop, soft and gentle, floating slowly to earth. I removed my goggles hoping for better vision, but there was too much water in the sky, so I was forced to put them back on and peer through the opaque plastic.

The cloud base was at two thousand feet, so as I flew through it, the airport became visible below. I could feel the winds buffeting my canopy, as I looked down at the wind direction indicator on the ground and began to plan my landing. I was perfectly positioned, up wind of the landing area and I estimated the wind to be about thirty knots, as the flags shook furiously and the windsock remained horizontal.

I was flying into the wind and still going backwards at an alarming rate. At one thousand feet I turned down wind and approached the landing area and the ground literally flew past, as my speed was combined with the speed of the wind. At five hundred feet I was directly over my landing spot and I turned my canopy into a vertical dive.

The ground rushed up to meet me and at the last instant I flared and brought the canopy back to horizontal flight, moments before I touched the ground. My feet touched and as they did so, the canopy wanted to be blown away with the wind, taking me with it. I pulled down hard on one steering line and instantly it turned up side down and flew into the ground behind me, removing the force of the wind from the parachute.

My hands were sore from the impact of the ice and rain, but upon my face and those of my friends, were huge smiles - as we thought of the dance we had done in the sky.

Dancing on Raindrops was no longer only a state of mind - the ability to dance upon adversity, - to take control of your thoughts and thus your emotions, and even though it might be 'raining' in your life, to rise above it in your mind and dance with a smile on your face. Now it also had a physical meaning.

A NEW DIMENSION

With over fifteen hundred skydives behind me, I was beginning to think about B.A.S.E. The acronym is for Building, Antennae, Span and Earth - each of the four objects used to launch from. BASE jumping is very different from skydiving. With a skydive you launch from an aircraft at a great altitude and open your parachute at around three to five thousand feet, almost a mile above the surface of the earth.

Although it may not seem like it to the first time jumper, altitude is one of the contributing factors that makes skydiving so safe. Should you have a problem with your first parachute, you still have plenty of time to cut it away and deploy a reserve. Most countries in the world mandate that one has to have two parachutes in order to jump from an airplane. Another added safety factor.

BASE on the other hand, is limited to the height of the structure you have chosen and most often its participants carry only one parachute. A BASE jump from only three hundred feet means that seconds, or more like milliseconds, can make the difference between life and splat. In addition, having only one parachute requires that it has to open perfectly every time and you know about Murphy's Law. Today's equipment however is excellent and rarely is there a problem with the gear. Any error is most likely to be caused by the user.

I had hoped that by pursuing skydiving, I would overcome my fear of heights, but I was wrong. It did however enable me to conquer my fears of jumping out of an airplane and falling through the sky. Now I looked forward to every skydive with the anticipation of being able to fly once more.

I stepped off the plane in Stavanger, southern Norway and caught the bus into town. Clean and green, that was my first impression. I checked into a small bed and breakfast close to the water and headed into town to take in the sights. The air was cold to me, but many people were walking about in only a light shirt, enjoying the last rays of the summer sun.

The town was buzzing with tourists and those from warmer climes, like me, were dressed to the hilt to ward off the chilly wind. The harbor was a hive of activity as ships and ferries came and went, but as soon as the sun dipped below the horizon, the chill became too much, so I headed for a restaurant to try the local fare.

Early the following morning, I boarded the ferry bound for a small village at the end of a fjord, Lysebotyn - BASE heaven. It was a five hour journey and the further up the fjord we headed, so the cliffs became higher and steeper. The water was clear but dark and as we neared our destination, the boat stopped and all eyes glued upon the mammoth, vertical cliff above, where jumpers were waiting to provide a show for the passengers.

Three thousand feet above, I could clearly see people exiting from the edge of the cliff. My heart raced as they fell, small dots, oh so close to the cliff. Then the parachutes opened and my fellow passengers let out a communal sigh of relief and tossed their comments about.

"Crazy; mad; not me; never." That seemed to be the general opinion. For me, I simply stood and watched, fascinated by the sheer size and beauty of the cliffs and tried to imagine myself doing the same thing. That made my heart beat even faster. It was strange how even the thought of a BASE jump would increase my heart rate.

Sometimes lying in bed at night I would think about jumping and that was it, up went the heartbeat and sleep would not come until I had removed the images from my mind. I guessed that was the price I was paying for having such a fear of heights.

Dancing on Raindrops

Walking off the ferry at the end of the fjord, I made my way to the small campsite where the air was full of excitement. I checked in at the office and was informed that first time jumpers needed to go through a course before jumping, and that was fine by me. I needed all the instruction I could get, so I pitched my tent and set off to find my instructor.

There were perhaps two dozen jumpers in the camp and some were packing parachutes on the grass, while others relaxed in the afternoon sun. I bumped into a few people I had met in different drop zones around the world, and it was good to unexpectedly meet old friends once again.

Yuka, a young man from Sweden, was to be my instructor. He had done several hundred BASE jumps and came here every year to jump these cliffs and enjoy the long summer days. We went through exit procedures, emergency procedures and landing procedures. I practiced the exit over and over, trying to get the exact sequence firmly embedded into my mind and body. The key was not to go head down, so by picking a visual point above the horizon and focusing on it at the moment of exit, that would help keep my body in a horizontal position as I picked up speed after launch.

Eight seconds was the magic number. If for some reason you were unstable and close to the cliff, you had eight seconds to impact. However, by tracking away from the cliff, your time was increased to over fifteen seconds. The more you tracked (horizontal distance covered), the longer you could stay in freefall, as the further down the talus you flew.

Next we repacked my parachute and although I had packed thousands of skydive rigs, it was different. Neatness and exactness were key. Every fold and twist had to be perfect and as soon as I got the hang of things, I was ready to go.

It's not hard to imagine that sleep did not come easily that night. It was impossible to get the image of launching off a cliff out of my mind. Over and over it would repeat itself, and each time my heart would start to race and I would try to replace it with another thought. I think exhaustion was the cause of sleep, as I certainly did not have much joy with removing the vivid images.

At nine o'clock the next morning, I boarded the minibus that would take us part of the way up the mountain. A fifteen minute drive and from there on it was by foot. A two hour hike. First came wake up hill, then warm up hill and finally hell hill. Aptly named, but I was awake minutes after rising, I was warmed up before I even got into the van and so by the time I had made it to the top, my legs were weak and my shirt wet from sweat.

From here on it was a gentle walk for about an hour. It was a barren and desolate landscape with not a tree in sight, but walking at the edge of the fjord gave spectacular views of the water below. In some parts the water was apparently as deep as the cliffs were high. Patches of snow

Dancing on Raindrops

remained on the mountaintop and one small stream that had to be crossed, was still covered in a layer of solid ice.

Soon we made it to the exit point and began to ready ourselves. Everything that was carried up had to be taken back down on the jump, so I stuffed my excess gear like water bottle and rig bag into my jumpsuit and zipped it up. I checked my rig, making sure that the two pins that held the container closed were properly inserted and that the pilot chute handle was easily accessible. I put it on my back, tightened the leg and chest straps and I could feel the adrenaline start to rise.

My turn - so I put on my goggles and helmet, turned on the video camera that was mounted on the side of my helmet and stepped towards the edge, as I tried to stop my body from shaking.

Scared? You bet I was - in fact close to terrified. My hands were sweating and it was hard to concentrate on anything but the fear. Slowly and cautiously, I moved to the edge. I could feel the blood pumping in my head and it was all I could do to stay focused. I glanced below and could see the vertical face of rock; it seemed so huge.

Far in the distance, out on the fjord, the rescue boat waited in the morning sunlight. My toes were right at the edge and the feeling of vertigo was strong, so I picked a visual spot above the horizon and took a deep breath.

Boom, boom, boom, I am sure the noise of my heartbeat could be heard on the other side of the valley.

"Stop it!" I shouted out to myself. "Stop the fear!"

Taking a deep breath, I began to concentrate on the positives and to convince myself that I was going to be okay. It was time. That was my moment. That was the culmination of hours and hours of lost sleep, and heaps and heaps of fear.

"Ready," I said as I focused on a point in the sky above the horizon and began my practiced routine.

"Set," my heart went into overdrive. The fear level reached a peak. I could still back out, but I knew that I would not.

"Go" and I leaned forward, beyond the point of no return and leapt as hard as my weak legs would allow.

The moment of nothing; suspended in space and time, an instant where the world stood still in silence. Babies were born, people died and the world went on the same. But not for me - I was alive, so alive I'm sure my heart had stopped beating!

The moment was simply that, a moment and then I was in the arms of gravity and the fear monster had gone. Just like that, in the instant after I launched, there was no more fear.

I kept my eyes fixed on my point in the sky and pushed my hips forward in an arch, as far as I could to help my stability. My legs were wide apart and bent at the knee, my arms at right angles to the side of my chest and bent forward at the elbows, with my hands about a foot away from my ears.

I looked down and the cliff face, oh so close, rose up towards me and disappeared behind. I could feel the acceleration and as the seconds ticked by, so the wind increased and its noise became louder and louder. I was counting to myself –

One thousand, two thousand, three thousand. Three long seconds and at last I was in a familiar situation, as the wind was strong enough to steer by. So I brought my legs together, hands to my sides and started to track - to fly my body forward through the sky. That was the easy part, for it felt natural for me to track across the sky, as I had done on hundreds of skydives. As I picked up vertical speed, so the faster my track became and the louder the wind began to roar in my ears.

Six thousand, seven thousand, eight thousand and by then I was well away from the face and heading towards the water. The ground seemed to remain the same distance away, only moving underneath me, as I concentrated my

efforts on powering myself forward. The bushes and trees near the water's edge were no longer tiny dots in the distance, now they had form and shape.

Ten thousand, eleven thousand, twelve thousand and I reached terminal velocity of about one hundred and twenty miles per hour. I was most of the way down the talus and the ground seemed to be moving up towards me at an incredible speed. The rocks and bushes below were visible in great detail.

Pull, pull, pull. As my right hand moved back to grab my pilot chute at the base of my container, so my left hand came in front of me to keep my balance. I clasped the pud securely and threw it out into the rushing wind.

Come on baby, come on, I thought as I went back into a stable arch and waited. That was it, I had done all I could and time again slowed, as I waited for my pilot chute to inflate and pull my main canopy out of the container.

The ground was rushing towards me, when all of a sudden it opened.

Whack, and there I was floating above the water, alive. I unstowed my steering toggles and headed for the small patch of green grass at the edge of the water.

My BASE parachute was twice the size of the one I used for skydiving and I seemed to float in the air, hardly moving forward. It was like driving a bus as opposed to a Ferrari, but right then accuracy was more important than speed. Out over the edge of the water I turned, headed into the wind and tried to judge my approach height.

Too low and the cold waters of the fjord were waiting to welcome me. Too high and I would fly right over the small landing area, into the fjord's wet and chilly arms. Spot on, that's the way it was as I went into full brakes and lightly touched down in the center of the small, grassy area.

"Oh yea, oh yea, oh yea," I shouted, as the endorphins rushed through my body, creating a high quite unlike anything else I had ever experienced. What a rush, I had done it. Perhaps my greatest fear - that of heights - had lost that round and I had won. I turned and looked back up the cliff as a group of three exited, they looked like tiny dots against a sea of granite. I could see them pick up speed and then start to gain some forward motion. Down and down they came, slowly growing larger and then in the moments before impact, canopies opened and a shout of pure joy echoed down the valley.

*Fear is the greatest thief of all,
for it robs you of your dreams.*

Dancing on Raindrops

A FOR ANTENNAE -
T FOR TERROR

The aeronautical chart listed its height at four hundred and twenty feet. In the acronym of BASE, that would be an A, for Antennae.

It was mid-afternoon, when we decided to make a jump early the following morning. Hanne and I had done several skydives that morning and being my mentor, she decided that we should take a few hours off and practice the exit for the next day's jump. We used an old metal gate to simulate the railings around the top of the antennae. I climbed over the gate and put my heals on the middle rung. Balancing there and leaning slightly backwards to keep my calves pressed against the top railing, I went through the routine in my mind.

Focus on a point above the horizon, count and go, launching up towards a point in the sky and throwing my pilot chute soon after leaving. I was careful jumping off that gate, trying to make sure I did not fall on landing and hurt myself.

Time and time again I practiced with my rig on my back and soon the balance required to climb over the railing was coming naturally. The whole sequence of events was imbedding itself into my mind. As I leapt onto the ground, I simulated the canopy opening, releasing the toggles and landing. I was almost ready and I was excited.

It had been several months since my last BASE jump, so I took the rig into a hangar and repacked it with meticulous care. I removed the slider, a cloth device that slows the opening of the canopy. Now when it deployed, it should inflate immediately and sooner was better than later. I was happy with the finished result and confident that it would open correctly. I'm sure there are few things worse than having second thoughts about your pack job, the moment you are about to launch. Ouch.

Yes, of course it was hard to get to sleep that night. The monster I had left behind on the huge cliffs in Norway had returned. I drifted off and woke holding the alarm clock. Two minutes until four it said, two minutes to wake up time. Well, I was wide awake; a quick call of Nature, a brushing of teeth and I was ready to go.

Hanne and the rest of the crew, drivers, photographers and watchers were all ready, so the entourage set off in search of coffee. By the time we arrived at the end of the road that led to the tower, the night was still pitch dark and the sky was covered in a light fog. Everyone was excited and high fives abounded as Hanne, Mr. T, our photographer who would be taking photographs and video from below, and myself, left the van and started the short walk to the base of the tower. The van was then driven around to the other side of the tower, to get a different angle from which to photograph the jump.

The air was still and the fog gave reason for concern. We would not be able to jump if we could not see where we were going. It was only a five minute walk to the base of the tower and we were in no hurry. For most of it we walked in silence, each preoccupied and content with their thoughts. What looked like a lighter section of sky began to appear in the east - the dawn was coming.

There was no wind on the ground, but that is not where we needed it. As the canopy deploys, it is safest to have a steady breeze blowing directly between the wires and in the direction of your exit. That is to say jumping with the wind to your back and heading between the guide wires that hold up the antennae, one to the left and one to the right. With no way to figure what the wind was doing higher up, we decided to take a climb and find out. We handed our rigs over the fence and once inside the enclosure, donned our equipment and headed for the base of the antennae.

Dancing on Raindrops

The steps were in the middle of the tower, a small circular latticework of steel surrounded us and as I looked up, it seemed to carry on forever. They were about a foot apart, so that meant four hundred and twenty steps, or more than a forty-story building!

The climbing space around me was very small and meant that I had to keep myself close to the steps, pulling my body in with my arms. Halfway up we stopped and reassessed the situation. A light breeze had begun and it was blowing in the right direction. The fog was starting to thin and the eastern horizon was the brightest part of the sky. After a much needed break, we continued up. My forearms were taking strain, as Hanne climbed on ahead of me, my pace slowing the higher we went. I took my mind off how far I still had to climb and began a mechanical approach, putting one hand up, then one step, one hand and one step. It still seemed to go on forever.

The last step was a beautiful sight and I rolled onto the platform, tired and sore. In a few minutes, they would be fine, but my arms needed rest. The layer of fog stopped half way up and all we could see from the top, was the earth as a blanket of white. Far in the distance, a smokestack rose up through the cotton wool surface and more smoke floated down from its chimneys. It looked as though it was making the stuff. Fortunately the tower was not in service, so that meant we would not be bombarded by the powerful radio waves.

As the sun pushed its orange glow over the horizon, we were ready to go. Final gear checks complete and the blood returned to my arms, it was time. The gentle breeze was blowing directly between the wires and the fog had started to break up, as soon as the sun's rays touched upon its fragile surface. I took a deep breath and as I did so my heart began to beat faster. Now was the moment - the moment of now.

The hand railing around the tower was much the same as the fence I had practiced on the previous day, but still my movements were slow and deliberate. I stepped up to the railing and took the top rung firmly in both hands, trying to still my mind and concentrate on the precarious climb to the other side. I stepped over the top pipe and put my heels on the middle ring from the outside, and leaning back more than I'm sure was necessary, I turned to look out at the view in front and below.

Standing on the outer edge of the platform, with nothing but air in front of me, the fear monster screamed. For someone who was afraid of heights, that was a scary experience and I felt dizzy. In some ways the ground was so far below, but on the other hand, it was so close. I crouched and held on to the top rung behind me, as I steadied my body and my mind.

My pilot chute was ready in my hand, as I cautiously stood upright and looked towards my spot in the sky, high above the horizon. Having to force strength into my legs to stop them from buckling, I knew it was now or never. Taking a slow, deep breath, I filled my lungs and held it for a second, then slowly exhaled and at the same time I started counting to myself.

"One…two…three." My world went quiet and somewhere far in the distance, a dog barked.

"See ya," I said as I slowly leaned forward and crouched over, my hands arcing back behind me. I went beyond the point of no return and continued over a little more, just enough to lower my angle of launch to get me as far out as possible. I threw my hands in front of me and used my legs to launch as far away from the edge of the tower as I possibly could; my eyes still fixed on my point in the sky.

For a moment once again, there was nothing. The world stood still and not an atom moved, but in the next, as I felt

gravity take a hold of me, I threw my large pilot chute out to my side as far as I could, then waited.

Out of the corner of my eye, I could see the metal cross structure of the antennae, rushing by in a blur of speed. My exit was good and my body was slightly head-high, pointing directly at the gap in the wires in front and below. The lower set of stabilizing wires rushed up on either side and behind my back, the open nose of my canopy caught the wind and in a moment it was fully inflated above me. The corresponding jerk was sharp and sudden, but there was no doubt that my descent had been slowed. Now was the time for fast reactions.

Depending on which direction my canopy opened, that was the instant to adjust course if I were heading into the wires, or the antennae itself. I reached up and took the toggles in my hands, as soon as the excess gravity from the opening shock had subsided. My large red, yellow and green canopy was open and flying in the right direction, so I made a sharp bank to the right, trying to turn myself into the wind before landing. The canopy ride was only a few seconds, so as soon as the turn was complete, I flared and touched down softly on the long grass, my world beginning to fill with elation.

I looked up as Hanne launched a perfect exit. She threw her pilot chute and as it filled with air, it stopped and pulled the main canopy out of the bag below it. A bright bolt of cloth tore from her back and as the suspension lines pulled taut, the cloth caught the wind and inflated. Again, a sharp turn and she too landed softly and safely.

A kind of euphoria had set into my head, as I looked up at the tower. My body was filled with adrenaline, but my mind was crystal clear. The weakness in my legs had long gone.

Dancing on Raindrops

6. SECRETS TO YOUR SUCCESS

FAITH and FEAR

FAITH

 **T**o a large extent your thoughts create and influence your faith, but it is through the use of your faith that you are able to keep your thoughts focused on your dreams. No matter how great an obstacle may appear in the distance, as you get closer it will change its appearance. If you approach with the right mindset and a clear vision, you will find a way; be it over, under, around or through.

From the moment you believe, your faith will become stronger and it is this power that will enable you to focus your thoughts, and become undistracted by the deluge of negative influences. It is doubt and fear that can deny your faith its power - and to deny your faith is to lose it.

- When I get on an airplane with a rig on my back, I have faith that my parachute will open correctly; but more importantly, I have faith in myself that if it doesn't, I will be able to deal with the problem, or cut away and open my reserve.

- Leaving on my first ocean passage took a huge amount of faith in myself. There were moments during that first storm when I held on for dear life, not knowing what to do. I was cold and wet, vomiting over the side and I certainly had fleeting doubts about my ability to cope with the situation, but it was still faith in myself that allowed me to leave.

• To accumulate the faith necessary for my first BASE jump, I did almost two thousand skydives. Yes, BASE still stirred extreme emotions, but I had acquired some of the necessary skills and that definitely added to my confidence. However, standing on the edge of the cliff, with my heart thumping and my body filled with adrenaline, it was still faith in myself that enabled me to jump.

• Writing this book took a gigantic leap of faith. Through the long hours and sleepless nights, it was with faith that I continued, for I knew that you would enjoy reading these adventures - and I eternally hope that you will apply these principles to your life.

"Such is your faith - you will get."

Dancing on Raindrops

FEAR

Fear is nothing but a thought. It is only a result of experiences and perceptions and because of this, any fear can be overcome. Removing the fear thought is actually not removing it at all, but simply removing its influence and replacing it with a more powerful thought.

Overcoming fear has four steps:

1. Identify the fear. Be sure that this fear warrants your attention and that its removal will make a positive difference to you. When overcome, will it leave you feeling stronger and good about yourself?

2. Make a decision. With this decision has to come a commitment, because the path ahead may change its direction at any moment. Are you willing to put in the effort required to at least try and control your thoughts?

3. Do it! Depending on your attitude, this is the part where many people fail. Often it is due to a lack of belief in yourself, or a failure to clearly visualize the end result. Fear can often prevent you from seeing benefits or any positive consequences, but if you can honestly see the benefits that overcoming a fear would give you, then don't give up. Don't become a quitter – you know what happens to them! Take small steps. NO, take tiny steps! Become successful with each step and this string of success will help you maintain a positive attitude. Lack of knowledge is so often the core of fear, so be sure to educate yourself in the fear you wish to overcome, and place yourself in the company of those who do the

things that you are afraid of. The added knowledge will increase your power.

4. <u>Repeat</u>. Yes, anything you do often enough will soon become quite normal. Just as the repetition of affirmations focuses your thoughts and clarifies your vision, repeated action is essential to your success. This is sometimes hard, because your fears are still your most dominant thoughts, but with repetition, a new thinking takes hold and the more it is repeated, the stronger it becomes.

I know first hand what it is like to be down and out, lacking for friends, food and shelter. It is hard to imagine anything but fearful thoughts, let alone to believe that you are in control. However with belief and practice, there are few things that you cannot accomplish, as long as your faith is greater than your fear.

Jabula spent a season in Venezuela and it was there that I found myself in one of the scariest of situations I have ever been in. Once again fortunately I found the faith to stay still and the will to control my fear.

BE AWARE OF THE POWER OF YOUR FAITH.

* For more information visit:
www.dancingonraindrops.com

GET IN THE TRUCK!

Puerto la Cruz was a friendly town, on the northern coast of Venezuela. We were there for the winter, living and working on a large yacht, moored at one of the fine marinas on the edge of town.

Jabula, was a one hundred and twelve foot sailing yacht. (Two different boats shared the same name – the first was ninety-eight feet.) Magnificent in every aspect, she carried a permanent crew of seven, and we normally spent summer in the south of France and winter in the northern Caribbean. That year however, we found ourselves a little farther south than usual.

Crime being what it was in the area, we were all given an identity card by the marina. That would give us access to the facilities and allow us in and out of the front gate, where a guard was on permanent watch. The bolivar was typical of any South American currency at the time. Very weak against the dollar, thus making it an inexpensive country, as long as you had dollars in your pocket. During the day, the seven of us worked on the yacht, cleaning and maintaining her, but at night it was party time. Bars, restaurants and nightclubs, we tried them all.

One such night, my friend Kurt and I were in party mode and had been out for dinner, then after a couple of bars, had found ourselves in a nightclub. Beautiful women were in abundance and drinks were cheap. Dancing to the local music, a sensual affair that only the Latin people seemed able to master. The time flew and soon it was three in the morning, we had both had enough and decided to return to the boat.

The night air was warm and humid, as we started to walk towards the beach about six blocks away and from there we would get a taxi to the marina.

A bit of a walk would do us good, I thought as we left the brightly lit main road and strolled into a much quieter part of town. The streetlights were no more and the buildings and alleys were dark. The distant rumblings of the city filled the night as we walked onward. Up ahead, four girls were waiting at a bus stop and we stopped to chat.

The Venezuelan people were so friendly, that our smattering of Spanish did not matter and soon we were laughing and talking together. Amazing how communication is still possible without any knowledge of the other person's language, a bit of mime and laughter, and the conversation was well on its way.

Without warning, two of the girls jumped up and ran off down the street, disappearing into the night. The two remaining girls seemed very worried about something, as they spoke in short terse sentences to one another. At that moment, a military truck appeared at the intersection and sped over towards us, its headlights cutting through the night as we stood in the beams like dazed rabbits. The truck stopped in front of us and six armed soldiers jumped out of the back and surrounded us with weapons pointed.

The passenger side door opened with a squeak, as the officer in charge climbed out and walked over to us. He was speaking very fast to the girls and Kurt and I could only understand a little of what he was saying, but there was a lot of energy in the air. The officer shouted questions, as the frightened girls replied and handed over their ID cards. The man looked at them and then looked at us.

"Show me your identity cards," he said in Spanish, as he motioned with his hands.

Kurt reached into the back pocket of his pants and retrieved his card from the boat yard. I simply stood there, for I had forgotten mine. These cards were all we used for identification, as it had our photograph on the front and carrying a passport was too risky late at night. The staff at

Dancing on Raindrops

the boatyard knew us by then, so the pass was no longer essential for getting into the marina, but I had neglected to bring any identification with me what so ever.

Taking Kurt's card, he looked at me and repeated his order. All the while the soldiers kept their attention on us, as if we were about to make an escape. I double-checked each of my pockets.

"No I don't have it on me, it's on the boat." I said in English and then tried to convey in my best Spanish, that we were off a boat in the marina and I had left my ID behind.

With his reply, I knew that it was to be considered a very serious offence, so I tried once again to explain that we were off a boat, a boat that was in the marina. He was not happy.

"Get in the truck," he said to me. That was not what I had envisaged our night out to become, and the notion of spending time in a Venezuelan jail was all too much at the forefront of my mind.

This is not going to happen, I thought to myself. *There is no way I am getting on that truck.* I looked into the dark chasm, under the tarpaulin of the five-ton truck. *No.*

"Listen, if you have to get in the truck, I'll come with you," Kurt said. A true friend, but my mind was made up.

Six soldiers could easily have picked me up and thrown me into the truck and I half expected 'the man' to give that order, because by that stage he was ranting and raving, so I sat down on the bus stop seat and shook my head.

"No way," I said looking him square in the eyes, trying to read his next move and willing him to let it be.

Get back in your truck and go away, I repeated silently to myself and before I knew what was happening, he pulled his handgun from his holster and cocked the automatic weapon. The cold metallic sound sent a shiver up my spine, and then the officer took one step towards me and put the barrel against my head. I froze. This had gone too far, too fast.

"Get in the truck," he shouted once again. The steel was cold on my temple, as my world became still.

Would he really blow my brains out, right there on the sidewalk? Surely the intelligent thing to do would be to get in the truck, but I had made up my mind and was not willing to do that. The skin on the back of my skull tightened and it felt as though my hair was standing on end. The adrenaline began to rise and I could feel a tightening in my chest, an involuntary shake beginning in my hands.

Don't let your adrenaline show, I thought. I had learned that in Africa. Multitudes of thoughts were rushing through my mind, one then the next, so fast I was not able to contemplate even a single one. That had to stop, so I began to focus my mind on positive things.

He will go away, I will be fine.

How long we stayed like that, I have no recollection, but I remembered seeing the look on Kurt's face and thought that it was one of shock and horror. Out of the corner of my eye, I could see the officer's face. He looked deadly serious. I noticed that the guards had not moved and they still had their rifles pointed in our direction. I could not see the girls because they were behind me, but everyone was silent.

Yes, you are going to go away. Yes, you are going to get in your truck and drive off, I kept repeating in my mind.

Something in the air changed and I noticed it immediately. Tensions eased off their peaks and as I looked at the man who had a gun to my head, his energy began to lose its snarl. Without a word, I felt the pressure of the barrel ease and a smile came over his face as he lifted the gun from my head. He turned, shouted an order at his troops and walked away, back to the open door of his truck. He climbed in and closed the door without once looking back. The troops clambered into the darkness and a moment later, the truck roared off down the street, leaving four relieved people in its wake...one especially so.

*If life is whatever you make it,
then you may as well
make it whatever you want.*

PRESENT DAY

The clock on my desk says it is eleven p.m.

Enough for one night, I think to myself. I have six points in the order that I want and all the relevant information to cover them, all that remains is the seventh and final concept. I turn off my computer, pick up the empty plate and glass and then switch off the light as I leave the room.

After a quick shower I head for bed, but before sleeping, I repeat my affirmations aloud to myself and ask for the seventh point to be revealed as I wake in the morning. Minutes later I am fast asleep.

ALONE ON THE MOUNTAIN

The smell of human dung and rotting garbage filled the air, as I stood outside the Puerto la Cruz bus station having purchased my ticket to Merida, a small town in the Andes Mountains. Jabula was not going anywhere for a few weeks, so I decided it was time to see some mountains.

With a life on the ocean, one gets to see plenty of water, but not much in the way of real mountains. So there I stood, rucksack beside me, waiting for the bus.

The afternoon was hot and humid and I was looking forward to the air conditioning that the bus would provide; the lack of putrid smells would also not be missed. Soon enough the bus arrived and I put my rucksack into the storage compartment underneath and made my way to my seat.

That was one of the first class busses with air conditioning and not a chicken in sight. Into the evening sunset we drove and as soon as it was dark, the bus assistant came around and closed all the curtains, so the inside of the bus was plunged into total darkness.

It did not take me long to find a light switch for the reading lamp above my head. I flicked the switch and no sooner had I done so, the conductor started yelling at me in Spanish. My fellow passenger, who spoke a little English, informed me that lights were not allowed.

"Banditos," he said. To lessen the risk of hijacking, the bus was kept in complete darkness and for some reason the air-conditioning was set to maximum. Why, I never did find out, but I was informed that to stop was impossible. I had only brought a light sweater with me on the bus and my warm gear was still in my rucksack. So I froze, as I watched the other passengers cover themselves in blankets and thick jackets.

Around two in the morning we stopped for fuel and a chance to stretch our legs. I of course made a beeline for the storage compartments and retrieved my warm jacket, thick socks and a sleeping bag. The rest of the night was going to be warm; I was making sure of that. The rest of the night was indeed warm and uneventful - we saw no banditos.

The bus began to make a grinding sound around lunchtime on the next day and when the driver saw another bus pulled onto the side of the road, we screeched to a halt in front of it. No sooner had we stopped, people jumped out of their seats, grabbed their belongings and made a frantic rush for the door. I was trapped in my seat and so I decided to wait for the madness to end. A line of people had formed at the door of the other bus, a 'second class' bus, with chickens and goats in cages on the roof. It seemed as though our ride was to go no further and that would be our transport from here on. We all squeezed in, people and their luggage filling every available space.

Later in the afternoon, this bus too gave out and after a three hour wait another arrived to collect us. That one gave us the shortest ride of all and not two hours later, we were once again on the side of the road, waiting for bus number four.

It was before the dawn when we made it to Merida, my destination high in the Andes Mountains. Merida is renowned for having the world's longest and highest cable car. As I walked from the bus station, my sleepy legs were strengthened by the dawn. Mountains began to take shape, huge mountains and they surrounded me. Clouds covered their peaks thousands of feet above and below, the valley was still drenched in darkness. I sat on my rucksack, leaned against a stonewall on the edge of the village and enjoyed the air at five thousand feet. The light slowly streaked across the sky and ate up the shadows, then, as the town began to wake, it was time for some coffee.

By noon I had found a place to stay, a small pension in the old part of town and I spent the next three days getting maps and provisions; acclimatizing to the thin air and wondering what it would be like up on the mountain. The basic route I had elected to follow, put me well above fourteen thousand feet in many places, so I tried to keep as little weight in my rucksack as possible.

A sure way to turn forty pounds into eighty is to carry it on your back at fourteen thousand feet!

Dozens of times I must have packed and repacked, trying to keep the weight down. Tent, sleeping bag and warm clothing took up most of the space, but food accounted for most of the weight. I was not able to buy dehydrated foods and since I had not brought any with me, I was forced to shop in the supermarket. Fortunately they had some sort of protein bars and I thought they would be a good source of energy for not much weight, so I stocked up on them. Canned food and dried fruits, water, flashlight, thermal blanket, maps, GPS and all the other little things that are essential on the mountain.

One afternoon, I was in a small coffee shop and noticed that the young lady behind the counter was using an abacus to add up a customer's order. She would quickly move a couple of beads and have the answer at a glance. I was fascinated. We wrote a list of ten numbers, some with six digits and decimals in varying places. The idea was to see which was faster, a modern calculator, or the ancient abacus? Ready, set, go and my fingers started to fly on the keyboard. Concentrating furiously, I could hear the clicking sounds of the abacus, as she flicked the beads from one side to the other. As I started the third line of numbers, the clicking stopped.

"Finished," she said quietly. She then wrote the total on a piece of paper, as I continued to plod on through the rest of the calculations. The answers were the same.

I was ready to go. My body felt strong, as the excitement of a new adventure ran through my veins. I headed out to the cable car early one morning and ordered myself a ticket to the top, but I was informed that the top station was out of order. They were only operating as high as the third station, Loma Redonda, a height of thirteen thousand feet. The cable car has four stations on its almost eight mile journey to Pico Espejo, the top station at fifteen and a half thousand feet. That meant that I would have to climb the difference, for I wanted to see the statue at the top. The Virgin of the snow. (Virgen de las Nieves.)

The first part of the ride took me over the valley, with its lush vegetation and a river coursing through it, over to the foot of the mountain on the other side. As we went up, the vegetation became sparse, the ground barren and by the time we reached our destination, the mountain was bare except for a few hardy bushes surviving in the thin air. Up above, the rest of the cable was visible only a short way and then it ran into the clouds, thick and dense clouds.

For a while I sat on the edge of the path, soaking up the feeling of being there and enjoyed the magnificent view. Across the valley and far in the distance, I could see the other mountain, its peak also enshrouded with cloud. Before my body had a chance to cool, I stretched and picked up my rucksack, attached it securely around my waist and started walking. Up, it was always up.

Frequently I would stop to get back my breath that the high altitude had taken away and to keep track of my course, or remove a layer of clothing as my body temperature increased. I would plot my position on the chart from the GPS reading (Global Positioning System) and take a little time to enjoy the beauty of my vista. It took me several hours to climb the two thousand feet to the ridge and as I climbed, so the cloud layer rose with me.

The going was tough and the rocky path never reduced its steep angle, but at least the sky was clearing and by the time I made it to the top, I could see Pico Bolivar, Venezuela's highest peak at over sixteen thousand feet. The clouds had gone and there too was the statue covered in snow.

I crossed the ridge and started down the other side. The afternoon sun was sinking in the sky and in the shadow of the mountain the air began to chill quickly. I knew that within the next few hours I had to find a place to camp. All around me the slope was too steep, so I kept on walking. As I went further down into the valley, I came across a stream and off to one side was a patch of flat green grass, about twice the size of my tent. There was my first camp at eleven thousand feet.

I pitched my tent and then sat by the stream, my hot and tired feet cooling instantly in the frigid mountain water. For dinner, I heated a small can of beans and a can of tasteless meat like substance, the two heaviest items in my food supply. The 'heat sticks' I had purchased in Merida were dry and old, so the impregnated cardboard did not burn too well, but it was better than nothing and the warm food helped offset the coming night chill.

The air was still and the mountain silent, as the evening shadows raced across the valley and up the other side, all the while the sky growing slowly darker, until Orion's Belt was clearly visible above. Stars were everywhere. Some, I had seen for years out at sea as a faint glimmer of light, but that night they were bright in the sky and the high altitude made the heavens seem so close. Far in the distance and way up the valley, the lights of a small village shone dimly. That would be my next stop.

I slept like a dead man on that first night and woke as the sun touched the peaks of the mountain above me. My body was stiff and sore, not used to the exertion and altitude, as I bent over the river and scooped a little water onto my face. The air was cold and as I broke camp, I heated a cup of water for tea and used that to wash down a couple of energy bars. I stretched, soaking up the morning sun, easing my body back into another day and another mile. My mind however needed no easing anywhere, the views were magnificent and the air clean and fresh. It felt good to be out amongst the mountains.

Around noon, I had lost a lot of altitude and was making my way along the contour of the hill. Thick bushes were on the high side of the small path that I followed and on the lower side, was nothing but a view of the valley below. The temperature had risen throughout the morning and I was walking in only a light shirt, stopping frequently for small sips of water.

The sound of breaking branches tore through the silence. Up above me and in amongst the bush, something large was moving quickly through the undergrowth. With every second it sounded closer and louder. The beast was in a hurry and was moving directly towards me. I looked for an escape route. There was a cliff edge twenty yards away down the sloping hill and all the trees were too small to climb. Whatever it was charging towards me had caught me exposed on the trail with nowhere to go.

A large black bull tore from the undergrowth in front of me. It was a huge beast, followed by two old men, being dragged along behind with a rope that was tied around the bull's neck. Out onto the trail he ran, then stopped abruptly. The two old men picked themselves up off the ground and then noticed me.

Apparently the bull had been out on the mountain and they were taking him back to the village they told me. They invited me to walk with them and once there, I was to stay in their house. That crazy gringo out on the mountain alone. I accepted and began to walk towards them, when they shouted at the bull and it set off in the direction of the village. The two men, heels digging into the ground, were dragged along faster than I could run and soon they were out of sight around a bend; but I could still hear the occasional sound of breaking branches - anything that was in the path of the bull was flattened.

I continued on at my own pace and by mid-afternoon I made it to the village, a picturesque little hamlet. Positioned on the side of the mountain, its tall church spire pierced the crystal clear sky. As I entered the outskirts, one of the old men who had retrieved the bull from the mountain was

Dancing on Raindrops

there to greet me and he showed me the way to his house. I must stay with him, he insisted.

His house was made of stone, the walls about two feet thick and the ceilings low. Off to one side was a spare room. It had a mattress and a shower, perfect. That however, was all it did have. For two days I stayed there, spending most of my time taking in the sights of the old village, or sitting on the banks of a small river, far down the valley. The church, the most prominent and largest building in town, was deserted every time I walked by. I had to guess that it was used only on Sundays. The streets were either cobbled, or in most cases dirt and all the walls were in need of a coat of paint.

Early each morning I was woken by the smell next door, as the baker's bread began to rise in the oven. By the time I was dressed and ready to go outside, the bread was done, so I bought a loaf, a couple of sugary buns and a pint of milk, then walked to the top of a hill above the town. As the sun started to light the surrounding mountains and the icy-cold air of the morning turned my breath to steamy clouds, I watched the beginning of another day and I ate my breakfast.

I left the village after saying goodbye to my new friends and stocking up with a couple of loaves of bread, then made my way along the edge of the valley, heading for a village on the far side of the mountain that lay ahead. The sun, not yet visible, cast huge shadows on the mountainside.

I walked on, trying all the while to keep as much altitude as I was able. Switching from one trail to another, up, once again it was always up. The walking was easy as the ground cover was sparse, only small shrubs and rocks were in my way. Occasionally I crossed a stream and would stop to rest and fill my water bottle. Each stream had a different taste it seemed, some heavy with the fragrance of moss and some clean and almost tasteless.

It was when I was stopped for lunch that I noticed a pain in my knees, both knees. I had been bending over the stream, washing my face in the cool water, when I felt a sharp pain pass through them. It went away as quickly as it arrived and while I walked about on the bank, my legs felt as strong as ever. I put the experience down to a nerve and thought nothing more of it, as I enjoyed some of my fresh bread and an energy bar for lunch.

Looking at the map, I knew I would not make it to the village that day. My progress had been far slower than I had expected due to the steepness of the hills, so I decided to keep on going and then start to look for a place to camp before sunset. I was in fine spirits and loving being amongst such huge mountains. That was what I had come for, my mind was clear and I took the time to ponder where I was going and where I had been with my life.

It happened at about four o'clock that afternoon. I was at the base of the ridge trying to negotiate a steep rocky section, when I put one foot forward and my leg began to collapse under me. To stop myself from falling over, I moved my other leg to take the weight and keep my balance, but that too gave way and I collapsed in a heap on the narrow ledge.

The pain was excruciating as I pulled my rucksack off my shoulders and tried to straighten my legs in front of me, but I had no control of them. Using my hands, I straightened each leg and leaned back against the rock face, waiting and hoping that the pain would ease off. It did not, and one hour later, after several unsuccessful attempts to stand, each of which saw my legs buckle under me, I began to ponder my fate. There I was, on the face of some unknown mountain, with a pair of legs that seemed as though they were incapable of taking me much further.

About a hundred feet below was a flat ledge, large enough to pitch a tent, so I began to head towards it by sliding myself over the rocks with my hands and arms. Moving forward a little at a time and then reaching back and dragging my rucksack behind. The face was almost steep enough to let my rucksack fall in front of me, but I decided that was not a good idea, in case it fell beyond the flat section and I might be unable to retrieve it. Gone was the crystal clear head of a few hours ago – as my thoughts were clouded in pain. Each movement was an ordeal, so it was late in the afternoon by the time I arrived at my destination on the little flat piece of ground.

Still sitting, I removed the tent from my rucksack and laid it on the ground, then I dragged myself from corner to corner, while trying to put the tent pegs into the rocky surface. Fortunately there was just enough soil to allow the pegs to grip and once it was erected, I sat in the opening and began to think about my situation. The nearest village was still some miles distant and over the other side of the thirteen thousand foot ridge, below which I was stranded.

The pain would not go away. It had increased from my knees up the outsides of my thighs, as well as down into my calves. When sitting still, it was a loud throb, but as soon as I tried to move, it became sharp and intense. As darkness fell, I heated a cup of water for some tea, hoping that would provide at least a little mental therapy. My appetite was non-existent and although I tried to force down a protein bar for dinner, it was too much effort, so I gave up and enjoyed my tea as best I could.

I laid out my sleeping bag, rolled myself into it, zipped it closed and tried to get some sleep; but I slept fitfully and each time I woke I seemed to be thinking about my knees; my knees and my predicament.

The best sleep came in the wee hours of the morning, but even that was not for long. When I woke, I stretched to loosen my body and before even trying to stand I massaged both my knees and thighs. Although they hurt somewhat, most of the pain had subsided and I had high hopes of continuing on my way, even if it was slowly.

I tried to stand and as I put more weight on my legs, the weaker they felt. I managed to get upright by holding on to the tent pole and stood there for a while, not daring to move. Then, still holding on to the pole, I began to stretch each leg and tried to get the blood flowing. Soon I was hobbling around, bent over with my bum in the air, but each step was still painful. I had decided that if possible, I would try to make it to at least the top of the ridge that day. Whatever was wrong with my legs, might not get better by sitting there and may in fact even get worse.

Things were not looking good. My first job was to get the tent down and as I bent over to pick up a peg, so both legs collapsed on me. The pain was awful and I knew right then that I would not be going anywhere that day. It was as much as I could do to drag myself back inside the tent without passing out and for the next few hours I lay there, immobile and watched the sun rise over the eastern peaks.

I had about a gallon of water stowed in and around my rucksack, for I had filled all my containers at the last stream, in preparation for the big climb that lay ahead. It seemed a lot at the time and even more when I had to carry it, but under those circumstances it was only a tiny amount.

For food, I had about a four-day supply. Six protein bars, a small loaf of bread, two packets of dried fruit, a bar of chocolate and a packet of sticky sweet things that had melted in the heat and formed a multi-colored blob in the bottom of the packet.

That whole day I lay there in pain and by the time evening came, either I was becoming acclimatized to it, or my condition was improving. I had decided that I would rest for the following day also, hoping that it would give my legs at least a chance of making it up the hill.

Once again I slept fitfully and by morning I did not feel well enough to go anywhere, so besides dragging my butt out of the tent to relieve myself, I spent all day lying down. For hours I massaged my legs, but the only effect I could feel was sore and tired hands.

The second day was much better than the previous and although I did not walk around at all, the pain was at a level where I could begin to think clearly. I knew that I could not stay there much longer than two days; for I had no idea how long it was going to take me to get to the village. With a good pair of legs it would only be a few hours to the top, then I guessed the same again on the other side.

Dancing on Raindrops

However if I was forced to drag myself there, it could take several days.

What to take and what to leave behind was my mission for the afternoon, as I emptied the contents of my rucksack onto the tent floor. I had to keep weight to an absolute minimum, so I was merciless in my sorting. Food and water were the only two absolute essentials, and I was left with about half my original stock. Tent, sleeping bag, GPS, mirror, light thermal blanket and a waterproof jacket, was all that made it to the end of the selection. Extra clothes, cooking pot, fuel sticks, flashlight, spare batteries and even my spare sunglasses, were amongst the pile to be left behind.

I was awake well before the dawn and spent the next hour massaging and stretching my legs, while lying down. When I tried to stand, I was pleasantly surprised, for my legs took the weight and the pain did not soar. Although they felt a little weak, they were working and I sat back on my butt, as I broke down the tent.

For breakfast, I had a half a cup of warm tea, a protein bar and a piece of chocolate. Breaking camp was easy in comparison to putting the pack on my back and my legs felt as though they could collapse at every step. The light was beginning to increase as I was ready to leave and the dawn was once again cold and still. I walked hunched over with my hands on the front of my thighs, using them to help steady my knees.

It was make or break time. I had to make it to the top, or else I knew I might well have a problem. I stopped often to rest my legs and drink some water, as the sun rose in the sky. In my mind I kept repeating to myself that I could do it, I would make it to the top and giving up was not an option.

Progress was slow and the pain was high. It was well after noon before I reached the ridge and could see the village far below. I had fallen many times as my legs gave way beneath me and my knees were sore and streaked with dried blood. Each time I fell, I would stop and rest, cussing all the while to take my mind off the pain, massage my legs and then battle to get up and rekit myself.

From here on every step will be down. How will my legs handle this? I wondered. Not well, I was soon to find out.

Climbing up hill I could use my arms for support, but down hill I could not bend forward and consequently I spent most of the time on my butt. I tried dragging my load behind me on the flatter sections, but that took even more effort, as it kept getting stuck on the stones and bushes. What worked best, was when I could find a steep rocky section, then I was able to sit and use my arms to take the weight of my body, as I dragged myself inch by inch downward, pulling my rucksack beside me.

I found out that there was indeed another way to turn forty pounds into eighty - drag a rucksack behind!

The village never seemed to get any closer. My hands were bloodied and my jeans torn from my numerous falls. The pain was intense. Each step seemed harder than the one before, but I refused to stop, knowing that if I did, I might not be able to start again. On the flat areas I made the best progress, as once again, I was able to use my hands to support my thighs and stop them from buckling outwards. One step, two steps, tiny little steps. It seemed as if it was going to take forever.

Darkness came and with it the temperature plummeted, the town a dim array of lights far in the distance. It was late as I hobbled painfully across the deserted town square, towards a most welcome sight, a sign saying Hotel. I stayed for two days. On the first day I hardly left my bed, but on the second I was able to walk a little, so I asked the lady at the front desk how I could get back to Merida. As luck would have it, she was going there herself the next day and would gladly give me a ride.

Once I was immobile in Merida, I began to heal quickly, but it was still five days before I felt strong enough to undertake the journey back to the coast.

Dancing on Raindrops

Success is a progressive realization of worthwhile, pre-determined, personal goals.

- Progressive realization. Your success is a journey - not a destination. Once you set off on the journey you are successful and the only way you can possibly fail is by giving up, or by not taking that next little step.

- Worthwhile. It has to be worth-your-while to change. If your dream is not worthy of your efforts, then at the first obstacle you will stop. Be sure to have a strong motivation, a reason for action.

- Pre-determined. Know where you want to go. Even a simple road trip requires directions. On your highway of life, know where you want to go with such clarity, that the map is engraved into your mind.

- Personal goals. Your goals have to have meaning to you. They have to be close to your heart because this is the only way in which to create the faith necessary for action.

Dancing on Raindrops

7. SECRETS TO YOUR SUCCESS

YOU

Leaving the world of dreams, I wake at seven-twenty with the sunlight pouring in through the open curtains. As I become conscious, the first thought I have in my mind is the word *YOU*.

You are who you are, because you are you. You truly are unique. I open my eyes and slowly they adjust to the light. *You are the one. Every one of us is a YOU.*

After a quick shower to wash away the cobwebs of sleep, I dress and wander into the kitchen to make some coffee. Impatiently I wait for the machine to brew enough for one cup, add a little milk and walk to the office to get my thoughts onto paper.

My knees work well these days, the thought enters my mind - but Alone On The Mountain was the beginning of three years of knee problems. I visited some of the finest specialists all over the world, but no one seemed to be able to find the cause of the problem. For weeks my knees would be strong, then without warning they would collapse and once again I was returned to the world of pain and a wheel chair. It was only once I left Jabula that the pain suddenly went away. Why I don't know, but after a while of living on land my knees seemed to heal themselves.

With all the things I have ever done, and of course ever failed to do, it seems as though at the outset of any new adventure, a most important ingredient is determination. Without it even the most vivid of dreams seem to fail. It is more than a thought, more than a vision; it is something within you that must refuse to give up. Determination and faith go hand in hand, for when you believe without a doubt in the positive outcome, your determination will carry you over the rough times.

Hannibal comes to my mind, with his legendary march from southern Spain into Italy. He had to fight his way through a Roman army before crossing the Pyrenees, (a large range of mountains in the north of Spain), then fight more Romans on his way across southern France, only to have the Alps stand between him and Rome. Searching for a route over the Alps he is reported to have said, "We will either find a way - or make one." That is the essence of determination.

You are what you choose to be.

Dancing on Raindrops

Thoughts for you:

- Is your dream so strong, that it can withstand the negative forces that your conscious mind sees as facts? Remember that in your subconscious mind there are no facts; there is only information.

- In everything you do, give more than you receive and you will receive so much more than you gave; not only in money, but in as many forms and variations as you choose to create.

- Teachers hold the keys to our future. A teacher who can inspire with these principles, has the ability to make a huge difference to our world. Everyone is a teacher, you are a teacher and you can impart your goodness - no matter how little it may seem - to everyone you meet.

- Nurture your faith in yourself and believe that your dreams are in the process of being created, then use your action and your determination to make them happen.

- Every encounter in your life has the potential to be what you want it to be.

- Don't hesitate on your journey of success for a lack of ability, because when you arrive at the point where you need that ability, have the faith that it will be given to you.

**Apply the principles of the 7 secrets
and you will succeed - you cannot fail!**

1. <u>Attitude.</u> The way you choose to look at life. The choice is yours.

2. <u>Thoughts and visualizations.</u> The thoughts you hold in your head create your reality, and combined with the power of focused visualization, you set into motion powerful creative forces.

3. <u>Words and desires.</u> The words you speak, even to yourself, affirm your future. Say it is so!

4. <u>Love.</u> One thing in life you cannot truly succeed without.

5. <u>Action.</u> All your thoughts, desires and faith are for naught without action. It is the catalyst that sets the entire process of creation into motion.

6. <u>Faith and fear</u> are opposites. The stronger the one, the weaker the other.

7. <u>You.</u>

"It's all up to you..."

BE AWARE OF THE POWER OF **YOU**.

* For more information visit:
www.dancingonraindrops.com

Dancing on Raindrops

PRESENT DAY

I glance at the clock and am startled by the time. Ten thirty - oh my, time to get going. It is a good half an hour's drive to town and the seminar starts at twelve. I had already put my notes into the computer, so I press ctrl-p and as the printer springs to life, I head for the bedroom to change.

Yes, the black slacks and the black leather shoes. I throw my T-shirt into the washing basket and put on my Lucky Mike shirt; a white shirt dashed in colors of red, yellow and green - my favorites. I brush my teeth and return to the office. The printer has finished, so I shut down the computer and collect the notes on my way out.

Ah, don't forget a bottle of water from the fridge, I think as I put my hand on the garage door, so I make a quick detour to the kitchen. The car purrs to life and I close the electric door behind me. Down in the valley, I join the highway and soon I have the sunroof open and a breeze in my hair. I put my hand up into the strong wind and my mind makes a connection to a time when the wind was very strong indeed; so strong that I watched houses explode and yachts tear free of their moorings and crash onto the shore. Everyone in our little group realized that their lives were about to change.

Dancing on Raindrops

BIG WIND COMING

Life was close to perfect, as warm summer breezes blew over a Caribbean island. It was the quiet season and most of the people in Oyster Pond were locals. Some lived on yachts and some in rented apartments; all finding work amongst the growing charter yacht industry.

I had opened a bar and restaurant on the water's edge, The Dinghy Dock. It was the only bar for miles around, so it was here that everyone would congregate for happy hour after work. All drinks were only one dollar and with a mixed drink, you were given a frozen glass, the bottle of alcohol, can of mix and a bucket of ice. You mix your own. That way you get your drink exactly the way you like it. Perhaps the only rule of the bar was - everyone mixes their own.

That unique method of bar service caught many a traveler on the first night, as they would fill their glass with rum and not leave much room for the mix. Then, usually after waking the following morning and feeling oh so close to death, they would thereafter pour their drinks the way they liked them, not too much alcohol.

Days came and went, everyone looking forward to the end of hurricane season and the influx of new tourists, the lifeblood of our economy. Saint Martin is half French and half Dutch, a unique combination for so small an island.

The French capital of Marigot was like being in down town Paris. French fashion and cuisine, even the franc was the official currency. Daily flights to and from Paris kept the town filled with the latest and freshest goods.

Philipsburg, the Dutch equivalent, was a little more American. The mighty dollar took preference to the Netherlands Antilles guilder and of course no one wore clogs, but KLM, with its daily flights to Amsterdam, kept the island stocked with Dutch delights.

Throughout the season we would track the tropical depressions, as they crossed the Atlantic all the way from Africa, usually making a beeline for the Caribbean. On the first of September 1995, we were watching one such storm as it grew to hurricane force, a thousand miles south east of us. All talk soon centered on the approaching hurricane, as it grew in strength and size. Would it hit us or wouldn't it? There was no way to know for certain.

A hurricane requires sixty-four knots of sustained wind (74mph.), that is then known as a category one. From there it builds all the way to a category five, a monstrous living thing. Luis was its name and as the next few days passed, it grew and grew, until it reached category four. (131-155 mph.) It was a large hurricane and the inside diameter of the eye was over forty miles. Everything in its path would be sorely tested by those mighty winds.

On the fourth of September, we knew that we were directly in its way and everyone was preparing for the big wind. Those who lived on yachts were putting down more anchors and removing sails, anything to reduce the windage. The house folk were boarding up windows and buying supplies of food and water. I was kept busy emptying the restaurant's stock room and taking the contents up to my house, a solid concrete structure on the top of a hill overlooking the water. The Dinghy Dock was only three feet above sea level and I was concerned that the water might rise and flood everything.

Six hours to go and we were still on a collision course, like standing on a railway line watching an express train coming towards you. The boat people decided that to stay aboard in such conditions, would not only be futile, but also extremely dangerous. So they secured their vessels as best they could and made their way up to my house. Even the three little pigs knew the advantages of a concrete house, when the big bad wolf started to huff and puff. A terse excitement filled the air.

Dancing on Raindrops

Fear and hope mingled, as we sat on my balcony and watched the storm approach. Coincidentally, it was the fifth of September 1995 and the Dutch side telephone area code was 5995.

The ocean was the first to signal that something monstrous was on its way. The swells increased in size and the water turned to a muddy brown. On most days the sea was fairly flat, or had only a little chop on the surface, but now it had turned into a frenzy of moving water. The swells seemed to come from all directions at once and would collide, then rise up into the air in a spectacular display, sometimes reaching twenty or thirty feet. The wind tore at the airborne water and turned it into a horizontal streak of spray.

On and on the wind increased and the sky became darker. The wispy clouds at the outer edge soon disappeared and made way for the dark gray, water-laden clouds. It began to rain and within a few short hours, the wind had picked up to over seventy knots; the barometer continued to plummet.

The boats on anchor began to strain at their moorings and the sheltered waters of the pond (a small enclosed bay of about three hundred by five hundred yards), soon showed its anger, as the wind ripped over the surface and created swells large enough to bury their bows. Short and steep, the swells would rush towards a boat and engulf it, the spray accelerating and leaving a wispy trail of water, as the boat bucked and rolled while trying to keep afloat and shed the water that covered its decks. All the while we stood in the shelter and watched. People's homes were fighting for their lives and we were helpless to assist.

Darkness came early and we huddled in the lounge and listened to the sounds of the storm. The large glass sliding doors bowed and strained to the force of the wind, even though they were covered with plywood. Each door was open about an inch or so, to allow the pressure to equalize in the house, as the gusts of wind forced their way in.

Hopefully that would prevent the glass from exploding, as a gust would come by then abruptly stop, leaving a high pressure in its wake. If the house was closed tight, the air would have nowhere to go but out through the glass.

Not long after dark, the lights went out. People huddled together on the settees or on blankets on the floor, trying to get some rest. It was bound to be a long night.

All of a sudden our world was torn apart by a huge crash and a second later, a third of our roof disappeared into the windy night. The rain began to pour in and the wind entered as an uninvited guest. Every second, more roof would be torn from the beams and more water would come in. The lounge was filled with spray and our first priority was to find somewhere else to sit out the storm, as the house had become a useless shelter.

My house was built on the side of a hill and underneath the swimming pool, was a small room. No more than thirty feet by ten, with a six foot ceiling; it was completely surrounded with concrete, save the wooden door. Fifteen adults, three babies, two dogs and a cat made our way through the storm to the humble shelter.

It was not far to go and closer on a sunny day, for the pool that was then filled with outdoor furniture, was outside the back door. But that was no sunny day. The wind was over one hundred and forty miles per hour and the heavy rain hurt the exposed parts of our skin. Flying debris was everywhere.

I stopped in the shelter of a concrete pillar, to see why the roof had given way and embedded into the metal sheeting, were several pieces of lumber. Javelins for giants, wood that was not a part of my roof. Then I recognized the shape of the alien intruder - it was a part of a balcony. There was a row of small apartments about a hundred yards away and one of their wooden balconies had been torn loose, taken to the air and had smashed into the corrugated iron of my roof. Bits of metal flapped and screeched in the wind trying to tear themselves free, and

Dancing on Raindrops

when they did, they would instantly disappear into the night.

An hour later, we were safe in our new shelter, stuck in a cave with no escape. The effects of the storm were already beginning to show, as people became exhausted from too much adrenaline and began to doze wherever there was space. The two dogs and the cat, normally mortal enemies, curled up on the floor together and were fast asleep. The eerie glow of candlelight threw its dancing shadows on the walls and though sleep was difficult, we all managed to drift in and out of consciousness.

Long before the dawn most people were awake and listening to the angry wind, trying to stay warm and perhaps doze for another few minutes. During the night the wind had changed direction, as the storm rotated around us. Our door was then in the lee of the swimming pool, so it was possible to open it and not have the wind and rain pouring in. Apprehensive faces looked out to the boats in the pond, searching to see if theirs was still afloat.

A sight of devastation greeted us as we watched, at the dawn of the first morning. The home of one of my friends was battling for her life. A beautiful little thirty foot wooden boat with a black shiny hull and a carved bowsprit, was being mauled by a much larger fiberglass charter boat. The larger boat had dragged its mooring and was T-boned onto the bow of my friends home. Like a lion and its prey, the two would not separate as they tore at each other. Ploughing down into the troughs together, then up again, slowly destroying themselves. It was only a matter of time before the cleats that held the anchor chain on the little boat tore from the deck and both boats, still entwined, rushed for the beach.

Tears flowed and emotions were high as people's dreams were shattered and there was not a thing they could do about it. Masts pointed up from the brown waters of the pond, as yet another hapless victim of the storm had sunk below the surface during the night. One yacht had torn free of its mooring and was heading out of the channel, guided only by the raging wind.

On the other side of the pond, large expensive homes were being torn to shreds. The wind would come over the hill and form its own miniature tornado, hurtling all its force on anything in its path. As we watched, one such gust struck a multi-million dollar home and it exploded. The roof was torn off and instantly it turned to matchsticks. Seconds later, only a bare shell of stone walls remained.

No one will ever really know the speed of those gusts, as all the wind speed indicators on the island were torn from their mountings. When a gust of wind hit us, we could feel the pressure in our ears and a moment later, the pressure would drop and make breathing in difficult. People would be talking, then have to pause and try to get another breath of air into their lungs.

It was morning and everyone needed to relieve themselves. The electricity had died early in the night, but now the water supply had also gone. The guys escorted the women to the bathroom in the main house, keeping a wary eye open for flying houses and not letting go - not for an instant. We flushed the toilet by taking water from the pool. Do your business, flush with a bucket of water and then refill the bucket for the next person. A routine was being established; one that we would use for weeks to come.

Around mid-morning there was a huge crash and the foundations of the house shook as if from an earthquake. Outside my front door were the remains of a house. A friend, who fortunately was not in his house at the time, had a double story wooden building, one block away from mine. It had been torn from its foundations, airlifted over all the other houses in-between and deposited outside my front door. From this pile the wind scavenged and anything that could be torn away, was blown into the wet and wild distance.

Later in the afternoon we were all huddled in the tiny room. Some people were playing cards and some just content to sit in silence, listening to the storm. The two

Dancing on Raindrops

dogs got up and started scratching on the door, they both wanted to go out. Crazy animals; outside was death and inside was safety, why on earth would my Labrador and a local special want to go out now?

Meathead was the Labrador's name and he was a very intelligent dog, who in my opinion was making a very bad judgment call at that moment. They both persisted, so I opened the door and as I did so, the wind began to drop and within minutes, it was a beautiful day outside. The eye of the storm had arrived.

A vertical wall of cloud was visible all around, yet here in the middle, were clear blue skies and not a breath of wind. The dogs had somehow sensed the change before the wind had dropped and were eager to go out and play. The first half was over.

Those with boats made their way to the marina, to try to get out to their homes and check for damage. Chaffed mooring lines, cleats torn from the deck, all needed resecuring if they were to survive the next onslaught. It was like a beautiful summer's day and the birds that had survived took to the sky once again. The damage all around was devastating. Not one house that we could see was without some sort of damage and some were a total write-off. Sheets of corrugated iron littered the hillside; uprooted trees and fences were everywhere.

A small group of us stayed at the house and carried more water and provisions down to our haven below the pool. We also tried to resecure some of the plywood sheets in front of the doors and windows that were on the verge of coming loose. The hour of stillness passed all too quickly and soon the far wall of cloud was upon us. The wind started rising, first in gentle gusts, which quickly became stronger. Once again the rain came and by late afternoon we were all huddled back in our shelter, with well over one hundred knots of constant wind outside.

Far less chatter filled the room on the second night. People were exhausted. Some boats had survived the storm so far and their owners were hoping furiously to survive the second half. Some on the other hand were either totally shattered, or sunk completely and their owners, in contrast were devastated, as a long planned part of their lives had come to an abrupt halt. All their worldly possessions were lying below the muddy surface of Oyster Pond.

By the next afternoon the worst was over, although the rain had not let up at all and was still pouring from the sky. Salvage work had begun on the boats, pulling those that would still float off the beach. Some boats were piled three deep, so it was a long process to get the masts and rigging untangled, remove the anchor lines and check below to make sure the keel bolts were still intact.

During that time, I set to work at the Dinghy Dock. 'A dangerous place in a safe harbor.' That was our motto, however then it seemed to be more like, 'A safe place in a dangerous harbor.' Salt spray covered everything and with no electricity or tap water, I simply used buckets of rainwater to rinse off the salt. The structure itself had faired well, with only a few minor damages, however anything electrical was so filled with salt and moisture that it would all have to be replaced.

No electricity meant that two freezers full of food would soon go bad. It was time for a feast. Fortunately we had gas for cooking and it was not long before I had made enough to feed everyone. Free food, come and get it. Soaked, weary and devastated, these were my clients and my friends, most without a means to cook and some without a home. In the next few days as the rain began to subside, we covered part of the hole in my roof with a tarpaulin, dried out the inside of the house and it became home to more than thirty people.

Each day groups were sent out to see what they could buy or barter from other communities, or shops on the island. Most of the roads were still blocked or completely washed away, so our search area was limited, but still somehow we always had bottled water and occasionally someone would come in with a bag or two of ice. Gold to a bunch of thirsty sailors.

Dancing on Raindrops

All the provisions I had brought up from the bar, including cases of alcohol, were still intact. So every night was a party, a respite from the harsh realities that surrounded us. Sometimes people would sit for hours staring into nothingness; shell shocked, as surely as if they had come out of a war zone.

We lived like that for three weeks. Fixing boats and houses, making food and partying. Then the airport was reopened and many of our friends decided to head back home, some just to lick their wounds and some forever.

I took a short vacation to Canada, a place I had always wanted to visit, to clear my head and ponder my future. As the fall leaves turned to a magnificent display of color, my mind was made up. It was time for a change, time for a new experience. My future lay beyond those shores.

In my heart I longed for the carefree life on the ocean once again, so I returned to Oyster Pond and arranged for someone to take over the business; moved out of the house and bought a small wooden yacht to live on. I cruised to a few islands in the northern Caribbean and took a break from real life, to decide exactly in which direction I wanted my future to head. I even took up painting, something I had always wanted to try but had never made the time, hence it always went undone. After so many years of living on a boat but working on land, I decided that I wanted to live and work on the ocean.

One year after Luis, I was anchored in Falmouth harbor, Antigua and when I rowed back to my yacht one evening, there was a note, a small damp sliver of paper, under a winch handle in the cockpit.

"Mike, I need help to take a 98 foot yacht (Jabula) to Palm Beach, Florida. – Mark. Short and to the point but the timing was perfect. Only a few days earlier, I had begun putting out the word that I was looking for large yacht that needed help. The note was exactly what I had wanted to happen - and it was the beginning of a new adventure!

THE MOMENT ARRIVES

"**T**hank you Ed," I say as I shake his hand and look directly into his eyes. His introduction was eloquent and well spoken, and his face is covered in a huge smile. So much good and positive energy surrounds him, that I can feel it radiating outward. Coming from a life as a heroin addict, he is living proof of the power of the **7** secrets.

Turning away, I walk on the polished wood to the front of the platform and look at the crowd of people, allowing them a moment to gather their thoughts. My body feels alive and my mind is crystal clear, rather like standing on the edge of a cliff about to jump.

"Top of the afternoon to you all Ladies and Gentlemen. Today I would like to speak to you about the **7** secrets to your success." I pause. "Who came here today to learn how to create more success?" I say in a loud and clear voice, as I raise my right hand to my shoulder and watch as my audience does the same.

"How about a lot more success!" I shout and raise my hand high above my head. There is energy created in that moment, when everyone lifts their hands towards the ceiling, some even standing to raise them higher. As they settle, I inhale a slow, deep breath and savor the moment. Looking at the attentive faces, a thought comes to me; it is so clear, as if it has been spoken.

"You can become anyone you choose to be and you can have anything your heart desires – but first it has to be created from within."

* * * * *

Dancing on Raindrops

The more I travel, the more concerned I become with the plight of hungry children on our planet. That is why one dollar from the sale of each and every book, will be used to feed and educate the little people and may well be enough to change the world. For it is not the money that is supremely important - it is the vision...

Every person who lives on this planet should have access to food, water, shelter, clothing and education. There *is* abundance for everyone."

Lucky Mike

www.dancingonraindrops.com

THANK YOU

Ann Lewis
Brian Delport
Dave Cole
Ed Schreiber
George Oakley
Hanne Svensson
Ian Boxshall
Joycebelle
Joan Suttle
Kurt Eder
Liz Barker
Lucille Fry
Mark Boxshall
Mary Jane Berry
Olav Zipser
Patrick Booth
Peter Heath
Robert Allen
Sally Ponton
Steve Siebold
Teresa Barker

Thank you
for helping my dream to come true,
but most of all, thank you for being you.

INDEX

Dancing

on

Raindrops

EXTREME ADVENTURES
REVEAL THE 7 SECRETS TO YOUR SUCCESS

To order the audio version on CD,
send a book to a friend,
or have Lucky Mike talk to your group –

Visit www.dancingonraindrops.com

Or write to:
P.O. Box 740852,
Boynton Beach, FL.,
33474 - 0852.

Dancing on Raindrops